Also by Susie Kelly

BEST FOOT FORWARD
TWO STEPS BACKWARD
A PERFECT CIRCLE

all published by Bantam Books

THE VALLEY OF HEAVEN AND HELL

Cycling in the Shadow of Marie Antoinette

SUSIE KELLY

blackbirdebooks
London
2011

The Valley of Heaven and Hell
Cycling in the shadow of Marie Antoinette

A digital original publication by blackbirdebooks 2011
© Susie Kelly 2011

ISBN-13: 978-1463644666
ISBN-10: 1463644663

The moral right of the author has been asserted

Cover design by Fena Lee at http://pheeena.co.cc
Bike image by Hector Herrera Jr at deviantArt

ACKNOWLEDGEMENTS

My thanks are due equally to:

Fena Lee for her skill and patience in producing exactly the unique cover design that I was looking for.

Deborah Rey and Carole Morrow for their feedback in the early stages of the manuscript.

Jeremy and Lynette Yonge for pet and house-sitting, thus enabling us to make this journey.

Keith Wheeler for his very kind permission to quote the passage written by his father, Harry St Clare Wheeler.

The International Sommelier Guild for permission to quote the interview with Bernard de Nonancourt.

The Tourist Office at Dormans for their permission to use the postcard scene of WWI.

Stephanie Zia, my editor, for having faith in *The Valley of Heaven and Hell*, for her diligent editing, and her enthusiasm, unfailing patience and good humour. It has been a joy to work with her.

And, of course, Terry for his (almost) perpetual good humour, for doing all the heavy work, coping with my tantrums and being the perfect travelling mate.

CONTENTS

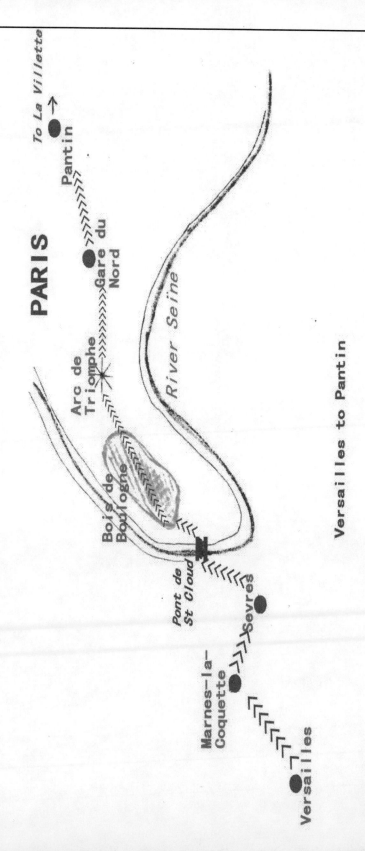

Versailles to Pantin

INTRODUCTION

Get a bicycle. You will not regret it if you live."

Mark Twain

IT is 3.00 pm in a small back road in Versailles. I am straddling my bicycle, cold, frightened and growing wetter by the minute, courtesy of a delicate but determined drizzle. Our waterproof clothing is carefully rolled and stowed at the bottom of our luggage, because when we packed our panniers this morning the clear blue skies had given no indication that they would only be of a very temporary nature. We are setting off to cycle first to Paris, and then half-way across France. An undertaking for which I recognise only now, at this very late stage, that I am totally unprepared mentally, and unsuited physically. I am angry with myself for agreeing to it in the first place, and even angrier for feeling so feeble about it now. I open my mouth to call out to Terry, a few metres ahead of me, to say I've changed my mind about this venture. Just as I do so he slings his leg effortlessly over his bike, waves his arm above his head and bellows over his shoulder "Forward ho!" I am reminded of John Wayne saddling up and moving out a wagon train. He shoots away like a rocket as I screech at his receding back; but he's already vanished around the corner.

Quickly checking that the baking tray behind my saddle is firmly secured, I hesitantly launch away from the pavement. The bike wobbles and whirrs forward, down to the junction with the main road, which is teeming with traffic. Our three months of training for this expedition have been on quiet country lanes where we count the traffic as heavy if more than four vehicles pass in an hour.

By now a hundred metres ahead, Terry has stopped and is looking back. Taking one hand from the handlebars, and nearly falling off as a result, I raise my arm authoritatively, to signal that he must stay just where he is, not move another inch. Misinterpreting my message, he understands that all is well. Away he pedals again, leaving me muttering dementedly, using alternate cuffs to wipe the rain from my glasses - a futile effort - and cringeing as convoys of coaches pass mere inches from my handlebars; from steamed-up windows rows of pink face-blobs peer out into the murk. I envy them their safety and comfort. The spray from passing vehicles unites with the drizzle to force itself through my clothes right down to my skin. Wheels in the gutter, elbows clenched to my sides, this is my first ever experience of cycling in heavy traffic. I am not enjoying it yet.

Terry is now 500 metres ahead; through the underwater effect of my glasses I can vaguely discern the blurred red shape of the panniers on his bike. Every traffic light in Versailles changes to red as I approach, further widening the distance between us. I'm forced to dismount and make a new wobblesome beginning each time the lights switch to green. I imagine a malevolent little man sitting in a traffic control box, watching my progress and gleefully pushing a button to make things as difficult as possible. The red panniers are almost out of sight by now.

On the outskirts of town we begin to climb a long hill, and the gap between us closes as my electric bike shows its muscle and begins to haul Terry in. At the crest of the hill I draw almost level with him and shriek at him to stop; over his shoulder he shouts something that is caught up and swept away by the noise of passing traffic. Again I yell, but he is unstoppable, inexorably rolling on like Ole Man River, while I bob along in his wake like a waterlogged paper boat. He turns onto a quiet lane winding through silent, dripping woods and zooms away down a steep hill. With all hope lost of being able to bring him to a halt, I have no choice but to follow, and we are travelling at exhilarating speed, slicing through the driving rain. My fingertips are a striking shade of mottled pink and purple and I'm virtually blinded by the rain on my glasses. It's terribly exciting and quite terrifying.

Shortly we arrive in Marnes-la-Coquette, a discreet village

mid-way between Versailles and St Cloud. This is where the good, great and sufficiently wealthy have made their homes over the centuries. Surrounded by hectares of park and woodland, it enjoys the highest per capita income in France. Napoléon III owned property there, and, seduced by the charms of the village known until then simply as Marnes, he added "la Coquette" (the Flirt) to its name, and the Imperial eagle to its coat of arms. Later Louis Pasteur used the property as a centre for his research into rabies. The other residents of the village, who objected to the several dozen dogs, rabbits and guinea pigs housed in the grounds and destined for laboratory experiments, did not necessarily welcome this. The snarling dog on the coat of arms is a tribute to Pasteur's successful development of a rabies vaccine.

I had planned a surprise for Terry in Marnes-la-Coquette - a visit to the Memorial to the Escadrille Lafayette, built to honour the volunteer American airmen who had flown and died for France during WWI, before the United States entered the war. With their squadron insignia of a screaming native American Indian, and with two live lion cubs as their mascots, the wild bunch were heroic pioneers of aerial warfare, and I know that this is somewhere Terry, with his passion for military aviation, would find fascinating. However, he is always several metres ahead of me, pedalling as if our lives depend upon reaching an imaginary finishing line. Regardless of how hard I try, I cannot get close enough to signal him to stop; he cannot hear the pinging of my tinny bell, nor my frantic shrieking. The elegant bijou village is just a smudge on the landscape as we shoot into, through and out of it, missing not only the memorial, but also the turning to St Cloud that would lead us to the Bois de Boulogne. Instead we arrive in the centre of Sèvres, which is heavily congested with impatient traffic.

Sèvriens appear to have scant regard for cyclists, and try to kill us by a variety of methods: by turning abruptly across us in either direction without signalling, slamming on brakes with no warning, or opening their car doors just as we are drawing level with them. It is every man or woman for him or herself. There are multitudes of traffic lights, all of which change to red just as Terry hurtles through, leaving me on the wrong side and standing in the gutter inhaling fumes from revving engines. Terry's bike, like him, is quick and nimble. Mine is cumbersome and awkward, and unable to squeeze past the cars waiting at the lights, particularly as, tied to the baking tray that is tied to the luggage rack, are two sleeping bags and a rather wide tent which protrudes further than the handlebars. Each time the lights change to green, I have to wait for all cars to be clear before I move off, because until the bike gathers sufficient momentum, it wanders suicidally all over the road, and I do not want to be squashed without seeing Paris first.

The gap between us widens again, and although Terry looks back from time to time to check that I am still there, it does not cross his mind that I am following from necessity and not desire. We cannot afford to lose contact, firstly because Terry doesn't know which hotel I have booked in Paris, and secondly because I have no money on me. Without each other, we will be truly in the mire. Our one mobile phone is in Terry's jacket. There is no means of communication between us, so I grit my teeth and squeeze my elbows tighter into my ribs. The rain is harder now, dripping off my cycling helmet, running simultaneously down the back of my neck, and my face, and into the collar of my jacket. Still, this discomfort is forgotten because of what happens next: after a brief respite from traffic we are suddenly on a vehicle-infested dual carriageway, approaching a miniature Spaghetti Junction. Above us is a fly-over, supported on huge concrete pillars. We must turn left, across two lanes of fast traffic, filter into the path of thundering trucks coming from the right and make it across another two lanes of traffic coming from the left. This is so terrifying that I give up trying to think, and instead pedal mechanically, mindlessly, eyes fixed on the red panniers, and surprise myself by reaching the Pont de Sèvres intact. A Parisian contact from a cycling forum has warned of the dangers of cycling on bridges, and recommended dismounting and pushing the bike over, which I do.

Terry has already reached the far end and at last has dismounted and is waiting for me. This is our first opportunity to speak to each other since leaving Versailles.

Wet, but clearly elated, he asks: "Well – how did you enjoy that?"

I am seething and shaking with inner fury, but do not wish to have a full-scale row in this public place nor at this early stage. "Not a great deal," I reply with what I consider great restraint. "I have been trying to ask you to stop since we left Versailles."

"I thought it was great!" he enthuses.

Yes, indeed, there are few things I enjoy as much as being concurrently cold, wet and frightened.

"Where do we go from here?" he asks.

"Through the Bois de Boulogne, up to the Arc de Triomphe, and then to our hotel near the Gare du Nord. And tomorrow morning, you'll have to go back and pick up the car. I'm not going to do this trip on a bike."

"What on earth are you saying?"

"Never mind for now, let's just get to the hotel and get ourselves warm and dry. We'll talk about it then."

CHAPTER ONE

Paris

"The first thing that strikes a visitor to Paris is a taxi."
Fred Allen, comedian

I TAKE out the small folding map of Paris with all the cycling lanes marked on it and we follow the banks of the Seine until we can find an entrance into the Bois de Boulogne. Immediately I forget the horrors of the last couple of hours, because we have the whole beautiful park almost to ourselves. The only other wheeled vehicle we see is a pram pushed by a young woman; an occasional panting, chap-kneed jogger shuffles past. Twice we ride past Longchamps racecourse; several times we pass places that we have already passed. The map is no help and begins to dissolve. As lovely as the park is, cycling around it endlessly in rain begins to lose its appeal. As the racecourse comes into view yet again, we find a sad-faced man standing under a tree and ask him how to reach the Arc de Triomphe. He stares at us in astonishment, as if we are asking for directions to the lost city of Atlantis.

I repeat "L'Arc de Triomphe."

"L'Arc de Triomphe?" he echoes, his voice raised in bewilderment.

"Oui," I say, forcefully.

"But ... it's a long way! At least two or three kilometres!"

Yes, but we are not ants. We are people on bicycles. Two, or even three kilometres is within even my meagre capabilities.

With obvious misgivings he points out a route, which we follow to a large roundabout, where the rain abruptly stops. Ahead of us Avenue Foch glistens in pale sunshine. Diamond raindrops shimmer and drip from the trees lining the wide road, as if they are weeping for Napoléon, who would never march through the great triumphal arch, but instead would die in lonely exile. It's a shame about Waterloo, in a way. I feel sad for Boney.

Mixed with this sadness is great elation, because I have, against all my misgivings, cycled from Versailles to Paris, and am now standing, for the first time in my life, in the luminous city, just a few metres from one of its greatest landmarks. Little congratulatory tears spring to life and slither down my cheeks.

Our destination is a hotel of slightly dubious reputation, but cheap, at the Gare du Nord, from which we are separated by the Arc de Triomphe and several kilometres of busy Parisian streets. With new-found and misplaced confidence I follow Terry as he happily plunges into the utter chaos of twelve roads heaving with traffic, all converging onto "l'Étoile" at 5.00 pm.

He instantly disappears between two trucks, and is swallowed up from sight, and I scream as a coach squeals to a halt in my path. Other cyclists whizz past. I am in a maelstrom of noise and vehicles, like a baby lamb in a Wild West show, straddling the bike and standing in the road, not knowing where to go next. I recall how all our French friends had reacted when we told them we would cycle through Paris. "But you will be crushed! It's too dangerous. You must not do it." I wish I'd taken them seriously, instead of shrugging them off in my most blasé manner and assuring them confidently that we English with our bulldog spirit were not easily deterred once we had made up our minds to do something.

Nobody seems to care that a woman and her bicycle are trapped and helpless amongst them; they weave around, glaring, blaring, or staring in disbelief. I turn the bike and drag it to a pavement. I start pushing it around the great circle, hoping that I will find Terry soon. He cycles up beside me, heedless of trucks and taxis and sightseeing buses, and commands that I mount my bike and just follow him, and I will be fine. But no thank you, I am content to plod along in a wide arc, heaving the bike up and down the kerbs, until reaching the Avenue de Friedland where there is a generous cycle lane painted onto the road.

Shaken, and a little stirred, I climb aboard and follow Terry, who is constantly waving his hands around pointing out interesting sights. I catch fragments of comments "...... fantastic ...." "Did you ....?", but all my concentration is needed to keep inside the cycling lane and watch for the traffic lights. Sometimes I shout back "Yes, fabulous!" to be polite. I have assured him that if we keep cycling, sooner or later we'll see a sign for the Gare du Nord, and this is indeed what happens.

We cycle through the shopping mecca of Boulevard Haussman. Whilst Terry is goggle-eyed at the great department stores (I can only imagine this, as he is always several metres ahead of me, but I know his passion for shopping), I concentrate on cycling. My clearest vision of hell, after trying to cycle around the Arc de Triomphe at 5.00 pm on a Thursday evening, is traipsing around department stores. If I never had to buy another garment or piece of furniture for the rest of my life, that would be just fine by me.

Unlike dignified Boulevard Haussman, Rue La Fayette seems to be having a temper tantrum. Most likely this has been provoked by a series of diversions that have caused a total gridlock in the traffic. Nobody can go anywhere. Traffic lights might as well switch themselves off and go home, because nobody can obey them even if they wish to. Vehicles are bumper to bumper, and in one case a car has actually mounted the pavement in an effort to escape. Drivers are standing next to their cars, shouting and waving their arms around, or klaxoning each other. In this utter pandemonium, the pedestrian is king. Terry isn't doing too badly either, and has disappeared into the distance. There is no room to cycle in the road, because the vehicles are interlocked like pieces in a jigsaw puzzle. There is no way for me to thread my bike through them, so I heave it onto the pavement and use it as a battering ram against oncoming pedestrians, forcing some of them to allow me a little headway which otherwise they would not. When the end of the world arrives, this is how it will be, I imagine.

The red panniers are my beacon, guiding me through this mad chaos. When we eventually reach the Gare du Nord, the road is trembling beneath roaring machines gouging up the tarmac around the station. Temporary wooden walkways have been set up to allow pedestrians to move from one place to another; however, they are rather narrow, with sharp bends around which it is impossible to steer a bicycle carrying a wide load such as mine, as I discover about half way along. This means wheeling the machine backwards, against the oncoming crowds, the most difficult challenge so far on this afternoon of trials. The pedestrians hurrying to catch trains are not impressed by my efforts, nor sympathetic to my dilemma.

Directly over the hotel's entrance - a narrow slot almost hidden between two cafés - dangles a menacing iron bucket full of chomped-up road surface. The machine to which it is attached growls and rattles, making conversation impossible. By grimacing and miming Terry and I agree that he will stand under the bucket with both bicycles while I go to check in and try to find somewhere to park them safely overnight.

As I walk into the lobby of the hotel, I am confronted by a weird, cartoon character. Legs encased in clinging black trousers, like Max Wall; upper half fighting to escape from a Lycra black and Day-glo green jacket; a round face, bright red and reflective with rivulets of perspiration running down it, crowned with a repulsive crimson cycling helmet. Betty Bumpkin, the cycling clown, I think as I stare at my reflection. What a holy mess. I cannot believe I look like this. I am truly aghast, and very angry at the hotel for placing a full-length mirror in such a thoughtless position. Before I knew what I looked like, I was relatively happy. Now I am utterly mortified, and forced to face several truths: not only am I a really crap cyclist. I need to lose weight. Skin-tight Lycra does not suit me. Neither does the helmet.

A smiling receptionist (I wonder, is he actually laughing, rather than smiling?) asks if he can be of help. I introduce myself and point to Terry and the bicycles, and ask if there is somewhere that we can safely leave them overnight. The receptionist, whose name is Ben, picks up a telephone – I hear the words "*anglais*" and "*bicyclettes*." With a dramatic flourish he replaces the receiver and announces that the patron is on his way, and will deal with the bicycles. Terry is impatient, and signalling to know why I am taking so long – it has been all of three minutes since I left him on the pavement. Ben skips up a very narrow winding staircase, beckoning me to follow. He flings open the door to a small room decorated in multi-shades of glowing orange. The effect is like being inside a carton of juice, but it is clean, dry and warm. Most importantly to me, there is a small wrought iron balcony overlooking the front of the historic Gare du Nord railway station. Ben shows me how to switch on the lights and plug in the television mounted on a bracket near the ceiling. He picks up the hair dryer from its pocket in the bathroom and points it at his head, making whooshing noises. No doubt my appearance has cast doubts as to my mental capacity.

Remembering my husband is still under the bucket, I thank Ben and spiral down the stairs, and find Terry playing an indignant tug-of-war with an elderly gentleman wearing carpet slippers. He has hold of my machine and is trying to push it across the road. Terry is trying to stop him from doing so. They are evenly matched: Terry is younger, but has to try to balance his own bike at the same time as holding on to mine, whilst keeping in contact with all the bags and bundles he has unloaded onto the pavement. The two tuggers are talking to each other, each in a language that the other does not understand.

"This gentleman is trying to help," I explain to Terry. "He is the owner of the hotel. He is letting us put the bikes in his garage overnight." I introduce us both to his adversary, who has a small boy in tow, who politely shakes Terry's hand, and kisses me on both cheeks.

"Please, follow me." Leaving obliging Ben to carry the luggage up to our room, the patron ushers us over the road, waving a scornful hand at the diversions and diggers and wooden walkways.

"Terrible. No idea at all. London is much better, Mr. Livingstone knows what he's doing. Look what a terrible mess Delanoë," (the mayor of Paris) "is making. It was perfectly fine before he started playing about. Now see what's happened." The traffic is still at an effective standstill and the noise of drivers and vehicles is deafening.

Our new friend unlocks a metal grille beside a shop, and the door slides upwards at the top of a long steep slope leading to an underground car park. We have to lean back and dig in our heels to stop the bikes dragging us down. At floor number minus 2 he unlocks another metal door, and reveals a very large, powerful, expensive shiny motorbike that he pats and strokes lovingly.

"Is it yours?" Terry asks.

"Yes, of course. At the weekends I ride it out into the country."

It is an incongruous image, that of this stately and aged gentleman roaring around the French countryside astride a machine that looks more suited to a bearded, tattooed, horned-helmet Hell's Angel.

Once our bikes are stowed safely and locked up, we climb back up the long slope; Bertrand walks very slowly. He tells us that he is nearly 80, and has had a heart by-pass, and is not as fit as he used to be. He calls himself "Le Comte de Paris," he laughs, because his surname is Comte. He certainly has the aristocratic looks, bearing and manners to go with the title; he wishes us a happy evening as we part company.

Up in the radiant room we take it in turns to bathe, and then stand out on the balcony in the dusk. Now that the digging machines have closed down for the night, and their clanking, grinding noises are silenced, the traffic is no more than a rhythmic buzz, broken just once in a while by a brief peep, an occasional shout, a door closing. The street lights awaken, illuminating the full havoc caused by the roadworks. We have an unhindered view of the magnificent Gare du

Nord, an example of industrial design from an age when buildings were not only built for functionality, but also for beauty and elegance. Three *tricolores* flutter on the roof. The central elevation is topped by nine female statues, representing major international destinations. At the next level down, and spanning the left and right flanks, sheltered in cosy niches are 14 male statues dressed in flowing robes - they could be apostles, saints or kings, it is difficult to say - and they signify major French cities. To make it unmistakably clear which station this is, the word "*Nord*" is engraved in the stone eight times on the upper front elevation of the building, and again at ground-floor level. For good measure, "*Chemin du Fer du Nord*" is carved on the side of the wings.

Bertrand had mentioned that by the time the original station was completed in 1846 it was already too small to serve the booming railway traffic. It had been meticulously dismantled and transported to Lille where it is now known as the station of Lille Flandres. We are looking at La Gare du Nord mark II.

The station has always been a place of excitement and romance in my imagination, a haunt of spies, star-crossed lovers, and shadowy figures in long raincoats dragging on cigarettes and lurking with intent. We go to see if this bears any resemblance to reality, and I avoid looking in the cruel mirror in the lobby, because I really don't want to see what I look like in my little chiffon skirt and black top. Limited by the available space in our luggage, I team my "going out" wardrobe for the trip with a blue cycling jacket (to ward off the chilly evening air and scattered raindrops), and the gold moccasins which seemed the ideal footwear when I was packing, but look quite inappropriate now.

What is most noticeable about the concourse of the station is its cleanliness. The floors and the platforms shine as if they have been polished for hours. So do the trains standing with their noses buried in the colourful plants clambering from flower boxes beneath the buffers. The half a million passengers who use the station daily haven't left any trace of their passing: not a sweet-wrapper, not a cigarette butt, not a dropped ticket in sight. With its shops and cafés and escalators the station resembles a skyport terminal, nothing like the vaguely sinister and murky sort of place I had imagined.

We decide to come back after we've eaten, when maybe the globe lights on their iron posts will add a romantic glow to the building that the weak ambient light from the glass roof fails to do.

Multitudes of bars, brasseries, cafés and restaurants surround the station, and we select one where a lone waiter copes efficiently with a dozen tables and still manages a smile, and the food is fine.

Seen from a full stomach, half a bottle of rosé and two generous Baileys, in retrospect our journey today doesn't seem nearly as horrifying as it did when it was happening, and tomorrow there's only a short distance to negotiate before we will be out of town and into the countryside. I am pleased with myself for having come this far, and I realise that in some rather twisted way, I had quite enjoyed being terrified.

Even by lamplight, the interior of the Gare du Nord is too clean and bright to be romantic, and there are no signs of any shadowy figures or anguished lovers. Terry photographs a number of trains, until a burly, armed policeman politely stops him when he points his camera at the maroon and silver Thalys. The appeal of looking at trains has until now escaped me, but I cannot imagine that there exists a more exquisite engine that this svelte, bullet-shaped beauty that links Paris with Brussels, Amsterdam and Cologne.

"Plan Vigipirate," (France's anti-terror alert system) explains the *flic* a little apologetically.

When we arrive back at our hotel after 11.00 pm, Ben is still on duty, fresh as a daisy, and bright as a button. Breakfast, he explains, can be taken in our room, or in the cellar – he points down at the floor.

It takes me a long time to fall asleep because of the continual noise from the streets below, something I haven't heard for many years, living as we do in a small hamlet in the

13

middle of rural France. Later, I wake disorientated, sure that we are in London and must get back to France as soon as possible. Terry reassures me that we are exactly where we are meant to be, and that I should go back to sleep.

CHAPTER TWO
Versailles

"Eat, drink and be merry, for tomorrow we die."
Ecclesiastes 8:15

WHEN some new friends, animal lovers, had volunteered to care for our menagerie for three weeks, we leapt at the rare opportunity to take a holiday. Two places we particularly wanted to visit were the palace of Versailles, and Epernay, the spiritual home of champagne. The Marne valley, one of France's least publicised, yet most historic areas, links the two towns, roughly 250 kilometres distant from each other. Travelling by car is a poor way to get in touch with the countryside, and Terry didn't want to walk – a shame as walking is my major accomplishment. Ruling out boats, camels and horses as too expensive, impractical and restrictive, we had settled on cycling, albeit more than a little reluctantly on my part.

I still harbour bitter memories of the daily cycle ride to school when each new day, it seemed, brought a puncture, snatching brakes, snapping cables, or a greasy chain falling off and covering my legs with black marks. The bike was my enemy, making life as difficult, uncomfortable and dangerous as it could, and the prospect of riding one for 300 miles or more was not one that filled me with extreme delight, but it would be the most practical way to travel, allowing us flexibility and the opportunity to enjoy and explore the countryside in a leisurely way. I'm a slothful creature with chronic back problems, and for the previous two years a trapped sciatic nerve had been causing unpredictable spasms of exquisite pain. To compensate for these personal shortcomings, I'd bought an electrically-assisted machine. It wasn't a moped, it still needed to be pedalled, but the 36-volt battery delivered a fair boost, as if somebody was giving the

15

bike a helping push, as my father had done when I was a small child. Managed carefully, a fully-charged battery would last for up to 70 kilometres; all it needed was plugging into an electric power point for a few hours to recharge. Beginning at Versailles, after visiting the palace we'd cycle to Paris – a thought that I had pushed into the deepest recesses of my mind. From there we'd travel through the Marne *département* in the Champagne-Ardennes region.

There seemed to be a dearth of information about the area; at the university library in Poitiers books about the Marne were remarkable for their non-existence on the shelves. The librarian searched her catalogue, to no avail. No, there wasn't a single publication dedicated to *département* 51. Our French friends pulled faces when we announced our plans to explore there, saying they were dubious that we'd find anything at all of interest.

While gathering information for our trip – something Terry was more than happy to leave to me – I noticed we would be following the same route as that taken by King Louis XVI and his Queen, Marie-Antoinette in their legendary attempt to escape from the wrath of the French Revolution. Where they had been, we were going, in their footsteps and wheel-tracks, and so I planned to try and integrate our journey with theirs. Hoping, of course, that for us it would have a less dramatic ending.

With our bikes loaded onto the car, we drove to Versailles on the last day of May, a month that had been far from merry, each day having been uniformly grey and cold. That morning the skies had shown a promising hint of blue, but the nearer we came to Paris the gloomier appeared the clouds hanging over the capital. A few timid raindrops splattered onto the windscreen and by the time we arrived, Versailles was beneath a blanket of purple clouds and surrounded by rumbling thunder. We checked into our *chambre d'hôte*, swaddled ourselves in waterproofs, and cycled to the park, which we planned to explore today, visiting the palace tomorrow morning before leaving for Paris.

16

Five minutes later the clouds collapsed beneath their weight and exploded into a deluge, turning the roads into rivers and driving icy rain down the backs of our necks, up through our sleeves, and into our shoes. Together with a huddle of similarly soaked people we sought shelter in the nearest and only dry place, the park's lavatories, where a motherly lady promised that in a few minutes the sun would come bursting out. She was well-meaning, but quite wrong. We stood eating a packet of miniature doughnuts while pebble-like raindrops battered the road and the cars parked along it. We discussed how we would cope if this weather lasted for the whole three weeks of our journey, as French friends had predicted it very likely would. Once the torrent had dwindled to a heavy drizzle, we rode around the park stoically, slashed by blades of freezing wind. I felt quite furious, absolutely enraged, that after an already overlong winter and dismal spring, the weather was still so disappointing on this, the last day of May, when it should have been at least spring-like, if not almost summery. After twenty minutes we admitted that we were not at all enjoying ourselves, so we changed our plans and went to visit the inside of the palace, queuing with a small group of other wet people waiting to get into the building that Marie-Antoinette had once so desperately wanted to get out of.

The Palace of Versailles peered out through a robust network of scaffolding that could not hide its vast splendour. Louis XIV, the Sun King, disenchanted after five years of civil war, wished to relocate from Paris, so that he could collect his devious aristocracy under one roof where he could keep an eye on them. So he decided to transform his father's simple hunting lodge, known as the House of Cards, into the most legendary and opulent palace in the Western world. The cost was unimaginable. No expense was too great, neither in terms of money nor human life, for the solar monarch's self-glorification.

We began our visit in the chapel, an astonishing confection of gleaming gilt and bright white marble, sculpted stonework and fluted columns rising twenty-five metres to a vaulted and magnificently painted ceiling.

It was here that 14-year-old Austrian Archduchess Maria Antonia Josepha Joanna of Habsburg-Lorraine, more familiarly known now as Marie-Antoinette, took the first step towards the scaffold, when she married the lumpen 15-year-old French "dolphin" (the hereditary title of the French heir apparent, dating back to the 11th century,) who would fairly soon have the misfortune of becoming Louis XVI of France.

If you believe in omens, you may find it significant that the Archduchess was born on the day following the cataclysmic Lisbon earthquake of 1755, which left an estimated 90,000 dead, and is still regarded as one of the world's most devastating natural disasters.

A high-spirited and poorly-educated tomboy, the young girl was a sacrificial offering made by her mother, Maria-Theresa, Archduchess, Queen of Austria, and Holy Roman Empress, to preserve Franco-Austrian harmony. Despite maternal misgivings as to the future awaiting the girl, Maria-Theresa packed off her daughter to the French House of Bourbon, for what use were children if not to extend one's power base and protect one's borders? Anyway, she considered that her daughter should be more than satisfied to become a queen. Expecting happiness as well was just plain greedy.

It had taken many months for Austria and France to thrash out the fine points of the marriage contract between Louis and Marie-Antoinette, down to the most tedious of details. How many of this, how many of that; where, when, who, why and how. Protocol was everything. En route to her new life, the girl was ceremoniously handed over from Austria to France, and symbolically stripped of all her clothing, servants, pet dog, and even her name. From now on, she was exclusively French property.

Her bridegroom was dull, uncouth and most definitely not eye candy; his interests were limited to hunting, fiddling with locks, and eating. He noted laconically in his diary, when his bride, having arrived in a great cavalcade, was introduced to him: "Met the new wife." On his wedding day: "My marriage. Apartment in the gallery. Royal banquet in the Salle d'Opera." A few days later: "Had an indigestion." He could not be accused of being a romantic.

What were these two children, selected to be mated like animals, thinking about, I mused, during their marriage ceremony? Was Louis wondering how soon it would be over so that he could go hunting? Was the bride missing her mother and siblings?

To celebrate the royal marriage, a grand firework display was held at the square called Place Louis XIV in Paris. A fire broke out; the crowd stampeded to escape the flames, and 132 people were trampled to death.

Another bad omen? Twenty-two years later, that square would have been renamed Place de la Revolution. It was the last place the newly-weds would ever see.

But let's not worry too much about that just now. It's a long way off, and we have far to go.

From the chapel we trundled on along with the crowd from one gold-plated room to the next. There was not a square inch of floor, wall or ceiling that was not ornately adorned. It looked to me (and I have to admit that unlike Terry, I am not a lover of fancy furnishings, frills and flounces,) as if successive inhabitants had tried to see just how much decoration they could cram into the available space. From one room to another we all shuffled, past marble pillars, gilded doors; glittering chandeliers, polished candelabras and porcelain jars; bronze busts, oil paintings, marble sculptures, mirrors, tapestries, vases, chairs and sofas that looked uncomfortable, and ugly, heavy cabinets and tables with hard edges. Very bad Feng Shui. We gawped at painted ceilings until our necks ached. Overwhelming opulence, wild profligacy, the triumph of excess over moderation, it seemed to me a beautiful example of more is never enough.

The air smelt of damp clothing and hair, and chewing gum, but it was not offensive. During the 18th century, for all its splendour, one thing had been notably lacking here - proper sanitation. In the absence of lavatories, people answered the call of nature wherever they happened to be at the time the need arrived, both outside and inside the palace, and the stench of urine and human faeces pervaded the air.

Ahead of us a band of solemn Japanese tourists listened intently to a gentleman holding a microphone and waving a bright orange flag on a long stick, as he shepherded them from room to room. Behind us a group of giggling American teenage girls were more interested in sending text messages than looking at the rooms and their contents. They would have been about the same age as the young Archduchess when she arrived at Versailles, and I wondered how any one of them would have reacted if she had been told that she was to be married to somebody she had never met, and who had neither good looks nor charm but with whom she would be obliged to share a bed and produce children. I doubt that any of these young American girls came from a particularly affluent or influential family, but each of them would certainly have more control over their own destiny than the unlucky, beautiful and rich little girl whose scheming mother was one of the most powerful women in the Western world. Those were my thoughts as I watched the girls nudging each other, whispering behind their hands, and sharing photos on their mobile phones.

Where life at court in her native Austria had been relaxed and informal, and morals were strict, in contrast at Versailles etiquette ruled and morals were almost non-existent. Combined with the stifling, small-minded formality of the 17th century French court, where a misplaced step in the minuet was cause for gasps and gossip, I thought that living in the palace of Versailles must have felt like being imprisoned in a constantly turning kaleidoscope.

The teenage Archduchess was entrusted to a lady of great virtue and an impeccable knowledge of court protocol. Her task was to ensure that the new arrival understood exactly what to do, when, how, where, and with and to whom.

Nothing must be left to chance – a head-dress worn at the wrong angle was sufficiently scandalous to provoke a fainting fit.

The Dauphine's day was occupied by prayers, rituals of dressing and having her hair dressed in public, more prayers, visits with Royal family members - in particular her aunts (the granddaughters of Louis XV), dining in public, needlework, music lessons, more family visits, reaching a crescendo of excitement with late night games of cards. A particular trial was the custom of dining in front of an audience of people who came to Versailles specifically to watch the royals eat. While her husband could nonchalantly demolish as many dishes as were put before him, and his grandfather had delighted spectators by his skill at decapitating his egg with a single swipe of his fork, the new Dauphine must have made for poor entertainment, as she had a modest appetite, and washed her simple meals down with water.

Louis XV gave his daughters - the Dauphin's aunts - affectionate nicknames: Pig, Tatters, Mite, and Rubbish. Madame Campan, Marie-Antoinette's first lady of the bedchamber, describes Sophie, aka Mite, as a person of the most unprepossessing appearance: "...she walked with the greatest rapidity; and, in order to recognise the people who placed themselves along her path without looking at them, she acquired the habit of leering on one side, like a hare."

Louise (Rubbish) moved into a Carmelite convent and became a nun.

A disinterested and gauche young husband, a licentious grandfather-in-law, four odd aunts and a strict disciplinarian guardian: what fun it must have not been.

Amongst the gilt and gloss and glitz of this museum I had difficulty in imagining it as a home, where men and women had lived and loved and schemed and dreamed and worked and died, and looked out of the same windows that we were looking out of, at the same views. What stories the walls could tell, if only ....

Contemporaneous accounts suggest that despite her youth,

the new bride could be a bit of a handful when she chose. Until her arrival, the King's powerful mistress, Madame du Barry, had been the undisputed Queen Bee at Versailles. As a commoner, and in Marie Antoinette's eyes no better than she ought to be, etiquette decreed that the du Barry could not address her until she was invited to do so. Marie-Antoinette took it into her teenage head that she would not speak to the royal favourite. Du Barry waited; the King waited, the whole court waited for the necessary invitation; the King used all his powers of persuasion in various quarters, and the du Barry all but turned herself inside out in her efforts to win her over, but Marie-Antoinette continued to ignore her. Her stubborn refusal threatened to have serious consequences far beyond the walls of Versailles, reaching into the intricacies and intrigues of Eastern European politics. As Russia, Prussia and Austria were busily dividing Poland between themselves, the Polish king was appealing to the Western European powers for help. The last thing that the Dauphine's mother, Empress Maria-Theresa of Austria needed was for the French to go to war on behalf of Poland. But the King was becoming increasingly angry and losing patience with his daughter-in-law; who knew what the repercussions might be. Maria-Theresa wrote to her daughter in such forceful terms that the girl finally agreed to bend her neck.

"There are a lot of people at Versailles today," she said, addressing the du Barry for the first and very last time. Those few words represented a victory for the King's mistress, a defeat for the Dauphine, a source of mixed delight and disappointment for the Court, according to whose side they had supported, and they sealed Poland's fate.

While the young couple were still in their teens, Louis XV contracted smallpox, and was dying a gruesome death - "the whole surface of his body coming off piecemeal and corrupted" was the unpleasantly graphic description by contemporary historian, Jean-Louis Soulavie. The King's priests would neither receive his confession nor administer the last rites as long as his mistress was living under the roof of the palace. So Madame du Barry was bundled off, and the King mercifully died, in a state of grace and decomposition. It was customary for monarchs to be embalmed, but the chief surgeon was not prepared to risk his own certain death by fiddling with the infectious remains; when ordered to do so by the First Gentleman of the King's bedchamber, the surgeon responded that he would obey if the First Gentleman would hold the royal head, as his position required him to do. The matter was dropped, and the defunct monarch quickly whisked away for burial without any of the usual pomp, leaving two mismatched adolescents the new King and Queen of France and heralding the promise of a new golden age under the reign of Louis XVI.

We arrived at Marie-Antoinette's bedroom, which is sandwiched between a dining room and a gaming room. Whether it was always so, I've no idea. Seems a bit odd. But in any case she enjoyed very little privacy, even in her own bed. Each day when she woke it was to a room full of courtiers elbowing each other aside for her attention as she performed her toilette. It was the privilege of the highest-ranking lady present to help the Queen into such items of clothing as she chose from a gold or silver tray. Should a lady of superior rank arrive during the dressing ceremony, then she would take control of the garment, while the Queen had to wait patiently for it to change hands until it reached her so that she could finish dressing. To preserve her modesty when bathing, she wore a flannel gown that enclosed her from neck to ankles; and with the same modesty she went to bed wearing beribboned corsets with lace sleeves.

There was no privacy, either, in the very depths of the intimate lives of the royal couple. Marie Antoinette had not been given to France as an ornament. Her function was to produce an heir, something that required the active participation of both parties; but Louis didn't appear to be active; or if he was, he was not effective, and no fruit was forthcoming to add to the family tree. Spiteful courtiers pointed cruel accusatory fingers at the young bride. It was plainly her fault. Despite her best efforts, and the explicit advice given to her in letters from her mother, the future Queen was still a virgin seven years after her marriage. Her sex life was public property, openly discussed by family, friends, foes, foreign ambassadors, and the ladies of the bedchamber, right down to the lowliest washerwomen. Everybody knew that the marriage had not been consummated. Differing explanations were given for this unsatisfactory situation, depending upon who was doing the explaining. Either it was a small irregularity in Louis' equipment, which needed a minor operation to enable him to function, or it was a serious disproportion between the couple that made the process too painful. Whichever it was, once things were finally working correctly, Louis confided in one of his aunts that he had discovered a source of very great pleasure, and regretted that it had taken him so long to do so. It seems somewhat unusual that a young man should discuss his sex life with a maiden aunt, but anyway, it's good to know that he enjoyed his marital obligations. We don't know whether his wife shared his enthusiasm, but she certainly did look forward to having children, and had sometimes wept in private over her inability to become a mother whilst her sisters and sisters-in-law were regularly churning out infants.

Of the crosses she had to bear, surely the Queen's domineering mother must have been one of the heaviest. During the first seven barren years of her marriage, she had not only to endure the contempt and disappointment of France, but also relentless pressure and advice from her mother, who had casually produced a litter of sixteen little Archdukes and Archduchesses. Each month, the unfortunate girl wrote to her mother, apologising that she could not give her the news she wanted. Each month, her fecund parent wrote back with admonishments and advice as to how her daughter should behave in the bedroom. Unlike her daughter, Maria Theresa was fortunate enough to have been in love with her husband, so she would not have known what it was like to have to regularly climb into bed with somebody with whom she had nothing in common, purely for the purpose of mating.

His mother-in-law strongly disapproved of Louis' preference for sleeping alone. She disapproved of him tiring himself out hunting, and prayed that bad weather would keep him indoors. She disapproved of her daughter staying up late at night gambling. And she never hesitated to express her disapproval in her endless nagging letters. Even after the birth of Marie-Antoinette's first child, a daughter, the bombardment of letters kept on coming.

"We must have a Dauphin!" wrote Maria Theresa in June 1780.

In August 1780 again she wrote: "We must have a Dauphin!"

It is an indication of the obedient and good-natured character of her daughter that she wrote to "*Madame ma très chère mère*," with never-failing courtesy and patience. A less dutiful daughter might well have written: "OK, mother. You're the expert. You come and do it."

Once her royal spouse had mastered the necessary technique, over the following eight years Marie-Antoinette became dutifully pregnant five times, and produced four live children.

By tradition, royal mothers gave birth in public, and when the Queen went into labour for the first time in December of 1778, it was in front of a huge and motley crowd who rushed into the bedroom, clambering on top of the furniture in their determination not to miss an exciting moment of the spectacle. Producing a baby whilst surrounded by such a commotion caused the Queen to develop life-threatening symptoms, and she had to be bled.

And after all that, it was only a daughter.

By an unkind stroke of fate her manipulative mother died three years later. Only thirteen months after her death, Marie-Antoinette triumphantly produced a son, the new Dauphin, who would, if things had worked out differently, have one day become Louis XVII of France. The King mentioned "my son, the Dauphin" at every opportunity, and there was jubilation throughout the land, although it was not shared by either of Louis' two younger brothers. Charles-Philippe, the Comte d'Artois, and the Comte de Provence, also confusingly named Louis, had each been rather hoping to have the crown for themselves.

Marie-Antoinette was a loving and devoted mother, set on bringing up her children sensibly, outside the rigid royal protocol. After the arrival of her first baby, she wrote to her mother:

"The way children are raised now, they are much less fussed over. They are not wrapped up the moment they can go outside, and, as they gradually become accustomed to it, they end up spending most of the time there. I think it is the best and the healthiest way to raise them. My child will stay downstairs, with a little barrier that will separate her from the rest of the terrace, where she can also learn to walk sooner than she would on the parquet floors." [1]

We shuffled on to the Hall of Mirrors, which was in the throes of restoration, but even with only half of it visible, this room sparkled. In Elisabeth Feydeau's book "The Scented Palace," she describes the weird colours that were created for fabrics during Marie-Antoinette's reign: "flea" which came in shades of young, old, belly, back and leg. Face powders bore names like "Dauphin's poo" and "Goose-shit." Beauty spots shaped like stars, crescents or hearts were used to signal the mood of the wearer depending on whereabouts they were placed, or alternatively used to cover up a "sapphire," more commonly known as a pimple. Like peacocks the men and women of the court minced around, prancing and preening themselves. Hairdressers created ever more bizarre styles: towering structures stuffed with fruits, vegetables and flowers, birds, ships, dolls, ribbons, feathers and ornaments. Hats and hairstyles became so tall that the wearers could no longer travel in their carriages without either kneeling on the floor, or having the seats lowered. People lived to show off and out-do one another, and the Hall of Mirrors provided the

---

1   Memoirs of the Private Life of Marie-Antoinette, by Madame Campan

ideal setting for them to do so and to admire themselves.

To do justice to this extravaganza of extravagance of a room, it called for men in high-heels, curly wigs and hats crowned with feathers; ladies with powdered white skin and rouged cheeks, in big dresses with their bosoms spilling out; pet monkeys and peacocks, whispers and laughs, sly looks and fluttered eyelashes; it needed liveried flunkies carrying pyramids of exotic fruits, *petits fours* and *bonnes bouches* on golden platters; hothouse plants and rival scents. It needed lapdogs and hunting dogs, swords and beauty patches, baroque music, jewelled fans, and sycophants. Today's throng of scruffy 21st century tourists wearing woolly hats, backpacks, cameras, anoraks and open mouths, and a woman in Lycra with purple hair, didn't quite work.

In the Coronation Room we relished David's enormous painting of Napoléon's coronation. The artist had captured every sour and indignant line on the face of Pope Pius as the Emperor, already crowned by his own hand, places the crown on Josephine's head. His message was clear: there is only one top dog here, and it isn't the Pope.

The Hall of Battles was exactly that: one giant canvas after another depicting victorious French generals and armies engaged in battle with their neighbours. There may well have been some French defeats shown too, but there were so many paintings, and all of them such a mêlée of limbs, weapons and animals that it was difficult to see who was winning, and our fellow visitors stood in the way of the captions that might have enlightened us.

Not everybody who had lived at Versailles had done so in comfort or elegance. Some nobles had to make do with attics, but luckily a tour of these was not included in the cost of our tickets. Neither did I want to visit any more royal apartments. After admiring four or five rooms, I had already seen enough for one day, or possibly for a lifetime. The more I saw, the more I found them oppressive and suffocating. The concept of "Less is more" had certainly not intruded into Versailles.

Ranks of busts of French notables gazed blindly down their

proud marble noses as we made our way to the exit. Terry, who loves ornate decoration and furnishings, said he thought the palace of Versailles was magnificent, and was already suggesting new decorating ideas for our house. My choice leans more towards plain white walls and functional furniture that doesn't collect dust, and although I could appreciate the craftsmanship that had gone into the palace, I was relieved to get out into the uncomplicated cold grey air and pelting rain.

By the time we had cycled back to our *chambre d'hôte* we were saturated, and blue with cold. Watching the storm lashing against the windows that rattled with every crash of thunder, I felt vindicated and justified at having baulked at the exorbitant fees charged by the local campsite, opting instead for this dry, warm room where we could soak away the misery of the weather in a good deep bath.

Swathed in grey gloom, the town of Versailles did not seem to be anything out of the ordinary, apart from the palace and its grounds. To me it felt as if, after the beleaguered royals had been frog-marched off to the capital in 1789 by the Parisian fish-wives, the town had decided that it had seen enough excitement to last for the foreseeable future, and beyond, and now wished for nothing more than to sink into obscurity, peace and quiet.

For dinner we went to a piano-bar restaurant that advertised live music. When we were quite well into our meal, and no piano player had appeared, I asked our waiter what time we could expect this to happen. Apparently we could not, as we had chosen one of the rare nights when there was no live piano, but instead taped music – Michael Jackson, Zucchero, Garou; not exactly what we were expecting, but nevertheless very much to my taste, and acceptable to Terry. Simultaneously a large television, suspended from the ceiling, with the sound turned off, was showing an old black and white documentary about the development of jazz, jive and jitterbug. Watching the one, while listening to the other, was really a rather surreal experience, with its total lack of synchronisation of movement and sound.

28

A group of eight people at a table nearby were holding a meeting of some kind, dominated by one man with a very loud voice and strong opinions which he emphasised by standing up and flailing his arms around. He was either oblivious of, or indifferent to the fact that he was in a restaurant where people were trying to enjoy a meal, and the obvious frustration of his colleagues who were cut off in mid-sentence each time one of them tried to speak. Several times they gathered together their papers and stood up as if ready to leave, but were compelled to sit down again by the sheer force of his personality. Between the sound of the music, the jerky black and white images and the loud man, the atmosphere in the piano bar was not at all what we had anticipated, but the food and service were fine. Although we had only arrived in Versailles at 3.00 pm that afternoon, it felt as if we had packed quite a lot into the last seven hours.

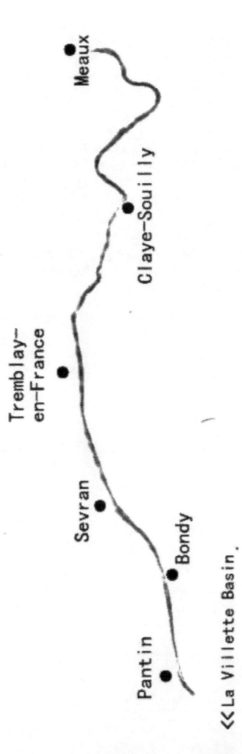

The Ourcq Canal from Pantin to Meaux

Meaux

Claye-Souilly

Tremblay-
en-France

Sevran

Bondy

Pantin

<<La Villette Basin.

CHAPTER THREE
Small is Beautiful, Less is More

"Have nothing in your houses that you do not know to be useful or believe to be beautiful."
William Morris

WE woke to brilliant sunshine, and the question of where to leave our car during our trip, which would last almost three weeks. Our hostess recommended the long-term underground car park. The manager there went to great trouble explaining the procedure for using the ticket, and the benefits it would heap upon us. He printed out an invoice, then a receipt, and then a ticket, and showed us how to put the ticket into the machine. Whether it was because we looked particularly witless, or because we were English and he suspected we might be fools too, he showed us again, just to make sure that we understood. He was absolutely charming and very handsome, and I said "You look very much like ..." but before I could finish he laughed and said: "Yes, I know, Zinedine Zidane – everybody tells me that."

While I was assuring him that we wouldn't lose the ticket, understood the repercussions if we did, and would remember how to use it, and thanking him for all his help, Terry had unearthed an exciting discovery in an underground workshop that was part of the garage: twelve Ferraris being overhauled. It isn't often you see a dozen Ferraris together. I think that for him this was probably the highlight of our visit to Versailles.

In a cheerful mood induced by the change in the weather, we packed our belongings carefully and cycled back to the park of Versailles. With our record of nearly always arriving at places when they are closed, we should not have been surprised that just as the palace was in the throes of renovation, so too were the gardens. All the ponds and fountains were empty; heavy machinery was digging up channels and laying new pipes, and there were mounds of muddy earth all over the place. There was nothing in bloom, and everything was either green, or path-coloured. We roamed around the gardens of the palace, down the side of the Grand Canal, along the endless, perfectly-hedged lanes, and through dozens of groves with their statues and empty ornamental ponds. Considering that the Sun King had enlarged his palace and herded his nobles under its roof so that he could keep his eye on them and nip in the bud any potential treachery, it seemed strange to me that there were so very many secluded places in the grounds where people so inclined could meet in secrecy. The labyrinthine layout was a perfect milieu for intrigue and clandestine encounters. If I had been in his high-heeled, beribboned shoes, I'd have had the whole place dug up and lawned so that nobody had anywhere to hide.

As a wedding gift, young Louis gave Marie-Antoinette the little palace known as Le Petit Trianon, originally built for Madame de Pompadour by Louis XV. Dignified, elegant and small enough to be homely, it became the Queen's refuge from the tiresome etiquette demanded at court. A sanctuary where she could let down her hair, kick off her shoes and entertain her friends.

Madame Campan describes in her "Memoirs of the Private Life of Marie-Antoinette," the relaxed lifestyle enjoyed at the Petit Trianon, where admission was strictly by invitation of the Queen, and where she and her close friends amused themselves with games or pastimes.

"There was but little room in the small château of Trianon. Madame Elisabeth" (the King's sister) "accompanied the Queen there, but the ladies of honour and ladies of the palace had no establishment at Trianon. When invited by the Queen, they came from Versailles to dinner. The King and Princes came regularly to sup. A white gown, a gauze kerchief, and a straw hat were the uniform dress of the Princesses."

Madame Campan continues that although the Queen was

notorious for her extravagance, this was unwarranted and she could in fact be rather stingy.

"...she amused herself with improving the gardens, without allowing any addition to the building, or any change in the furniture, which was very shabby, and remained, in 1789, in the same state as during the reign of Louis XV. Everything there, without exception, was preserved; and the Queen slept in a faded bed, which had been used by the Comtesse du Barry. The charge of extravagance, generally made against the Queen, is the most unaccountable of all the popular errors respecting her character. She had exactly the contrary failing; and I could prove that she often carried her economy to a degree of parsimony actually blameable, especially in a sovereign."

I don't know how many of the current materials in Petit Trianon are original, as the building had recently undergone extensive renovations, but as we walked up the marble steps of the staircase, I wondered whose feet had trodden there, and whose hands had touched the black and gold stair rail. Had Marie Antoinette, and later Napoléon, looked out of the same window to admire the colourful flowery gardens behind the house, just as we were doing? I put a light fingertip on a marble fireplace, in case one of them had previously touched it. *"Ne touchez pas!"* snapped an officious girl sitting in the corner on a chair. Too late, I already had.

Of Marie-Antoinette and Louis' marriage, Stefan Zweig, in his book "Marie-Antoinette – Portrait of an Average Woman" (Grove, 2002) says that despite the fact that the couple were absolute opposites in all respects, their union was a happy one. Louis was not physically attractive, nor quick-witted or extrovert, but he was well-read, courteous and kind, and paid his wife's bills. She dutifully produced four children for him, and to them he was a doting father. According to a letter written by her brother, the Emperor of Austria, she felt that after producing four children she had sufficiently fulfilled her obligations to France in the matrimonial bed and wished to be allowed to withdraw from it.

33

There has always been speculation as to whether or not Marie-Antoinette had an affair with the handsome Swedish diplomat Axel Fersen. She had long been accused by her enemies of infidelity, lesbianism and all manner of depravity; she might as well have been hung for a sheep as a lamb. Whether or not their relationship was more than platonic we will probably never know. We do know though, from letters that remain, that they were in love, but beyond that there is only conjecture. Madame Campan, like the loyal servant she was, never mentions their relationship. It doesn't seem that Louis was unduly disturbed by her retreat from his bed, and there is no record of him ever having any sort of involvement with another woman. I hope that the Queen did enjoy some boudoir pleasures with Fersen, in recompense for her dutiful coupling with Louis, so that she had at least some sweet memories during her future ordeal. That's what was going through my mind as we stood in the bedroom, looking at the exquisite, very small bed.

Originally the Petit Trianon garden comprised formal flowerbeds and massive, expensive hot houses where exotic plants and fruits grew. Under Marie-Antoinette's ownership up, down and out these were ripped, to be replaced with a bucolic landscape of a wiggling stream, lakes, waterfalls and grottoes, arbours and follies, meadows of wild flowers and beautiful specimen trees; a transformation to the simplicity which she craved but which, ironically, was only achieved at scandalous expense.

We followed a pathway towards the Queen's little hamlet, past a very ordinary tortoiseshell cat with a red collar curled up beneath a shrub, watching us through slitted eyes with a rather smug expression that clearly said: "Tourists."

Whilst we were walking around the quaint collection of timbered, thatched cottages where the Queen used to entertain herself pretending to be a milkmaid or shepherdess, a group of 6-year-old French schoolgirls surrounded Terry, jumping about and asking him questions in fractured English. He hadn't very much idea what they were saying, and they could barely understand a word he said, so each exchange sent them into an eruption of giggles. When their teachers ushered them away, they queued up to kiss Terry's cheek, then skipped away, stopping once or twice to wave at him, leaving him flattered and quite bemused. French children can be so enchanting.

In June of 1787 the royal parents lost their youngest child, baby Sophie-Beatrix, just before her first birthday. Almost exactly two years later they were mourning the death from tuberculosis of their eldest son, the seven-year-old Dauphin Louis-Joseph, frail, crippled and deformed. In her private letters, Marie-Antoinette expressed her hopes and fears for the ailing child. He was a little better, the fever had left him. Maybe it was only teething that was making him so ill. The physicians were worried again. The little boy had been moved to the château at Meudon, where his father, as a sickly child, had profited from the cleaner air – and just look what a strapping chap he had become. Louis-Joseph seems much improved. He is giving cause for alarm. The physicians don't believe he will last the night, but he rallies. The next day the little boy they had tried for so long to produce, and of whom they were so proud, dies.

Maybe the couple were so wrapped in grief that they failed to recognise the gravity of the situation as the political crisis that had long been brewing in France neared its zenith. Maybe that's why Louis hunted and Marie-Antoinette played at being a peasant in her twee hamlet. But all the while she was living her rural idyll, or treading the boards in her private theatre, and Louis was galloping around killing wildlife, the common people of France were getting increasingly hungry, and very angry. They stormed the Bastille. But in the palace of Versailles, nobody took much notice.

Nineteen years after Marie Antoinette's triumphant arrival to marry the Dauphin, a furious and vicious mob of knife-wielding harridans, several thousand strong, surrounded the royal family and those faithful friends who had remained with them at Versailles, and forcibly marched them off to Paris. The

King and Queen would not see Versailles ever again.

The morning was drifting away. We had to cycle to Paris that afternoon, so we began making our way back through the gardens to the chambre d'hôte to collect our luggage. As we passed the lake a shoal of carp, each large enough to make a meal for six people, surged through the water towards us and poked their heads up, opening and closing their mouths silently, plainly saying "Feed us." They followed us hopefully around the edge of the water, until they spotted some more people arriving, and splashed away to try their chances with them.

We stopped in one of the glades at a place selling drinks and fast-food snacks, and ordered a couple of coffees from a softly-spoken, smiling black man. While he was preparing them, an American customer came up to the counter and queried his bill – he thought he'd been overcharged. The black man listened politely, opened and checked the till, apologised to the customer and handed him a few coins. A swarthy man in a camouflage jacket, matching trousers tucked into black boots, and very dark glasses appeared from behind some shelves, and harangued the black man loudly. Although we were embarrassed, the man himself seemed quite composed and after a few minutes wandered off to chat to another swarthy person also dressed in para-military clothing. When we stood up to leave, that person yelled "Oi!" and pointed at the two plastic cups we had left on the table, and told us rudely to put them into the bin. He could have taken four steps and put them there himself, if he unglued himself from the wall against which he was lolling. Giving Terry an order is tantamount to tweaking Mike Tyson's nose and asking him what he's going to do about it. Before he had time to react, I picked up the cups and threw them into the bin: the swarthy man looked as if he was hoping for an excuse to pull out an Uzi and blow us away.

It left us wondering whether visitors to Versailles deserved mediocre refreshments from an enterprise that appeared to be run by some sort of Eastern European mafia who were rude to their staff and customers. Do pizza and Coke and plastic cups fit into the fabled sophistication of the place? Should there not be *tisanes*, *infusions*, hot chocolate and delicate savouries and pastries served by demure French wenches in Bo-Peep costumes, or deferential flunkeys in frogged livery?

By early afternoon we'd seen as much as we wanted, and the weather looked to be deteriorating, so after loading our bikes we had set off on the hair-raising ride to our hotel in Paris. I doubted that Marie-Antoinette could have been more terrified on her final journey from Versailles to the capital than I was on this, my first.

CHAPTER FOUR
The City of Blood

"If slaughterhouses had glass walls, everyone would be a vegetarian."
Sir Paul McCartney

THE next morning we were still asleep when the orange bedroom of our hotel was rocked by a mild tremor accompanied by sinister grinding and clanking noises, as if a battalion of tanks was surrounding the area. Terry drew back the curtains in time to see the earth-moving bucket gliding past our balcony. The road-diggers were back at work. Above the neighbouring rooftops the sky was decked with ominous grey clouds. I retreated beneath the covers. Terry was already dressing, anxious to be on the move.

With less enthusiasm than I should have felt, I squished into the Lycra cycling clothes. Photographs of cyclists generally show bronzed limbs, sculpted bodies and shiny, vibrantly-coloured clothing. When we bought our equipment for the journey, I had imagined that I would look like that, but six months of winter had left my face and limbs pasty-white, and six months of warming winter food had expanded my waistline beyond anything it had ever achieved before. The vibrantly-coloured garments clung cruelly, and emphasized every bulge. The gusset of our shorts and trousers were equipped with the thick pad of some sort of foam and called a "chamois," designed to ease the pressure on the most delicate area of the cyclist's anatomy. It was like wearing a sanitary towel, and reminded me of matron's weekly visit to the dormitory at boarding school, when she stood in the doorway with a large packet under her arm, heedless of any embarrassment she might be causing pubescent girls, shouting: "Who needs some bunnies' ears?"

Worst of all, though, was my disastrous hair, the outcome

of the hairdresser having an off day, coupled with a last-minute home colouring that had gone terribly wrong. The "golden copper" had turned out a violent shade of beetroot, and given my hair the texture of medium grain wire wool. The whole ensemble, from top of head to sole of foot, was utterly catastrophic. I believed that a crash helmet was vital, as I expected to fall off onto my head frequently; a friend had warned, however, that if I did, the helmet would not only fail to protect my skull, but its straps would snap my neck. Still, I wore it anyway. Flowing garments in large prints, and a wide-brimmed floppy hat would have been kinder to my image, but impractical. High-tech fabrics, although they don't come in large prints, are light-weight and quick-drying, and somehow manage to be warm when it's cold, and cool when it's hot. Magic, really. They also, according to their explanatory labels, "wick away moisture" to keep the wearer dry. I don't know what happens to the moisture, but I imagined tiny clouds of it following us across France.

As we went down to the cellar for breakfast we passed Ben in the reception area, back on duty again, and talking on the phone. He gave us a thumbs-up sign and pointed to a narrow iron grill like a portcullis at the foot of the stairs. It required a hefty shove to push it open, and the staircase continued down and into what was more of a dungeon than a cellar. A display of vicious medieval weaponry and a full suit of armour occupied one wall. The low vaulted ceilings and walls were of attractive dressed stone, but I had to fight back the desire to rush up the stairs, past the portcullis and into the daylight. A woman at the table behind us accentuated the dungeon-like environment. As thin as a rake, damn her, with a deathly white complexion, her elbow-length hair was straight and jet black. Long fingernails varnished black, with little silver stars on them; a long, thin black dress. Narrow, pointy-toed black shoes with long, thin heels. Masses of heavy black eye make-up. It was Morticia Adams in the slender flesh. Incongruously, her partner wore jeans, a checked shirt, high-heeled cowboy boots and a blonde forked beard. He looked like a latterday

General Custer. They could have been going to a fancy-dress party, except that it was 8.00 am, and they were studying a map of the Metro and discussing the places they were going to visit that day in Paris.

All of the other guests in the dungeon were Japanese, and they were all eating Japanese Pot Noodles.

We discussed our plans for the day. We'd cycle a couple of kilometres up the road to the La Villette basin. From there on we'd be on towpaths. We'd stop for lunch somewhere along the way, and spend the night camping at Meaux. A distance of about 50 kilometres in all.

We lugged our panniers and paraphernalia down the stairs, and Ben, after making us promise that we would take great care, and have a very good time, phoned the Comte de Paris, who arrived again in his carpet slippers and took us back to collect our bikes. By 9.00 am the skies had cleared from dreary grey to watery blue, but Bertrand wasn't convinced.

"If you were going south, or west, you'd be fine. But east – the forecast isn't very good. You may get wet," he said gloomily. "And it will be very cold at night."

"We'll be fine," I laughed. "We've nice warm sleeping bags." I patted them where they were strapped onto the baking tray. Bertrand shrugged, shook our hands, and stood watching as we pushed away from the pavement. He raised a hand in the air when I looked back, but I needed both of mine on the handlebars, so I waved to him by waggling my elbows up and down, like an ungainly bird struggling to take off.

Terry led the way along the Rue Lafayette with élan. I followed more cautiously. Although we had hit the morning rush hour, we managed to avoid any noteworthy incidents, apart from when Terry shouted at me to follow him past a traffic light that was turning red. In consequence I found myself surrounded by hostile, hooting traffic and whistling, hissing drivers. I had to climb off and trudge, mortified, weaving the bike through angry vehicles.

Very soon, though, we reached the new chic Bohemian area for artists and musicians. Centred around the Place de la

Bataille de Stalingrad and the Villette Basin, it's where three canals – the St Denis, the St Martin, and the Ourcq converge. We cycled beside the Ourcq canal along a tree-lined quay, past apartment blocks and moored leisure craft. A few walkers hunched against the cold nodded as we bounced by on the cobbles. From the City of Music and the French National Conservatory of Music on the opposite bank stray notes danced in the air and floated across the water, and a group of black-clad people practised the exaggeratedly slow movements of Tai Chi on a lawn. Small clouds in a sky of bright blue reflected from the metallic surface of the stunningly beautiful hemispherical Géode, which houses the Cité des Sciences.

A dredger chugged slowly past La Villette's leisure park, the largest green area in Paris, made up of a number of themed gardens and futuristic sculptures, and you either love it, or hate it.

I hated it, not for what it is now, but for what it had been until almost 50 years ago, when it was known as the City of Blood. It was here that the nine individual slaughterhouses which had until then served Paris were united into a centralised abattoir; for more than a hundred years, every year, two million animals arrived here by train at the market halls, and went from there directly to slaughter. The thought of the smells, the sounds, the sights and the mess that would have engulfed this area turned my stomach. In the latter part of the 19th century, Parisians even came here to drink blood as it was drained from the animals, in the belief that it served as a tonic.

It may be impossible for carnivores to appreciate quite how vegetarians feel about the whole process that brings meat to the plate, so I won't try to explain it. But I firmly believe that there will come a day, if the world lasts long enough, when people will look back on the killing of animals for food with disbelief and horror, on a par with cannibalism. Leonardo da Vinci said much the same thing 500 years ago. Pope John Paul II addressed the age-old argument as to whether or not

41

animals have a soul in 1990, when he declared that "animals possess a soul and men must love and feel solidarity with our smaller brethren." As far as I know, nobody has ever seen a soul, so there isn't any proof that any of us have one, but what I know for certain is that animals are capable of a variety of emotions, including fear and pain, which was in abundance here for decades. No amount of buildings, nor grass, nor benches, nor flowerbeds, nor entertainments can extinguish that for me, and I was anxious to cycle out of this area as fast as we possibly could. I hadn't even mentioned to Terry the history of La Villette, because I was quite sure he would have refused to cycle through it.

It should not be difficult to follow a canal, which is a big thing. But somehow we managed to lose it, possibly due to the cement factory that swallowed up the towpath and diverted us onto a small lane, which issued into a busy road in the midst of the bustling industrial suburb of Pantin. The largest cemetery in Paris is here, the final residence of a million dead people, among them a very much larger than life character called Jules Védrines. A pioneering aviator with a fierce expression and imposing moustache, he was the winner – in fact the only finisher - of the first Paris to Madrid air race in 1911, an event which got off to an unfortunate start when one spectator, the then French Minister of War, walked into a propeller and cut himself into slices. During the war Védrines flew secret agents to and from behind German lines, and in 1919 he thrilled Paris by landing his Caudron G3 biplane on the rooftop of the Galeries Lafayette. Sadly his luck ran out a few months later when he crashed and died on a flight to Rome, leaving him permanently grounded in Pantin.

Through the noisy, cosmopolitan streets, fragrant with spices and populated by colourfully-costumed people and honking traffic, we wove our way back to the canal, and crossed over a bridge to Bondy, an extensive no-go area of bandit-ridden forest until the end of the 19th century, when wealthier Parisians began moving there in search of cleaner country air.

With the development of train and tram links to the capital Bondy became a popular suburb, attracting more residents, and immigrants – firstly other Europeans, and later North Africans seeking higher wages and a better life than in their own countries. Bondy had achieved notoriety in the autumn of 2006 when the predominantly immigrant residents rioted for several days to express their disappointment that the Republican ideals of liberty, fraternity and equality did not seem to have extended to the banlieus. The then Interior Minister, Nicolas Sarkozy referring to the rioters as *racaille* – scum, hadn't done much to defuse the situation.

Before the arrival of motor transport, for anybody travelling east from Paris, Bondy was the first staging post where coaches halted for a change of horses. In the early hours of the morning on 21st June 1791 an enormous, lumbering carriage arrived at Bondy, where it was harnessed to a fresh team of horses. Aboard were "Madame de Korff," accompanied by her two daughters, their governess "Madame Rochet," and steward "M. Durand." In reality, the passengers were Marie-Antoinette and Louis, their children – the Dauphin dressed as a little girl - and the King's sister, Elizabeth. All in disguise, they were fleeing from the capital in the hope of reaching safety and the support of a loyal army at Montmédy, close to the Belgian border.

When you read about their escape plans, that they had even managed to reach this far seems miraculous.

After their violent removal from Versailles, the royal family were installed in Tuileries palace in Paris. Their captors did their best to make this dismal and dilapidated building fitting and comfortable for its new residents. Luxurious furnishings were brought from Versailles, and there was a substantial household of servants. Away from the rigid formality of court, the royal family made the most of their changed circumstances and were able to enjoy a more relaxed lifestyle.

Among the works of art brought from Versailles was a painting by Van Dyck of the English king, Charles I. It should have served as an ominous reminder to Louis that a crown offered no protection against a sharpened blade travelling at high speed towards the back of the neck, and that it might be a sensible idea to take heed of urgent warnings from those with more foresight than him, and to disappear while he still could. Sadly he did not seem to pick up this message.

He and his queen took their meals together and spent time with their two surviving children. They entertained those loyal friends who had chosen to remain with them at the Tuileries, amused themselves playing billiards, and were able to travel when they wished to the royal residence at St Cloud where the King hunted. If he had taken the prudent advice of well-wishers and people more astute than himself, he could have made a successful escape from there. Plans were made for the Queen and their children to flee in light, fast carriages, and the King to join them on horseback. But Louis didn't act. It would have been quite out of character for him to do anything decisive while there was still time to do so. Better sit tight, make the best of your situation, and see if things improved in time. In the meantime – tally ho!

For eighteen months life continued uneventfully for the residents of the Tuileries, but as the Revolutionary movement gained momentum the family's liberty became increasingly restricted. By the time they realized the extent of their peril, they had become closely-guarded prisoners. When they were physically prevented from travelling to St Cloud on Easter Monday of 1791 the King finally recognized that the only way they were going to achieve freedom was by their own efforts, and he left it to his wife to make the arrangements for their escape. She did this with the help of her devoted admirer, Axel Fersen. It was he who raised the necessary finance for the operation through personal loans and by mortgaging his own property; who negotiated with those who supported the royals, and smuggled correspondence to and from them past watchful guards.

The plan was for the family to escape from the Tuileries by night and flee to Montmédy. The fugitives would need disguises; Fersen smuggled these to them piece by piece.

When it came to the question of transport, Marie-Antoinette demonstrated her blondeness by spurning the suggestion of a light, fast vehicle; it would be both undignified and uncomfortable for such a long journey as they were undertaking. Instead she insisted on a stately carriage, the building of which was organised by the faithful Fersen. This vehicle, described by Stefan Zweig as "a sort of little warship on four wheels," was equipped with a well-stocked wine cellar, a silver dinner service, a clothes press, a cupboard full of food and a portable toilet. Beautifully upholstered and splendidly painted, it could not fail to attract attention. The royal retinue included the children's governess and the Queen's hairdresser, that creator of creations, Monsieur Léonard, who in the event contributed nothing apart from confusion to the whole project. Although it sounds as if he was something of a buffoon, it was essential for Marie-Antoinette to believe that she would reach freedom, and when she did so she did not intend to arrive looking a wreck. For the same reason, she had entrusted Madame Campan with the job of ordering a wardrobe of fine clothes for her arrival in Belgium, and these were also stowed in trunks in the carriage.

To escape from the Tuileries the King had to creep out of his bedroom without disturbing his valet, who slept attached to his royal master by a string tied to his wrist. Louis' sister Elisabeth, Marie-Antoinette and the two children had to be spirited out of the Tuileries without being seen by the National Guard; and they had to cross Paris unnoticed. After months of meticulous planning, they had to change the date for the escape at the last minute because the Queen was suspicious about the loyalty of one of her ladies of the bedchamber. Finally the time arrived for them to make their move.

Valuable time was lost in Paris due to various misunderstandings and wrong turnings being taken, so that by the time the royal entourage arrived at Bondy they were already two and a half hours behind schedule, but at least they were now clear of the city. Fersen would travel on ahead and wait for them in Montmédy. With the first and most difficult part of their escape plan behind them, they must have been feeling optimistic at this point.

During the next 24 hours Louis, Marie-Antoinette and their children were out of the public eye for the first and last time in their lives. Travelling as they were, incognito, secretly, urgently, the details of this part of their journey are very slim, and the only eye-witness account is found in the memoirs of the King and Queen's daughter, the Princess Marie-Thérèse, thirteen at the time, and the sole member of the immediate family who would survive the Revolution. Not until Varennes, more than 200 kilometres to the east, would they become public property again.

Ten minutes from Bondy the noise of traffic changed to birdsong, and the busy suburbs to fields of wild flowers. Apart from bridges spanning the canal, when the towpath climbed steeply up and down the embankments, the landscape had a timeless appearance. It had probably looked much the same when the royal runaways lumbered past here in their unsuitable carriage while Louis traced their route on a map. Their journey was giving him an opportunity to see something of the realm over which he had reigned so unsatisfactorily for seventeen years.

It was by design, not accident, that the majority of places we would visit were at intervals of about 30 kilometres from each other, as they had started life as staging posts along the road, the distance that a team of horses could be expected to travel before they needed to be changed. In contrast to the previous day, our cycling was effortless and peaceful and we were really enjoying ourselves by the time we reached the neat and quiet town of Claye-Souilly, the second staging post on the route from Paris.

Here Louis took advantage of the halt to round off his breakfast with a nice piece of Brie while a new team of horses was harnessed to their carriage.

By the time we arrived at 2.00 pm it was too late for a seat at the first two restaurants, but in the third the very kind lady said that although they were closed, she could see we were cold, tired and hungry, and she'd be happy to cook something for us as long as we didn't want anything fancy. She had two nice pieces of fish left if that would suit us. Although we are vegetarians, we do sometimes eat a little fish, so that was fine. There was nowhere in sight where we could safely leave our bikes, and as this would be our first experience of being separated from them without them being under lock and key, Terry was anxious. Our hostess suggested that we should park them on the narrow pavement outside the restaurant. This meant that every passing pedestrian had to step around them and into the road.

Opposite the restaurant was a small supermarket, where a delivery vehicle was parked outside unloading stacks of cartons. For twenty-five minutes, in an unhurried manner, the driver climbed onto the tailgate, pushed a button which raised him up, loaded cartons into a wire trolley, pushed the button to go down, wheeled the trolley to the door of the shop, unloaded it, wheeled it back, onto the tailgate, up ..... Unable to squeeze past the wide van, traffic built up. Drivers switched off their engines. Up and in and out and down went the unloading man, until the pavement was entirely blocked with cartons. Pedestrians were forced into the road on that side, too. It reminded me of a M. Hulot film. People leaned out of windows to watch. The Clayois seemed to be very tolerant folk and nobody showed the least sign of impatience or irritation.

During the First World War, Claye-Souilly was home to an American veterinary hospital. Vast numbers of equines were engaged in the war effort, and each of the armies had to provide treatment facilities for the horses, mules and camels whose misfortune it was to find themselves a part of the conflict. At one time animals wounded in battle would either have been destroyed or retired, but such was the scale of the Great War that every beast was a valuable commodity that had to be patched up and returned to the field to be used and used again until there was no use left in it. Statistics showed

47

that during the four years of the war, on average each equine in the French army would have been ill or injured seven times, and the mortality rate was 80%. If the appalling conditions suffered by the men makes harrowing reading, it doesn't come anywhere near to the nightmare existence of those animals requisitioned, or imported in their tens of thousands from North Africa and the United States, whose suffering was beyond description. With mechanised warfare still in its infancy, horses were needed in huge numbers as cavalry mounts or to haul artillery and machinery. Like the men alongside them, they shared the mud, mustard gas, mange, artillery wounds, fear, deprivation of food and water. The upper lips of mules were mutilated to prevent them from making a noise. Scabies and glanders (a highly infectious respiratory disease) were rife. Considering the logistical difficulties of supplying rations to the animals – the daily ration per horse was defined as 7 kg. of oats and 6 kg. of hay, plus 20 litres of water - it isn't surprising that they were quickly reduced to skeletons.

Ironically those animals unable to make it to the hospitals for treatment under their own steam were taken by motorised equine ambulances that collected and transported them from the battlefield. There was no anaesthesia for the patients. Those considered untreatable, or unfit for action, were sold for meat. Those that died of their injuries on the field were injected with a serum to prevent decay, and sold to dealers. When the war ended, the animals who had survived were sold off as meat or for labour. That was the fate of the equine slaves in the First World War. Their suffering added to that of the men beside them who witnessed their misery. I learned a great deal more than I wanted to know about an aspect of the war that I had not previously considered.

We'd have been happy to stay in Claye-Souilly overnight, but there was no campsite so we had to push on to Meaux for the night. Strangely, although we cycled for several hours through the lush, flowery pastures, trees and water that is the ancient Brie region, home to the King of Cheeses, we saw not a single cow all day long.

Just as the Comte de Paris had suspected, the rain caught us by mid-afternoon, and we were very wet by the time we reached the outskirts of Meaux. If cycling around the Arc de Triomphe had seemed daunting, it was nothing compared to Meaux at 5.00 pm on this sodden Friday evening. We found ourselves unwittingly, also unwillingly, swept into the frenzied excitement of motorists on the way in and out of the town at the start of the Pentecostal weekend. We were carried along by the traffic on a tide of bedlam, aggravated because we had no idea in which direction lay the campsite.

There was a man standing beside a pile of old furniture on the pavement and Terry shouted at me to GO AND ASK HIM, so I did, only realising just as I opened my mouth that it would be a fruitless venture, because he was plainly either drunk or the victim of some neurological disorder. His eyes were unfocussed and uncoordinated; like a chameleon, he seemed able to point them simultaneously in different directions, independent of each other. I said very slowly, and clearly, that we were looking for "*le camping*," and he interpreted this as an invitation to recite the story of his life in Meaux, detailing all the different addresses he had lived at over three decades, and the reason he had had to keep moving. Terry was very irritable, because he was getting hungry. Clearly the chameleon-eyed man was never going to tell us where the campsite was, but it seemed rude and uncaring not to listen to his tale of woe. Terry climbed onto his bike and rode away, shouting something over his shoulder, and leaving me listening to an episode that was something to do with a neighbour and cats.

A young man walked past and I latched on to him. He said that the nearest campsite to Meaux was a few kilometres down the road at Le Trilport. There was a choice of routes to get there – either through the traffic-ridden town centre, or by a longer but quieter route that he strongly recommended. Terry, reappearing from the opposite direction, irrationally tried to insist we cycled through the town. We had a furious row on the pavement, which I won by playing my trump card - a fit of hysterics - before pedalling off along the longer-but-quieter route to the site. By the time we reached there, instead of the fifty kilometres we had estimated for the day's journey, our cycling computers showed we'd covered seventy.

The *gardienne* at the campsite asked for our passports, and locked them firmly in a drawer. She had no change for the note we offered in payment of the camping fees. I suggested she kept the note, and gave us the change the following morning, but no, this wasn't possible: we would have to bring her the exact amount in the morning before we left. There was absolutely no other way. In the meantime, she said sternly, she would have to trust us not to leave without paying. She repeated this four times. I thanked her four times, and pointed out that with our passports locked in her drawer, her trust was unlikely to be misplaced.

As campsites go, it was just about adequate (despite an alarming claim on the website that the place benefited from "running water, sewage and electricity …") We pitched our tent, and Terry cycled up the road to where the *gardienne* had said, with a grimace, that there was a shop that stayed open late "because they are Arabs," her tone leaving no doubt that she didn't approve of other races.

Terry returned with a strange and mountainous assortment. Because most of the food in the shop was meat, and as we had no cooking facilities anyway, he had bought four kilos of various fruits and two large bars of chocolate. We crouched in the tent sheltering from the continuing rain, peeling, munching, and spitting out pips, before I changed into my nice new satin shortie pyjamas, and we settled down for what was one of the most miserable nights of my life.

When we had put up the borrowed tent in our garden, it had seemed large enough for two, but that was without the self-inflating mattress and all our bags and bundles. With these inside, there was almost no room for ourselves and our wet waterproofs. We were squashed together in damp steaminess. In the foolish belief that the nights would be quite

50

mild at this time of year, instead of bringing bulky sleeping bags I'd just brought along the thermal liners. We were both desperately cold. It is most unusual for Terry to be cold; at home I often have to shout at him to close the doors in the depths of winter, because he will happily leave the front door, back door and patio doors wide open all day long, in gale, hail, rain and wind.

After we'd shivered for an hour we writhed with great difficulty, in the limited space and pitch darkness, back into all our cycling clothes. Then we spread over ourselves an aluminium survival blanket, and over that our wet waterproof coats. The whole lot slithered about noisily every time we moved without noticeably adding any warmth, and our faces occasionally brushed against the damp and clammy walls of the tent.

There was continual noise from aircraft, trains, cars, roaring motorbikes and barking dogs. A family with several little whimpering children arrived after midnight and spent what seemed like hours pumping up inflatable mattresses, sounding like a convention of the chronically asthmatic. I lay awake for most of the night, shaking with cold, trying not to rustle and plotting how I could force Terry to buy a decent tent and some warmer bedding, because I couldn't survive another night like this.

CHAPTER FIVE
Cheese and Millstones

"Only peril can bring the French together. One can't impose unity out of the blue on a country that has 265 different kinds of cheese."
General Charles de Gaulle

WE awoke enveloped in a glowing yellow aura, to the sound of somebody beating a carpet. Digging our way out from beneath our damp and tangled heap of covers, we poked our heads through the tent's small entrance. The yellow glow was deceptive, simply an illusion created by the bright-coloured fabric of the tent; the skies were still grey, and it was drizzling. The carpet-beating noise was coming from two pigeons attempting to mate on the branch of a nearby conifer. They were attempting to mate at the extreme end of a branch far too feeble to bear their combined weight. Each time pigeon number one leapt upon pigeon number two, the branch dipped almost to the ground and sprung back up, launching them both into the air like missiles from a catapult and sending them into paroxysms of frantic wing beating. They appeared incapable of understanding why this was happening. Instead of finding a more robust branch, or even moving away from the tip, they just kept on trying and failing with much panicky wing-flapping. Obviously novices with much to learn before they would hear the flutter of tiny wings.

Our options were either to squat uncomfortably in the pokey tent, eating more fruit and chocolate, or to strike camp and cycle in the drizzle to find a hot drink and breakfast. While I curled myself into as small a heap as possible, Terry dressed; then he dismantled the tent around me while I contorted myself into clean clothes. With the change from last night's shopping we settled our camping fees to the satisfaction of the *gardienne* and retrieved our passports, then headed back to Meaux for breakfast.

En route, we passed a supermarket where they were most fortuitously selling large tents. Terry didn't need any persuading after the horrible night we had spent, and our new purchase was soon strapped to the baking tray. A few hundred metres further along the road destiny had planted a sports shop, where we added a thick polar blanket to our growing pile of equipment.

With twenty kilos in his panniers and five kilos in a backpack, Terry was already well loaded. He had fixed the baking tin to my bike rack, I should explain, to make a stable, lightweight support for the things I was carrying – the tent (two tents now), which were far wider than the handlebars, and the sleeping bags, none of which would have fitted into panniers. Plus our toiletries and a couple of books, whose combined weight was twelve kilos. On my handlebars was a wire basket holding maps and various small items that we might need along the way.

Still uncertain if it was safe to leave the bikes unattended, we sat beside them outside a café in the cold damp morning; my machine attracted a crowd of people who were interested to know how it worked, how fast it went, how much it cost, how far it would go and how the battery was recharged. The few "proper" cyclists, with their streamlined clothing, state of the art helmets and person-powered machines weren't impressed, unlike the old boys and a few elderly ladies with venerable heavy, black-framed bicycles, who looked longingly at my springy, cushioned saddle, array of gears and large battery.

Gradually the drizzle fizzled out, and after our restless night we were content to just sit for a while watching the world and enjoying coffee and croissants, then wandering around for a little window-shopping, or, as the French say, window-licking. You could smell the cheese emporium at the lower end of Meaux's pedestrian zone long before you reached it, and the whiff was both nauseating and irresistible. On the upper shelves English Cheddars rubbed rinds with

Stilton, Wensleydale and Double Gloucester; beside them Italian Mozzarella, Taleggio, Pecorino, Ricotta, Gorgonzola and Grana Padano looked down upon colonies of Dutch cheeses and Spanish cheeses, Danish cheeses and German cheeses. White, yellow, red, gold, mouldy-green, blue-veined, brown, firm, creamy, pyramids, cubes, cylinders, truckles, wheels and wedges, flavoured with cumin seeds, paprika, walnuts; cheeses coated in ash, dipped in nuts, wrapped in leaves or straw, dusty, gooey, smooth, wrinkled, they sat, sweated or oozed on shelves and counters. Of the innumerable French cheeses, some were familiar but many were unknown. The place smelt like a shoe-locker might if all the runners had tossed their old trainers in there at the end of a Marathon. You could sample a different cheese here every day for a year and still not have tasted them all.

In 1814, after decades of warfare and political turmoil in Europe, the Congress of Vienna met to redraw borders and restore order to the fractured continent. During this protracted event lasting many months, to enliven and lighten the proceedings, the French foreign minister, Talleyrand, proposed a competition between participating nations to find the best cheese. He was justifiably confident that his country's nomination would trounce the English Cheddar, Italian Gorgonzola, Dutch Edam and Swiss Emmental cheese, as indeed it did. Brie was proclaimed by the members of the Congress "the cheese of kings and king of cheeses."

Personally I think there are many other cheeses equally worthy of the crown, but with such an overwhelming choice, and given that we were in Meaux, home of the very finest Brie, we bought a weeping chunk, reverently wrapped in waxed paper, and a smaller lump of the notorious Black Brie, which I have heard described as the most utterly disgusting cheese in the world. Lengthy maturation gives this horror a brown and leathery rind, a tough chewy interior, and a bitter taste; aficionados dip it into milky coffee for maximum enjoyment. We couldn't resist buying some, out of curiosity, as we are both fairly adventurous when it comes to culinary experimentation.

The shop also sold stone pots of Meaux mustard, which the Benedictine nuns from nearby La Ferté-sous-Jouarre developed during the Middle Ages to mask the taste of tainted foodstuffs; but we had no need of unnecessary weight to carry, nor expectation of having to eat any tainted food, so we gave the mustard a miss.

A short walk up the pedestrian street leads to Meaux's Gothic cathedral, and the adjacent Bossuet gardens, mitre-shaped in keeping with their Episcopal ancestry. In pallid sunshine we picnicked on the Brie smeared onto a couple of crispy *ficelles*, throwing crumbs to a couple of timid kittens, and watching groups of students sprawled on the grass planning how to rule the world. Disappointingly, the Brie Noir was not nearly as horrible as we had hoped. That's not to say it was nice: it was not, but it was no worse than a very old Cheddar that might have been found stuffed down the back of a seat on a bus. We baulked at dipping it into coffee, though. After all, we wanted to experience it at its very worst; and we didn't want to spoil a good cup of coffee.

Terry stayed outside with the bikes while I explored Meaux's cathedral of St Etienne. The exterior showed considerable signs of distress. On the southern side, amongst gargoyled turrets, stood a row of ten saints, or apostles. They were all headless, a result of having been decapitated during the War of Religion between Catholics and Huguenots. I wondered how angry people must have been to break off ten life-sized stone heads, because it must have required a fair amount of energy.

For a relatively small town such as Meaux, the cathedral of St Etienne seems disproportionately splendid. The vaulted ceilings are very high; the columns supporting them are very slender; the stone is very white, the light very clear. There was a pervading and not unpleasant smell of bleach. Somebody was tinkling on the organ, sending haunting, delicate notes fluttering into the air. Instead of the usual sombre paintings depicting the fourteen Stations of the Cross, simple crosses cut

55

out of purple paper were stuck to the walls, marked with Roman numerals and titles. Number XIII bore the legend: "Jesus is taken down from the cross." An irreverent wag had written beneath: "He'll be back in five minutes."

Towards the rear of the church is a vast marble statue of The Eagle of Meaux, Jacques-Bénigne Bossuet, 17th century bishop, orator, statesman and writer. A notice explains that when the statue was delivered in 1911 it was originally destined to stand outside the church. Almost one hundred years later, it's still in the same place it was put temporarily. That is no great surprise, because it must weigh at least 20 tons, and how it was ever brought inside in the first place is a minor miracle.

During WWI, Meaux had its own angel, Monsignor Marbeau, the city's 70-year-old bishop. In September 1914 the German army was advancing rapidly towards Paris, driving back the exhausted French and British troops. With the enemy only a day away from Meaux, the town was expected to fall imminently. When news spread that the last trains were leaving, anybody with the necessary means fled, including all the local dignitaries. They left the town virtually deserted, doors and shutters closed, gas and water supplies ruptured, and bridges blown up to impede the German advance.

They also left behind some two thousand helpless women, children and wounded soldiers, all in need of food, medical attention, shelter, organisation and moral support. With no civic structure to look after them, it was the bishop, with a few helpers, who formed the "Committee of Public Interest" to care for these vulnerable people. The bishop summoned doctors and nurses, medicines and precious tobacco from Paris for the streams of wounded arriving hourly, and the committee requisitioned supplies of meat, vegetables, bread and milk to ensure that everybody was fed. They organised the cleaning of the streets, the putting to sleep of stray, starving and distressed animals, and the evacuation of the wounded.

Some of the wounded went by barge or wash boat to Lagny on the eastern outskirts of Paris; others by the newly-formed

Field Service of the American Ambulance, one of the three volunteer American ambulance services set up at the outbreak of war. With the bodies of their Ford ambulances made from packing crates, their very first mission was to rescue the wounded from Meaux and take them to the American hospital at Neuilly, in the charge of the admirable Mrs William K Vanderbilt, who "wore the white Red Cross uniform. Half concealed about her neck was a double string of pearls. Rose-coloured silk stockings were tipped with neat but serviceable white shoes, and in this attire she seemed to impersonate the presiding "good angel" of the hospital." [2]

In her book "*Le mouvement perpétuel, histoire de l'Hôpital Américain de Paris 1906-1989,*" Nicole Fouché described the pitiful condition of wounded soldiers of the African Rifles. In a foreign country, whose language they did not understand, maimed and traumatised they waited helplessly to be rescued and cared for. Many of them would die in the ambulances taking them from Meaux to Paris for medical treatment.

As well as taking under his Episcopal wing Meaux's needy citizens, Mgr Marbeau organised trucks to go daily to the front line, loaded with those items that would bring a little comfort to the troops there – pipes and tobacco, clean linen and clothing, blankets. He maintained the morale of his flock, drove around the surrounding area searching for wounded, and blessing the dead who lay in their hundreds, unburied, in what witnesses described as worse than a charnel house.

The busy bishop recognised that the situation gave him a valuable opportunity for a public relations triumph. Since the French Revolution, the Catholic Church and the State had had a difficult relationship. The poorer classes resented the politically powerful, massively wealthy clergy living in luxury, building huge churches and furnishing them with valuable works of art. All education was in the hands the clergy too. After the Revolution the State confiscated the considerable property and land belonging to the Church, and set up schools in every town and village under lay teachers.

---

2 Paris War Days by Charles Inman Barnard

Although the church subsequently regained some of its property, it lost all of its salaries when State and Church were legally separated in 1905. This loss of power was a crushing blow to the Catholics.

Now, however, as Mgr Marbeau reminded his dependent flock, at this terrible time they were all together in the same boat. Previously many of Meaux's citizens wouldn't have recognised their bishop; maybe some of them had even been hostile towards him, but now they were united by the tragedy of war. It was the same all over France, with 60,000 monks and nuns returning from voluntary exile to help their country in its hour of danger. Four Jesuits had cycled back to France all the way from Belgium. It was time to put any ill-feeling behind them and work together. The bishop was rewarded for his efforts by regaining the respect and affection of Meaux's citizenry.

But to return to the threat to Meaux and Paris. Whilst there were several thousand French troops in Paris, ready to deploy to Meaux to reinforce the exhausted French and British troops holding the enemy at bay, the overstretched railway network was unable to transport them. In an inspired and ingenious exercise, the military governor of Paris requisitioned the capital's taxis. Quenching their thirst with wine because water was in short supply, carrying five troops to a taxi, the Parisian taxi drivers drove the forty miles between the capital and Meaux, back and forwards through the night, their headlights turned off, delivering between 4,000 and 6,000 fresh men to the front line to support the beleaguered allies and give them the strength they needed to hold the line, and forcing the Germans to retreat in what was known as the first battle of the Marne.

Paris was safe, for the time being, and so was Meaux.

Spared the devastation suffered by neighbouring towns and villages, Meaux retains a number of medieval buildings, and all its provincial charm. After we had cycled around the town and ramparts, we headed down to the river Marne, which is born nearly 500 kilometres to the north-east, weaving its way south-westwards towards Paris, where it attaches itself to the Seine on the eastern outskirts of the city.

This was our first sight of the river that had once been a busy thoroughfare. Now the silky, jade green water was utterly peaceful; a few fishermen stood on the banks staring at their lines, and a flotilla of moored boats were so still that they could have been paintings.

Until the advent of the washing machine in the 1950s, it was on wash-boats moored in the river that local laundresses carried out their trade. They paid the boat's owner for space and the use of water heated by wood fires. On Monday they collected soiled laundry from their customers, taking it by handcart to the wash boat, where they washed it on the lower deck, first scrubbing it with hot water and ash – washing powder hadn't yet arrived - then beating it with poles, and rinsing it in the river. The clean linen was hung on the upper deck to dry, before it was ironed and returned to the customer on Wednesday. For the washerwoman it was hard work earning them a meagre living, but providing a valuable service for the townspeople. I wonder what happened to them once washing machines made them redundant?

Another vanished custom was the timber trains that once floated on their way to supply the insatiable appetite of Paris for building timber and firewood. Trees cut at the beginning of winter were thrown into streams in the spring, to be carried to the rivers, where they were collected and piled up to dry over the summer before setting off on their journey to the capital. Each wood merchant marked his timber at both ends with his individual stamp, so that it could be traced on arrival. For the final leg of their journey the logs were secured together into huge rafts. Steered by two men, and often carrying cargo and livestock, the rafts caused great upheaval to others who depended on the river for their livelihoods, such as fishermen and mill owners, and it was important that the timing of journeys was well-judged so that they passed as quickly as possible to minimise disruption. I thought what an exciting event this must have been for spectators, and what a shame it is that today the noisy great trucks and trailers rumbling along the roads laden with logs aren't worth a second glance.

We followed a well-maintained cycling path for a couple of kilometres into dark woods. Just as we were remarking what a fine track it was, it came to an unannounced and abrupt halt on the edge of a shallow ravine. Across a gulf of about thirty metres a group of workmen were breaking stones, and a merry voice shouted, unexpectedly, in English: "Jump!"

Terry and I smiled at each other, turned our bikes, retreated fifty metres down the path, and took deep breaths. Then, pedalling furiously, we hurtled towards the chasm, took off at the edge and sailed effortlessly through the air, landing with small thuds on the opposite bank, to the tumultuous applause of the workers standing there.

Of course we didn't. Not really. I'm just being silly. Instead we waved and turned back until we found a very bumpy track through the woods, culminating in a fallen tree over which we had to haul our bikes, and from there through a quiet residential area and back onto the main road. The river Marne makes a long sinuous loop northwards at Meaux, and following it to our next destination would have entailed an impractically long ride, so we opted instead to keep to the road for this stretch. Although busy with heavy traffic, it was wide and straight with good visibility, and forewarned by the bright day-glo orange flag that flapped from a one-metre-high pole behind my saddle, passing vehicles gave us plenty of room.

The sun came out. Our hideous cycling helmets offered no protection to our faces, and when we arrived in La Ferté-sous-Jouarre my upper eyelids were a bright powdery pink from constant dabbing at incessant tears caused by the wind in my face, and my cheeks were a glowing raspberry tone from a combination of sunburn and chapping. The differing shades blended harmoniously with my beetroot-coloured hair. There were only head-height mirrors in the campsite's washing rooms, for which I was grateful. I didn't want to see face and body in the same frame.

60

You couldn't find a cleaner, quieter, more peaceful town than La Ferté-sous-Jouarre. Sitting astride the river Marne and its tributary le Petit Morin, in a well-mannered, tidy way, with a pretty park and neat streets, it has the appearance of a sleepy place where nothing has ever happened; whose sole purpose might be as a commuter town for Parisian workers.

But for nearly 400 years, from the 15th century until early in the 1920's, La Ferté-sous-Jouarre had bustled with activity, producing the finest millstones in the world, exported all over Europe and as far as North America. The locally quarried stone was used to create French Burr millstones that, with their unique composition, were able to grind out all the goodness from the wheat, leaving virginally white flour. While quarry owners flourished and built fine houses, the lives of the workers were hard and frequently short. They worked with sledgehammers and crowbars extracting lumps of stone from the quarries in all weathers – except when it was too cold, when they didn't work, and didn't get paid - and if the stone-dust which clogged up their lungs didn't finish them off, the cheap wine they drank to drown their miseries probably did.

The quarries of La Ferté-sous-Jouarre did not yield sufficiently large pieces of stone to make whole millstones; instead the pieces were shaped into wedges, cemented together to form discs, and bound around the circumference with iron. Strangely, La-Ferté-sous-Jouarre does not make any apparent effort to advertise its heritage as the producer of the very best of one of the most useful items known to man. Had we not known about it before we arrived, we would have remained ignorant, because we didn't find any evidence or mention of the millstone industry in the town, apart from one large and very old specimen half-buried in grass at the entrance to the campsite.

What we did find is that the Fertois are the most hospitable people. The campsite *gardien* and his wife were warmly welcoming, and suggested that they charge my bike's battery in their office overnight, so that we would not need to pay for electricity. In the town centre we asked an elderly gentleman where we could find a supermarket. He seemed delighted to find himself talking to English visitors, and equally delighted that he was able to tell us the supermarket was no more than one minute's walk away. He grabbed our hands and pumped them energetically, wishing us *bon weekend* and turning every so often to wave as he toddled off into the distance. The cashiers in the supermarket were just as cheerful and friendly, and so were all the people we passed in the streets as we cycled around admiring the elegant three-storey houses, mostly built of flint tied in with red brick corners, and pointy slate roofs with spikes upon them.

There is also a pretty Byzantine building that was originally a synagogue, built in 1890 for the town's growing Jewish community as they migrated westwards from the German annexation of the Alsace region. Over the next few decades many of these early immigrants evolved from traders into professionals and artists, and moved to larger towns, or the capital. During the Second World War, members of the Jewish community were sent to German death camps, and after the war only a few Ashkenazim remained in the town. Orthodox Jews and Sephardic Jews arriving from North Africa preferred to worship in Meaux, and so La Ferté-sous-Jouarre's synagogue deteriorated from neglect. Now it belongs to the town and houses an art gallery and museum for the work of local artist André Planson, a painter of bold, vivid landscapes and equally bold females usually depicted baring their upper assets.

The afternoon sunshine was short-lived, and developed into a dreary grey evening. We were not greatly looking forward to the prospect of spending another long cold night under canvas. We killed some time cycling around the town again, and along the banks of the river, until just before darkness fell, when we set up our new tent. At least it was comfortably spacious, but even snuggled together beneath the polar blanket, the rustling aluminium blanket, our jackets and the flysheet of the borrowed tent, we were still shiveringly cold. Next morning we were slow, like reptiles emerging from hibernation, and it was eleven o'clock before we cycled out of the site in timid sunshine, entrusting the borrowed tent to the *gardien*, to be collected on our return in two weeks' time.

It started raining again. We cycled along for about 20 kilometres through open countryside with no distinguishing features other than its featurelessness, until we arrived in Viels-Maisons. On the face of it this very small town seemed like the sort of place that you would pass through without noticing that it was there. There were no shops, not even – *quelle horreur* - a bakery. Just a post office, a *Mairie* and a few houses. It didn't look as if anything notable ever had or ever would happen there. However, within the uninspiring bosom of Viels-Maisons is a treasure chest, a Pandora's box of delights. If you can find the sign, and follow it down a very narrow alleyway, you will find yourself at the magnificent gardens of Madame de Ladoucette, in the grounds of her château.

As we reached the entrance to the gardens two things happened simultaneously: Madame de Ladoucette arrived in an electrically driven golf cart, and the sun suddenly burst into life. Madame is a handsome woman with a very direct gaze, and I imagine a will of steel. I pictured her having a stern word with the Lord, reminding him that it was now early May. We'd already had several months of rain and cold and she expected him to do something about it, and quickly. It seemed that he had listened and obeyed.

Madame de Ladoucette guided a group of a dozen of us around her splendid estate, talking as fluently in English as in her native French. She had recently broken her ankle, and was encased in plaster almost to her knee, hence the golf cart, but she dismissed her injury as "Nothing – people have much worse." With the help of just one other lady she had created, and maintains a family of gardens living in harmony behind her white, classically elegant château. Of the original building only the portico had survived the Revolution, unlike the owner at the time, who had not. The château gazes lovingly at its reflection in the pond, framed by varieties of blue and white plants dipping their toes into, or sipping from the water.

Most of the ten diverse gardens appear deceptively natural – the kind of effect only achieved by carefully designed and knowledgeable planning and planting. Resplendent rhododendrons, leafy, quiet water gardens, arbours and herbaceous borders blended into one another. At the bottom of a slope is a cool, mysterious area of water and ferns; leathery ferns and feathery ferns; giant-leaved gunneras and slender reeds; in the dappled shade, on a floating piece of bark, a frog sat with a contented smile on his shiny green face.

The English garden consists of a number of flowerbeds, each in three colours, and each bed carrying over one colour to its neighbour. Next to the virginal white garden is an analemmatic sundial, an unusual and ingenious timepiece formed by a semi-circle of slabs set into the ground to represent the daylight hours, and a line of slabs on which are inscribed dates, which joins the semi-circle, like the trunk of a tree. If you stand on the slab bearing the current date, your shadow becomes the "dial" of the clock and points to the stone showing the current time. By adding an hour for summer time, and some extra minutes that are engraved on the slabs, the result gives an accurate reading of the time.

The most formal of the gardens is that of the Parish Priest. By tradition it contains seven elements: flowers for the church; fruit and vegetables for the priest's table; medicinal plants for the sick; water for the birds and garden; vines to produce the wine for Mass; box, the symbol of eternity, and a statue of the Virgin Mary. This garden is laid out in thirty-two equal rectangles contained within four squares, skilfully designed so that each square is a mirror of its geographic opposite in colour. Seen from a bird's perspective, it would resemble a tapestry of subtle pinks, blues and yellows.

In the introduction to her book *"Les Jardins de Viels-Maisons,"* Madame de Ladoucette writes of how she was inspired to create her glorious gardens as a means of attracting visitors to the family's beautiful but seldom-used 11th century church.

Together with a lady landscape gardener, she achieved her vision. Then the terrible storm that swept through France at the end of 1999 destroyed more than 500 trees in her garden. Entire roofs from nearby houses were blown into the flowerbeds causing absolute devastation. A lesser woman might have put their head in their hands and wept to see eight years of hard work ruined. But Madame is not that kind of woman. I have a vision of her rolling up her sleeves (she is a hands-on gardener, not one who leaves the work to somebody else,) and going round with a wheelbarrow shovelling up the mess, all the time writing a list of replacement plants to order. Replacing the 540 trees brought down in the pinewood would maybe have taxed even her determination. Instead she created her Grand-children's Wood where each girl has a spring foliage tree, and each boy one with autumn colours. This is explained on a small blackboard, on which the number of grandchildren had recently risen – twenty-two had been chalked out and replaced with twenty-three.

Although spending two hours walking round a garden would normally bore Terry, who has an exceptionally short attention span unless he's looking at engines of war, boats or aeroplanes, he found the gardens of Viels-Maisons a perfect place for photography, and didn't fidget once.

The adjective that comes to mind when I think of Madame de Ladoucette is "redoubtable" – the huge house, the enormous gardens, all those little children's names to remember. Plus she has time to spend talking to all the people who visit the beautiful gardens that are one of her great passions. If you would like to visit, it's only one hour's drive from Paris, and the gardens of Viels-Maisons are open from 1st June to 20th September, from 14.00 to 18.00, every day except Wednesday and Thursday.

I imagined that Marie-Antoinette would have delighted in the gardens of Viels-Maisons. With her love of informality and flowers, and Madame de Ladoucette's aristocratic bearing and easy confidence, they would have been entirely relaxed with each other, walking slowly around arm in arm, stopping often to admire and discuss the plants. The queen could have forgotten, for a little while, her troubles and the need for speed. But the gardens weren't created until two hundred years after Marie-Antoinette and her family passed by.

During their flight, they too had stopped at Meaux and La Ferté-sous-Jouarre, to change horses, and again at Viels-Maisons, where Louis stretched his legs around the town square.

When we had finished our exploration of the gardens the sun was blazing down and our clothes were steaming as we set off to the next staging post, Montmirail.

CHAPTER SIX
An Abundance of Railway Stations

"It is by riding a bicycle that you learn the contours of a country best, since you have to sweat up the hills and coast down them. Thus you remember them as they actually are, while in a motor car only a high hill impresses you and you have no such accurate remembrance of country you have driven through as you gain by riding a bicycle."
Ernest Hemingway

AS the wide-screen horizons of the plains morphed into a steeply undulating switchback we breathed hard hauling uphill, and laughed with excitement on the high-speed downhill swoops. While we cycled conversation with Terry was seldom possible as I couldn't maintain his speed, and he was usually far ahead of me. So I amused myself by speculating on the royal occupants of the great carriage as they trundled eastward. Imperturbable Louis, I imagined, would have been reminiscing about their triumphal journey along this road, in 1775, on the way to his consecration in Reims. He'd be recalling the fine meals he had enjoyed, and discussing the suitability of the landscape for hunting, while Marie-Antoinette listened dutifully, prompting him, behaving as if they were simply out for a joy ride, both of them conscious of the need not to alarm their children, whom the King's sister, Madame Elisabeth, would be entertaining with stories and games.

As a family they hadn't previously travelled any great distance - they didn't need to since everything that they wanted was right on the doorstep of Versailles. Within just a few kilometres were the Royal châteaux of Fontainebleau, St Cloud, Rambouillet, La Muette in the Bois de Boulogne, Meudon, Choisy, Compiègne and Marly. Whilst the Queen herded her sheep and carried milking cans around her little hamlet, her husband could satisfy his passion for hunting by moving from one château to another without ever going far afield.

Marie-Antoinette's brother, the Austrian emperor Joseph II, had criticised Louis for not travelling around his kingdom and introducing himself to its towns and people. Maybe if Louis had listened to that advice, and met more of his subjects he might not have aroused so much hatred. As they fled for their lives, the family must have been asking themselves and each other where they had gone wrong. Neither of them were unkind; there are no records of Marie-Antoinette slapping or pinching anybody, but many instances of thoughtfulness and generosity. Nevertheless she had made enemies in every quarter, and it seemed that she could do nothing right. Although she favoured informality, both in dress and behaviour, the court was scandalised when she dressed simply, and by doing away with much of the tedious etiquette she angered the *aristos* who lost their jealously guarded positions around her. If she wore extravagant clothing, all the ladies of the court aped her, and their husbands complained that she was driving them to ruin. When she retreated to the modest Petit Trianon to entertain her close friends in the simple way they enjoyed, those nobles who were not invited were resentful, and circulated slanderous and unfounded stories about her behaviour there. And, most unforgivable of all, she was foreign. Even as wife to the French king, and mother of the heir, she was and always would be an outsider. But the early, clumsy union of the two teenagers had developed into a relationship of genuine affection and, extraordinarily for the time, Louis was faithful to his wife. What had begun as a mechanical mating machine had become a caring liaison between two very different and mismatched people, united in their devotion to their children, and strengthened by their misfortunes.

He may not have been a very good king, but Louis was not a bad man. He was courteous to everyone, regardless of their rank. Nobody ever accused him of any act of cruelty – unless you count chasing wild animals to their death.

Frederic Grunfeld, in his "Treasures of The World: The French Kings," portrays a kindly, humane king who wanted to improve the lives of the poor and underprivileged. Louis XVI abolished the forced unpaid labour previously imposed upon the peasants. He banned the use of torture as a means of extracting confessions. Under his rule Protestants, discriminated against since the time of Louis XIV, were tolerated, and the hitherto harsh taxation of Jews was lifted. Unfortunately, his good intentions were too late to save him from the anger of his people caused by the excesses of his ancestors.

If the fates had been kinder to him, Louis XVI would never have been king, but it seems as if the gods were set upon picking off the French monarchy one by one. He was the last-but-one link in a chain of catastrophically bad luck for the House of Bourbon. It began with his great-great-grandfather, Louis XIV, the Sun King, who inherited the French throne at the age of five and reigned for 72 years. Louis XIV's son predeceased him – the first link in the chain of disaster - and so did his grandson, the second link. It was thus the Sun King's five-year-old great-grandson who ascended the throne as Louis XV. He had two sons, and in the normal course of events one of them would have taken over the reins when his father died after almost sixty years on the throne. But both his sons died before him – two further links in the bad-luck chain. The oldest of them left five sons, of whom the two eldest died in childhood – the final two links in the chain that left the third sibling to become the unfortunate Louis XVI on his grandfather's death. If all these characters had not been called Louis it would have been a great deal less confusing, and if tuberculosis hadn't been so rife during their lifetimes then most of these people would not have died when they did. Louis would have ended up as a minor prince far removed from the throne.

As it was, after Louis XIV and Louis XV had between them ruled France for more than 130 years, their legacy to poor

69

Louis XVI was a realm teetering on the brink of bankruptcy due to their profligacy and mismanagement.

History has depicted him as an inept simpleton with no thoughts in his royal head other than hunting and eating. Yet he was a keen student and very learned on the subjects of history, geography and astronomy, and also fluent in English. His apartments at Versailles housed collections of wood-working instruments, maps, globes, rare books, prayer books and manuscripts. He may have been indecisive and weak when it came to politics and government, but he wasn't unintelligent.

His portraits are proof that he most definitely wasn't any kind of eye candy. According to Madame de Campan: "The features of Louis XVI were noble enough, though somewhat melancholy in expression; his walk was heavy and unmajestic; his person greatly neglected; his hair, whatever might be the skill of his hairdresser, was soon in disorder. His voice, without being harsh, was not agreeable; if he grew animated in speaking he often got above his natural pitch, and became shrill."

I know people with voices like that.

Lovers of *gratin dauphinois* and *frites* have particularly good reason to be indebted to Louis, who gave 100 acres of otherwise useless sandy soil to a certain M. Parmentier, a botanist and chemist, so that he could plant potatoes. Until 1785 the French were strongly anti-potato, holding it responsible for, amongst other evils, leprosy. M. Parmentier, however, realised that the plant would be a valuable addition to the table if only people could overcome their prejudices against it. To pique the curiosity of his farming neighbours, he placed an armed guard around his potato patch. How could any red-blooded French farmer resist the challenge, when one night the guard was absent, of helping themselves to a few plants? Which is what they did, precisely as M. Parmentier had intended. The farmers planted their booty, his spuds, in their own fields, and the *frite* was on its way. What greater legacy could a king bequeath to his country?

A golden eagle soared into the sky ahead of us as we approached Montmirail. Perched on a tall column, the Imperial eagle is an unmistakable sign that Napoléon had been here. It marks the position from where Boney, outnumbered by two to one, gave the Russians and Prussians a good bashing during several battles in the surrounding areas during February 1814. Although the monument was intended as a tribute to those victories, it seemed to me that it's really more of a signpost pointing to the end of his career. Maybe his successes here restored his ego somewhat after the Russian campaign débâcle and his mortifying retreat, but the Bonaparte star was fading. Less than two months after the battle of Montmirail, Paris had fallen to the enemy, and the Emperor was forced to abdicate and exiled to the pleasant island of Elba, off the Tuscan coast. He could have lived there in comparative freedom and comfort. Instead he chose to escape and return to France, rally his troops and lead them to a thorough trouncing at the battle of Waterloo. It was all over for him, and he'd never return from his second exile home, St Helena, in the south Atlantic, hundreds of miles from anywhere. It was a sad ending for the belligerent little general who left such a legacy of orderliness in French law and life, even if it does sometimes make for tiresome bureaucracy.

Overhead a phutting microlight was making its final approach to land on a small grass airstrip. It looked like a deckchair held up by an umbrella and propelled by a lawnmower engine. The pilot waved to us. Did he, I wondered, ever think about Napoléon, or Louis and Marie-Antoinette?

Montmirail's municipal campsite was delightful. A vast area of perfectly-mown green grass which we shared with just one other family. A night's stay cost a negligible €2.80 ($3.90). The town centre emanated a rather defeated atmosphere and bore little resemblance to the description by Spanish war correspondent and travel writer, Señor Gomez Carrillo, who toured the area in 1914 as a neutral journalist. He portrayed "a vain and gentle little town," where the cheerful inhabitants went about the "busy monotony" of their lives, sipping aperitifs in the cafés, shopping in stores filled with elegant goods, and streets that were miniatures of Paris. And, furthermore, to the envy of neighbouring towns, Montmirail boasted three railway stations, serving the *Compagnie des Chemins de Fer de l'Est* between the Ourcq Valley and Esternay; the *Compagnie des Chemins de Fer Départementaux* linking La Ferté-sous-Jouarre and Montmirail, and *Chemins de Fer de la Banlieue de Reims* from Epernay to Montmirail.

Today, there is only one station in the Rue des Trois Gares, and the only passengers are those who travel on the tourist route between Mézy in the south of the Aisne departement, and Montmirail in the Marne. An association of enthusiasts *"Tourisme Ferroviaire de la Brie Champenoise à l'Omois"* operate the line, running a quirky Picasso railcar, so named because of the strange position of the driver's cab. Perched asymmetrically to one side on the roof of the train it looks as if it might slide off, like the noses on the artist's paintings.

Unlike the ruined and pillaged villages all around, Señor Carrillo found Montmirail untouched by the war. The German General von Bulow had established his headquarters there and had given an undertaking that his army would behave themselves as long as the inhabitants did likewise. A local inn-keeper related how German officers made use of his kitchen and provisions to prepare themselves fine meals, washed down with his best Chambertin and champagne. A good meal seemed to be the Germans' priority, and the inn-keeper remarked that if he hadn't been so angry at them for helping themselves to his produce, it would have been a pleasure to see how they enjoyed their food.

General von Bulow demanded 10,000 rations of bread a day for his troops. An impossible undertaking for the only two bakeries still functioning, so the local citizens had to roll up their sleeves and bake to fulfil the order. Luckily the Germans would soon be driven away in the first battle of the Marne, retreating with their tattered dreams of taking Paris, as well as some souvenirs of their stay in Montmirail to which they had helped themselves.

Now, a little more than 90 years later, wandering around the deserted town it was difficult to imagine it as a miniature Paris. And then, in the otherwise bleak and empty street – it was, after all, Sunday – we came upon a light, bright, airy, chic *salon de thé*. Standing in the doorway was a super-slim lady with flame-red hair (not beetroot like mine, but a true Titian) wearing a floaty, flowery chiffon dress that would turn heads on any Parisian boulevard. She smiled and beckoned us. "Come in," she said. So we did.

Charmingly, authoritatively, insistently, gently, she sat us down and extracted an order for one cup of coffee, and a hot chocolate that she assured us would be made in the correct, traditional way. Then she gestured to an enticing display of cakes and pastries that she had personally baked with love and skill, and which would go very nicely with our drinks. While she made the hot chocolate she explained, without any conceit, that she was a perfectionist in everything she did. Watching her elegant hand blending the rich brown squares of chocolate into scalding full cream milk and then adding fresh cream, I pushed the word "cholesterol" from my mind. I asked her cautiously why she had chosen Montmirail in which to be perfect and to establish her tea-room, because if there was something special about the town, it wasn't evident. She wrinkled her elegant nose disdainfully, and told us that she was a music teacher, who had been transferred to Montmirail from Meaux and it was not, sadly, a move which had given her any joy. Despite having a positive attitude and cheerful outlook on life, she could find nothing whatever to appreciate about her new home.

Just then there was an alarming noise outside, coming from a bunch of slack-mouthed, pimply youths fighting amongst themselves to climb onto my bike. Terry leapt through the door and the boys fled shouting, leaving the bike rocking on its stand but otherwise undamaged. Five minutes later they were back again, jeering raucously, staggering around and waving beer bottles, but they soon got bored. After yelling a few obscenities and giving us the finger they wandered away, bumping into and pushing each other.

"*Et voila!* That's what it's like here," said our hostess angrily. "It's the fault of the parents. Unemployment is very high, there's a lot of alcoholism, a lot of hopelessness. The parents don't care if their children are educated or not, so how can the children care? I don't understand this attitude."

Couldn't she move somewhere else, I asked. It wasn't so easy to get a job, she replied, and her husband worked in Meaux so they couldn't move far away. She felt like a prisoner in Montmirail, but tried to maintain her morale by opening her tea shop and baking fine cakes.

I admired her spirit and hoped that she would find sufficient custom in this depressed area to make her investments and efforts worthwhile, and that her bright little salon would survive. Although towns like Montmirail are not on the tourist trail, we found them interesting because they offered an insight into the reality of daily life in rural France far beyond the rose-tinted veneer that we see so often.

We weren't able to find very much to explore in the town so we returned to the tent and spent a few quiet hours reading before going to look for somewhere to eat. For a small town it was well supplied, with several pizzerias that only served plates containing meat, a few kebab houses that only served meat, or places that were closed and served nothing at all. Panic, nay despair, began to overtake us as we had no food with us. We had a short, bitter debate about which of us was to blame for this, but as we turned back to the campsite in hungry silence we came upon Le Vert Galant, (one of Henri IV's nicknames meaning "the indefatigable romantic") a hostelry that looked as if it had been there since the beginning of time. The owner/chef and his wife were welcoming and the food and service were unexpectedly good. I wondered if this was the same inn where the German officers had helped themselves to the contents of the pantry and wine cellar.

We drank rather a lot, hoping it would help us to sleep through the icy night. (It didn't.) One of Terry's stranger habits is carrying on silent conversations with himself and believing that he is speaking to me. At some arbitrary point, he begins to talk aloud, continuing the conversation where he had left off in his mind. He expects me to have picked it up telepathically. Quite often I do, but not on this occasion.

"Did they ever find out who did it?" he asked, in the darkness.

"Who did what?"

"Did they ever find out who killed them?"

"Find out who killed whom?"

"Those cyclists."

"What cyclists?"

"That British couple who were on a cycling holiday."

"Where?"

"Up in Brittany, I think. Years ago. They were found shot in a field."

"I think I remember something, vaguely. Why, do you suspect we might be murdered?"

"No. But I was just thinking about it."

"Let's try and go to sleep," I suggested.

Between the miserable weather, my eyes that had been watering persistently since we left Versailles, and private, growing doubts as to whether I was really up to cycling several hundred more miles after finding today's hills gruelling even with the help of the electric bicycle, I thought I had enough to contend with, without having to worry about being murdered, too.

By the next morning I could barely see; my eyes were swollen almost shut and still dripping incessantly, so we cycled back to town to find a pharmacy. Montmirail had come to life, and a busy market sprawled over the streets crowded with cheerful and noisy people wrapped in heavy coats and carrying bulky shopping baskets. We had forgotten that it was Pentecost Monday, and all the shops were closed, so the eyes would have to wait.

Providence had put in our path on the way to Epernay the Château d'Etoges, with a worldwide reputation for fine

75

dining, where I had booked a table for lunch. After cycling 160 kilometres, mostly in the rain, five days of effort, and three uncomfortable nights, a little luxury couldn't come too soon.

There isn't a great deal to see on the twenty-five or so kilometres between Montmirail and Etoges, apart from gentle up and down countryside beneath a carpet of lush crops.

For the benefit of anyone unfamiliar with the structure of France's administrative areas, these are divided into regions – of which there are twenty-one in mainland France - the Champagne-Ardennes being the one in which we were travelling. Each region is sub-divided into *départements*, and it is in the Marne, *département* 51, where we were spending most of our time. Although the Marne has been the theatre of some of the most terrible fighting man has known, and its name, like that of the Somme, will always be synonymous with warfare on an unthinkable scale, it is also home to the majority of vineyards producing that most quintessentially French of French products, champagne.

During the Middle Ages, the Champagne region was famous for its six great annual international trade fairs; merchants travelled from Italy, Spain, North Africa, Germany and the Low Countries to buy and sell leathers and furs, spices, silks, linens, livestock, precious metals and jewels. A crossroads of trade routes between northern and southern Europe, and from Eastern Europe to Paris and the Atlantic, the region was ideally situated as a major market place. Independent of the French crown, Champagne was ruled by powerful counts, under whose control the fairs flourished. The safety and security, both physical and financial, of merchants were guaranteed by strict rules, enforced by the "Guards of the Fair" and armed escorts provided by them.

Jewish money-changers conducted their business from benches; if one of them failed, his bench was said to be broken – "*banca rotta*" in Italian, and in English "bankrupt".

As well as a market place, the fair was somewhere for the exchange of intellectual and cultural ideas, and a great social gathering, but as financial transactions became more sophisticated, merchants began to conduct their business through correspondence, rather than travelling the long and arduous roads to the fairs. Wars in parts of Europe made road travel risky, and the Italians began to open up new maritime trading routes, so the great fairs fell into decline.

Then the Champagne region became known for centuries as "the lousy Champagne," a land fit for nothing except for grazing a few sheep; "...and we are in a hungry Champagne Pouilleuse, a land flowing only with ditch-water," wrote Thomas Carlyle. Sitting on a chalk bed 1,300 feet deep, it was long regarded as an impoverished and ugly place. Its geographical location makes it a natural bulwark to protect Paris from attacks from the east, so it was frequently a theatre of war.

"There is scarcely a region in all France where a battle could have been fought with less injury to property. Imagine, if you please, an immense undulating plain, its surface broken by occasional low hills and ridges, none of them much over six hundred feet in height, and wandering in and out between those ridges the narrow stream that is the Marne. The country hereabouts is very sparsely settled; the few villages that dot the plain are wretchedly poor; the trees on the slopes of the ridges are stunted and scraggly; the soil is of chalky marl, which you have only to scratch to leave a staring scar, and the grass which tries to grow upon it seems to wither and die of a broken heart." [3]

Pine forests were planted to hinder invaders; the towns of the Champagne were heavily garrisoned, and the rural population abandoned their homes to find work in Paris. Succeeding wars obliterated small villages; the land was peppered with shells and mines, and the forests destroyed by heavy artillery. Consequently, after World War II land here was cheap and plentiful, and its vast horizons ideally suited to mechanised cultivation. The porous structure of the once despised chalk acts as a sponge to bring deep water to the surface, belying the apparent dryness of the soil. Now the

---

3   Vive la France by E Alexander Powell, 1915

Champagne has become one of France's most productive areas for sugar beet, cereals and lucerne. And despite being the birthplace and homeland of the world's most renowned effervescent drink, symbol of luxury, nowadays the Champagne-Ardennes is still one of France's poorer and less known regions. It has about it an air of the land that time forgot. With its unspoilt provincial towns and gentle, undulating landscape the place seems at odds with its history of warfare. It's a popular choice for Parisians and people from the Low Countries looking for low-cost second homes. The sparsely populated and tranquil rural land that we saw today had once been a ruined wasteland ravaged and trampled by war. It is a most paradoxical part of the world.

Ten minutes before we reached our destination a light spitting of rain began to fall. Within seconds it became a substantial downpour leaving us soaked to the skin as we arrived in Etoges. The town comprises of a single street whose only commerce is a wine merchant, and the château. By the time we had cycled up the tree-lined gravel path and over the moat bridge the rain was cascading off us in runnels; we looked as if we'd been swept in by a tsunami.

In the shelter of an open-fronted out-building where mopeds and sports equipment were stored, we towelled ourselves as dry as we could and Terry changed his clothing. I didn't feel like struggling out of the tight, wet black leggings and frightening anybody who might be passing, so I took my little bundle of clean clothes into the château, and called at reception to ask for the ladies' cloakroom. As I stood quietly dripping onto the carpet, the receptionist looked at me with a mixture of wonderment and horror.

The cloakroom was roughly the same size as a telephone cabin. After I had writhed out of the clinging wet clothes like a python sloughing its skin, and changed into my chiffon skirt, blouse and gold moccasins, the reflection in the mirror was no different except for the costume and the fact that my face was even redder after my cramped exertions.

The décor of the château is spot-on. 18th century elegance

with rich furnishings, spacious, high-ceilinged rooms, marble floors, stately potted plants and statuary. In the dining room, which was filled to capacity, we sat by a window overlooking the gardens, beneath a chandelier and under the blind gaze of an undraped lady statue in an alcove.

Our four-course meal was flawlessly prepared and served, punctuated by several little unexpected surprises between courses – cheesy nibbles, an asparagus cream, a pear liqueur sorbet. The young *maître d'* was attentive but unobtrusive, courteous but not obsequious, and wore a huge smile. I was rather worried about him, though, because he was terribly thin, and as he was also slightly stooped he looked rather like an apostrophe. There was another, even younger man who seemed to be an apprentice, and when he thought nobody was looking he chewed his fingernails nervously.

We had never tasted a better bottle of perfectly chilled Sancerre, and rounded the meal off with coffee and a plate of *petit fours* taken on big squashy sofas in the grand salon. We agreed that the modest fortune we had invested here had given excellent value. If the royal couple had eaten here when they stopped for fresh horses, Louis should have been very well satisfied. Full, warm, dry and drowsy, how fervently I wanted to stretch out on the soft sofa and sink into the cushions for a couple of hours' sleep in front of the fire. But Epernay and its champagne cellars lay ahead and so, like Cinderellas at the witching hour, we changed back into our sodden cycling clothes and set off through the vineyards.

Immediately out of Etoges we were into the heart of the champagne country. The landscape changed dramatically from rolling green nothingness to the seriously steep hillsides of the Côtes des Blancs with their symmetrically ordered Chardonnay vines, and prosperous, flowery villages. No longer did we whirr along briskly, but rather kept changing down through our gears and pedalling faster for less forward progress. But at least the weather had taken a turn for the better, and the warm sunshine drew a steamy vapour from our clothing.

After hauling up one particularly challenging incline, we were glad to meet a friendly man dressed in white overalls and wellies. He spoke English and recommended a route to Epernay that was both scenic and level all the way. It took us through fields and woods, and finally into the heaving heart of the spiritual capital of the champagne world.

From Etoges the royal fugitives had continued their journey to Châlons. By this time things were starting to go wrong. Foolish Louis had insisted on walking in the sunshine for a while, and twice the horses had fallen, breaking their harnesses, causing dangerous delays.

CHAPTER SEVEN
The City of Effervescence

"Remember gentlemen, it's not just France we are fighting for, it's Champagne!"
Winston Churchill

CHAMPAGNE takes its name from the French region where it is produced, which the Romans rather unimaginatively christened "Campania," meaning fields or countryside. The drink was born by default rather than design. Although the Champenois had been making wine for two thousand years, they were never able to replicate the fine wines of neighbouring Burgundy, having neither the same climate, nor the same soil. Second-rate and erratic red wines were the best they could produce, and whilst these remained stable in their barrels through the cold winter months, as the temperature rose in spring, so did an unwelcome fizziness which the wine makers regarded with dismay. But - the bubbly drink was greatly appreciated by French royalty and the aristocracy, and at the court of Charles II in England, where it was introduced by the exiled French *aristo* the Marquis de St-Evremond (not to be confused, confusing thought it is, with the fictional evil Marquis St Evrémonde from "A Tale of Two Cities.")

Recognising a potentially lucrative market, the Champagne vintners were eager to find a way of stabilising their product and preserving its bubbles. The solution was to keep it in bottles, but at the time wine could by law only be transported in barrels. When in 1728 Louis XV issued a royal decree allowing bottled wine to be moved, the Champagne producers opened for business on a grand scale, together with manufacturers of corks and bottles, labels and *muselets* - the wire caps and metal plaques that lock the corks down.

It would still take many years of trial and error to perfect the bottling technique. Until the end of the 19th century workers in the cellars had to wear protective masks fitted with grilles to shield them from bottles that were liable to detonate unexpectedly.

In Roman times Epernay was a small fishing village known as Sparnacum, from which today's inhabitants take the name of Sparnaciens. The village grew into a town, with tanning the mainstay of the local economy until the explosion of the Champagne industry.

Due to its strategic position on the Marne, for fourteen centuries somebody or other was constantly waging war in and around Epernay or burning it down. After suffering the ravages of Imperial wars, civil wars, religious and world wars, the fact that the town is still standing at all is an indication of the resilience of the Sparnaciens.

During the Napoléonic wars the Cossacks looted the cellars, and after them the Prussians in the Franco-Prussian war. Even when there was a rare lull in human hostilities, a destructive new enemy attacked in 1888 - the ingenious phylloxera insect that wiped out half the vines. It's a nasty, minuscule creature not more than one millimetre in length, and takes many forms – from eggs to creepy-crawlers to winged beasts. The female lays two types of eggs, male and female, and these siblings mate incestuously to create a new generation. They attack the leaves and roots of vines with devastating effect, and are very bad news indeed when they appear. Early experimental treatments included drowning them with white wine, and burying live toads at the end of each row of vines. Neither of these strategies worked. The eventual solution was to graft the vines onto American rootstock resistant to the pest.

With that problem out of the way, next it was the turn of rioters to bring strife to the town. Under the 1891 Treaty of Madrid, sparkling wine could only be called champagne if it was produced within the Champagne region. In 1910 and 1911, the French government redefined the regional borders, which led to the exclusion of certain territory previously included. This caused violent riots between infuriated producers outside the new borders trying to squeeze in, and those inside fighting to keep them out. Epernay and the surrounding villages were sacked and burned.

Then along came 1914, bringing with it a new war on a vast scale. The German invaders ransacked the cellars: some soldiers would depart for the great battlefield in the sky with a bottle in their hands, bubbles in their belly and a song in their heart.

During the harvest that year, several women and children picking in the vineyards were killed by shells. The Préfet decided that the best thing for him to do would be to run away; so that's what he did, along with most of the municipal authorities and police, abandoning the citizens to their own devices.

At the time the mayor of Epernay was Maurice Pol-Roger, joint owner of the champagne house of the same name, and it was he who undertook the organisation and running of the town. Aside from caring for his flock, he also had to keep his business running, and to somehow harvest the grapes in between bombardments. The German army had an unquenchable thirst for champagne, and demanded it in great quantities. Maurice was quite willing and able to supply it, although for some mysterious reason the quality was unusually mediocre, and deliveries chaotic and unreliable. It is a fair assumption that he was not the only one to outwit the enemy. There are tales of misleading labels and inferior wines finding their way to the front line, whilst the best bottles were stowed away out of sight to await the end of the war. Four times Maurice was threatened with execution by the Germans, but he survived the war, remained Mayor of Epernay until 1935, and, when he wished to retire, was elected Mayor for Life.

Once the coast was sufficiently clear for the absconding Préfet to slink back to Epernay in safety, Maurice threw down the gauntlet and challenged him to a duel. During a vigorous battle with swords each sustained a modest injury and honour was satisfied. Personally I think the Préfet got off rather lightly.

By 1918, after years of bombardment, the Rue du Commerce was obliterated, the houses of Chandon and Chanoine destroyed, Mercier, and Moët & Chandon badly damaged. When the war ended, almost the entire town had been reduced to rubble.

Still, the inhabitants could look forward to twenty years of peace before the next blow. They regrouped, rebuilt and carried on regardless. A stoic bunch, the Sparnaciens.

The enemy was back in 1939, the Germans again anxious to ensure the continued production of champagne, on which their armies marched, and they therefore adopted a relaxed attitude towards the producers. But the chalky tunnels beneath the streets of Epernay were not only used for storing bottles; they were a hiding place for stock that their owners had no intention of handing over to the Nazis. They were also a useful place for meetings of the Résistance. At Moët & Chandon, Comte Robert Jean de Vogüé and Paul Chandon-Moët were both arrested by the Gestapo and deported for their involvement in the Résistance. Although the Comte was sentenced to death, he was instead deported to a forced labour camp in Germany. Paul Chandon-Moët was sent to Auschwitz-Birkenau, transferred from there to Buchenwald and Nordhausen and later Bergen-Belsen. Both men survived the war.

The Pol-Roger family were still doing their bit, too. Maurice's daughter-in-law Odette carried messages to Paris by bicycle, a 12-hour journey. That she was stopped and questioned by the Gestapo probably had something to do with the fact that she wore an RAF badge on her dress.

By the time we arrived on our bicycles, thankfully Sparnaciens had enjoyed more than 60 years of peace and were able to sleep soundly in their beds.

Epernay seemed reticent regarding the whereabouts of its campsite, as if it was ashamed to admit to having one. All those centuries of warfare, civic "improvements" and the building of the railway had resulted in the destruction and demolition of virtually every ancient building and all the town's ramparts, leaving very little of charm. Apart from the Avenue de Champagne, it's really rather a scruffy place. We might possibly still be looking for the campsite today if Terry hadn't forced a police car to halt by placing himself in its path on a busy roundabout. Once the two policemen had recovered they were kind enough to draw a map which led us by a long and circuitous route to the campsite. It was about as far away from the town as it could be without actually being in an entirely different town, but it was a very attractive site with excellent facilities.

We pitched the tent beneath an exotic tulip tree and spent another uncomfortably icy night. But when we woke the next morning it was to a glorious day of blazing sunshine, finally allowing us an opportunity to wash all our wet and smelly clothes and festoon them over the hedge of our encampment. Our hideous cycling helmets offered no protection from the sun. If my face became any more burned than it already was, it would fall off, so we went shopping and bought ourselves some big-brimmed baseball caps. Terry's was a manly dark blue, while mine was rather glamorous – black, with diamonds all round the peak and a diamond butterfly on the front. They probably were not real diamonds, because it only cost €3, but I did think it looked rather striking. I also bought a pair of very large sunglasses, which covered half of my face, and which I hoped would help to protect my eyes. The disadvantage of them was that without my corrected glasses the whole world was completely out of focus, but with my left eye half-closed the road was just about visible.

I do rather like champagne, but not sufficiently to venture into the sub-terrain to look at it, so Terry nobly volunteered to do so. We chose to visit the Mercier cellars so he could ride the little laser-guided train through the tunnels cut into the chalky underground rock. With perfect timing – a rare feat - we arrived just as the English guided tour was setting off, and Terry disappeared into a lift that plunged him into the bowels of the cellars thirty metres below.

85

The pretty receptionist was distressed to learn that as a claustrophobic I would miss the tour, but she invited me to wait upstairs, and offered me a free glass of bubbly as a consolation.

Eugene Mercier, the founder of the house, was a man of great vision, with big ideas and a genius for advertising. Prior to the Revolution most vineyards had belonged to the clergy and nobility. Now they were in more egalitarian hands. M. Mercier believed that champagne should be within the grasp of Monsieur and Madame Ordinaire, and not just the privileged classes. Everything he did was in the style befitting his product. The entrance hall to Mercier's establishment is dominated by the colossal oak barrel designed and built for the Paris World Fair Exhibition of 1889. Beautifully carved, with two semi-naked ladies gazing rather suggestively at each other while caressing a bottle of bubbly, the barrel has a capacity of 200,000 bottles of fizz. It took sixteen years to build, and it needed 8 days, 24 oxen and 18 horses to tug it from Epernay to Paris. A journey that would wreck roads and bridges and necessitated the purchase and demolition of five houses that were obstructing the barrel's progress.

I have never been able to find a definitive explanation as to why wine and champagne bottles are named as they are. The piccolo – a quarter of a bottle, is obvious. But it seems that the –ams and –zars were named for larger than life biblical characters simply because they were larger than life. The largest bottle of all is the 30 litre Melchizedek produced by Drappier, holding the equivalent of 40 standard bottles. Its price, not to mention weight, means it isn't a common sight.

After Terry resurfaced, he reported that the railway tunnel that took the bottles from the cellars to the specially built railway which carried them to market was more than just a passage: its walls are beautifully carved with nearly-naked ladies, frolicking bare cherubs, and scenes of Bacchanalian romps. It seems that for M. Mercier his product and mild debauchery were inseparable. Despite the ban on using the camera's flash because it could cause the laser-guided train to

86

career out of control, Terry had managed to take some very good photos of these carvings and some of the fifteen million neatly stacked bottles of bubbly. He had also captured a shot of the nearly-nude that had so scandalised Parisian society when it was displayed that it had been removed and placed in the tunnel out of sight of delicate sensibilities. Admittedly her clothing is revealing and a little dishevelled; she stands holding a champagne glass raised in her left hand, and a bottle in her right, and parts of her upper anatomy have popped out into full view. Granted that she does look a little the worse for wear, but by 20th century standards she is really quite demure. If nineteenth century Parisians thought that was shocking, how would they react to today's ladette culture and girls staggering out of bars and nightclubs smashed out of their heads?

When we had enjoyed a glass of bubbles, we cycled slowly down the Avenue de Champagne, previously named Le Faubourg de la Folie (The Mad Suburb), the part of town that really sparkles. Lined with grand, glittering 19th century mansions, each trying to outshine its neighbours, this is the visibly glamorous heart of Epernay, while it's beneath these streets that the real work takes place, and the bottles slumber awaiting their moment of glory. But the road surface has more potholes per square metre than anywhere else I've ever been, including the poorest suburbs of Nairobi. Really, the whole street was falling to pieces! As we cycled along I wondered how strong it was, and whether there was any possibility it would cave in, as it had done in 1900, destroying a million and a half bottles of Pol Roger.

This hot afternoon deteriorated into yet another glacial night, which gave birth to a day of molten sun. It was June 6th. By 10.00 am our bikes were too hot to touch, and we lay on the grass, happy to do nothing for a couple of hours before cycling on to our next stop, Châlons. An English couple parked next to us insisted that we really should go up to Hautvillers, "the cradle of champagne," where Dom Pérignon, the cellar master at the Benedictine Abbey, is buried. "It's about four kilometres," they said. "Only takes ten minutes."

Slightly reluctant to abandon the cool grass beneath the tulip tree, we nevertheless felt we should make the pilgrimage. As our neighbours had said, Hautvillers was no further than four kilometres away, but in that short distance the road climbs more than 100 metres, at an angle of about 45°. With the benefit of an air-conditioned car it would be a pleasantly scenic drive and the occupants would barely notice the incline. On a bicycle, in sweltering heat, with the soft, sticky tarmac snatching at our wheels, it was the next best thing to impossible.

I watched Terry's legs pedalling faster and faster, as he changed down to his lowest gears, and his bike moved slower and slower until he was almost stationary. Even with the electric assistance of my machine I was almost rolling backwards, and I couldn't change gears because my sweating hands slipped round and round on the handlebars. Soon we were both forced to dismount and push, stopping along the way at the observation points to recharge our energy and look out over the dozy, sunbathing vineyards and distant hills of this currently contented part of the world.

Heaving nearly 30 kilograms of red-hot bike up a steep hill on a roasting day was quite beyond my puny strength, so Terry and I swapped over bikes. His is so light I can lift it with one hand. Still, even then it was a challenge, and when we arrived in the village after almost an hour of shoving and panting past seemingly endless rows of vines, every muscle in our bodies was shaking.

It takes a great deal to sap Terry's almost infinite energy; in fact I can't remember a single instance in all the thirty-five years I have known him, but the haul up to Hautvillers succeeded. We had started out imagining that we would sit and sip a cool glass of champagne when we reached the village; the reality was that badly dehydrated, what we each wanted were several bottles of a fizzy, brown, sugary beverage that had never been anywhere near a grape, but which did quench our thirst and restore some of our energy.

88

At mid-day the pretty little streets of Hautvillers, with their immaculate buildings decorated with quaint wrought iron signs were deserted but for a lone tractor rumbling by, loaded with spraying equipment and covered with dust. The driver looked as hot and weary as we felt.

Hautvillers church is small and bright, with beautiful carved stonework and gleaming pews. In a secluded corner a stern old lady was lighting a candle to buy a blessing. I wondered who or what it was for. A couple of coach parties gazed reverently at the polished slab glistening in the sunshine pouring through the window, beneath which the Dom slept and dreamt of drinking the stars. The crowd listened intently while their guide described the work of the clever monk.

The name of Dom Pérignon is synonymous with champagne, but how many people link the name of Christopher Merret to the drink? While it is DP who is generally credited with the "invention" of champagne, if you read about the history and development of the drink, you will find many references to the fact that it was Mr. Merret, an English wine merchant, who first created a sparkling white wine in 1672 by adding sugar to still wine, and it was in England that the first bottles were invented which were sufficiently robust to withstand any explosion of their contents. It was not until a couple of decades later that Dom Pérignon took his place in history by perfecting the process and introducing the cork stopper. Still, the Dom gets the kudos, while Christopher Merret's name is known to few except amongst the champagne cognoscenti.

In the Père Lachaise cemetery in Paris another "Dom" Pérignon is buried: Dominique-Catherine Pérignon, a soldier, politician and Marshal of France, and nothing to do with champagne. Odd name for a man, isn't it?

Outside the abbey a couple of coach drivers were studying my bike with a mixture of interest and suspicion, the way somebody might examine a strange insect. I explained how it worked and offered them a ride, but one shook his head and the other just grunted, and they both moved back to the coach as if seeking protection from mad Englishwomen.

The killing slog up to the village was worth the exhilarating whoosh back down. Terry reached 53 kilometres an hour, only limited by the bends in the road, but I was more cautious, resisting the temptation to go flat out, conscious that if I flew off onto the tarmac, with no helmet and virtually no clothes on, it would certainly mean the end of our journey, so I followed more sedately, hitting 35 kilometres an hour, which was still quite fast enough to release the adrenaline.

CHAPTER EIGHT
A Small Epiphany in the Catalaunian Fields

"Isn't it enough to see that a garden is beautiful without having to believe that there are fairies at the bottom of it too?"
Douglas Adams

NEXT morning we set off towards Châlons-en-Champagne, site of a seminal event in the history of Western civilisation. In the 5th century, at the stirringly name Battle of the Catalaunian Fields, an alliance of Romans and Goths trounced the ferocious hordes of Attila's Huns in a savage battle that led to vast loss of life, but succeeded in putting an end to Attila's conquest of Western Europe.

The *gardien* of the campsite at Epernay recommended a pleasant route which took us through the top-notch, *grand cru* village of Aÿ - a tricky little name pronounced like a cry of anguish – famed for the quality of its wines long before champagne was invented. We stopped there for a late, light lunch and a glass of ratafia. I remembered this as a small biscuit, or an almond-flavoured liqueur favoured by old ladies in the Victorian and Edwardian eras, but the ratafia of the Champagne region is a blend of brandy and the champagne "must," resulting in a rich and rather sweet drink, very similar to our local pineau de Charentes.

We continued on our way through Tours-sur-Marne, home of Laurent-Perrier, one of several great champagne houses developed and managed by a widow; in fact in the case of Laurent-Perrier, two widows, one having bought the enterprise from another. We debated what it might have been that killed off so many champagne husbands. Flying corks? Exploding bottles? Too much of their product? Surely not wifely ambition? I thought it rather odd. Being the male head of a champagne house seemed to be an inherently precarious occupation. But didn't the widows do well? Bollinger, Clicquot, Roederer, Pommery, Perrier all flourished under female control, during the 19th century and through two World Wars. The widows' might, one might say. And yet women wouldn't have the right to vote in France until 1945!

Laurent-Perrier was sold by the widowed Madame Perrier to the widowed Madame de Nonancourt, whose sons, Maurice and Bernard were active members of the Résistance during WWII. Maurice helped to organise the escape from France of young men being sent to Germany for forced labour, but he was captured and deported to die in a concentration camp. Bernard, survived the war, and in an interview in 2004 described some of his wartime adventures. In Paris he was recruited into the Résistance by one of my personal heroes, Henri Groués, better known as l'Abbé Pierre. [4] Then he travelled to Grenoble for commando training, before joining the Leclerc tank division of the French army.

"I arrived at Maisons Lafitte announcing I wanted to fight and offered 100 bottles if I could be on a tank straight away. It's true that 100 bottles to get your head blown off might not sound like much. But I wanted to avenge my brother who was killed by the Germans at Oranienburg in the concentration camp's gas ovens.

"By the time we reached Berchtesgaden I was a tank commander. In that mountain Eyrie there was an incredible network of tunnels. As for the Eagle's Nest, the elevators had been blown up. We had to use ropes to get up there. My lieutenant then said to me that because I was from Champagne I was obviously the right man to take care of Hitler's wine cellar.

"We had trouble getting the underground doors open to enter the cellar. It was full of Rothschild. The Bordeaux were extraordinary, Lafite Rothschild, Mouton Rothschild. We had a binge. It was a soldier's just desserts and just waiting to be

---

4 Founder of the Emmaüs movement, an iconic French figure in his black cassock, with huge ears, a scraggly beard, spectacles and a beret. A tireless campaigner for human rights, his is a story all his own.

drunk. There were also bottles of Mumm and Pommery 28 because Von Ribbentrop had been a wealthy champagne merchant who represented the house.

"There was Cognac and Lanson Champagne from my own mother's house," (Madame de Nonancourt was a Lanson by birth) "including an unforgettable Salon 1928. What an experience! There was also a lot of unnamed champagne because at the time each producer had to provide the occupying forces with one third of its sales for the year's 1937. The Champagnes were category A, B or C. This famous 'third' was billed to the Wehrmacht and used to maintain troop morale." [5]

Terry remarked that the Eagle's Nest would have been more aptly named the Pillager's Perch.

We cycled beside the milky green Canal Laterale à la Marne, where ducks paddled and herons flapped backwards and forwards, and fishermen nodded over their lines. Sometimes a barge chugged past, disturbing the waters and sending them slapping petulantly against the banks, and a couple of men with a golden Labrador bobbed past in a dinghy, waving. In the shade of the trees overhanging the towpath it was deliciously cool, and a welcome respite to be cycling on level ground after the last few days of hills.

The canal leads right into the heart of Châlons. As we left the towpath there we met a stout French gentleman with a face like a rosy apple, wearing tartan carpet slippers and the ubiquitous dark blue-bibbed trousers favoured by French country men, pushing an antiquated bicycle up the path beside us. Usually Terry designates me to find directions, but I forestalled him and suggested this time he tried his luck. "And remember," I said, "it's pronounced 'comping', not 'camping.'"

First the gentleman pointed straight ahead, then bent his arm around in different directions, firing a rapid succession of "à droit", "à gauche" and "toute droite." We looked at him blankly, and showed him our map. He traced a route which seemed to

---

5 From an interview published in the International Sommelier Guild News, June 2004

go through every street in Châlons, then traced a different route, shaking his head and muttering all the time "*Pourtant, c'est très compliqué, très compliqué.*" We suggested that if he indicated the general direction, we'd ask somebody when we were nearer, but he shook his head again. We had asked for his help, and he was determined that he would get us to our destination, whatever and however long it took. When we still were no wiser despite all his efforts and gesticulations, he tapped Terry on the shoulder, climbed onto his bike, shouted "*Suivez-moi!*" and pedalled away straight across a line of brisk traffic. Terry managed to keep pace with him, but I had to cycle like a demon to keep them in sight.

That old boy's bike looked as if it might have come off the ark with Noah. It made a grating clunky noise as he pedalled, and had no gears, but it swooped around bends, flew along the roads, round the roundabouts, over the crossroads, past shopping centres and through housing estates, for ten long, fast minutes. I glued my gaze to the red panniers, disregarding all traffic in my fear of becoming lost forever, causing a few screeches of brakes and angry hoots as cars were brought to an unplanned halt by my passage. Finally our leader drew up beside a paddock where several horses were grazing. Ahead was the entrance to the campsite. "*Voila!*"

When we thanked this very kind gentleman for taking so much trouble, he shrugged. "It's normal to help visitors," he said. Away he pedalled on his clanking machine. The site was packed with caravans and camping cars, but there were only a couple of tents, leaving a large area for ourselves, and once we had pitched the tent we lay outside on the daisy-speckled soft green grass, pleasantly sandwiched between the coolness of the ground and the warmth of the sun.

During the early hours of the following morning we woke to find that for the first time on our trip, the tent was warm, and our jumble of covers could at last be cast off. I cannot remember another year when summer was so late arriving.

In the morning we went to explore the town. Standing in isolated magnificence on its outskirts is the stone archway known as the Porte Sainte Croix, originally built in honour of the young Austrian Archduchess on her way to marry the Dauphin. At that time it had been named La Porte Dauphine. The Latin inscription over the arch read: "May it stand for ever like our love." Marie Antoinette would see it three times during her life: on her way to her wedding, during her attempted escape, and on her return to her eventual death.

Known as Chaalons-en-Champaigne until the 16th century, then Châlons-en-Champagne with the arrival of the circumflex accent, the more plebeian Châlons-sur-Marne during the French Revolution, the town reverted to prestigious Châlons-en-Champagne once more in 1998. It is the regional capital of the Champagne-Ardennes and departmental capital of the Marne, although nearby Reims is a more imposing city, four times larger, with a much greater population. But Reims is also the city where traditionally the French monarchy were blessed, and the revolutionaries wanted to downgrade its importance, which they did by demoting it in favour of Châlons-en-Champagne, and so it has remained.

We thought Châlons a most attractive town, with generous, wide streets laced by a number of rivers and canals, bright, clean buildings, sparkling fountains, imposing Gothic and classical buildings. There are some wonderfully-preserved or restored medieval timbered houses – at least two of which had been transplanted, stone by stone, timber by timber, to new locations to conserve them during modernisation of the town. Strangers nodded and smiled, motorists stopped to allow us to cross the roads; the sun shone. It seemed like a township of which its residents are proud and where they are pleased to live, and we felt that, had circumstances forced us to stay permanently, we could have settled there quite happily.

Sitting in the sun, at a café, with a cup of hot chocolate and a croissant, watching the cheerful Châlonnais shopping and chatting could have been a pleasant way to pass the morning. But my eyes streamed constantly and my blotchy crimson face looked as though it was covered with first-degree burns. I

95

wondered how the human body manufactured tears, and what from. I must have leaked several pints over the last couple of weeks. "What does '*Maladies des yeux*' mean?" Terry asked, pointing to a polished brass plate on the wall next to where we sat. I looked at the plate. It belonged to an ophthalmologist. Surely this was a sign from the gods, an apology for the torment they had sent down upon me.

In the doorway stood a young woman in a white uniform. I asked her if she thought there was any chance I'd be able to have an appointment. She replied that she was only an ambulance driver, waiting to drive a patient home, but she would show me where I could find the doctor's secretary. She pushed a bell, and led the way into a gloomy waiting room, where the only occupant was a very old lady wrapped in a number of woolly jumpers and wearing a pair of thick, wrinkled stockings. She answered my "*Bonjour, Madame,*" with a weary nod of her head. The ambulance driver signalled me to sit down, and leant against the wall flicking through a magazine.

After a little while a door opened, and out came a dark-haired woman in an angry striped dress. Taking three firm strides, with one hand she banged on another door, which opened instantly. In that doorway stood a lady in a pink suit, and a man in a white jacket. Behind them the room was in darkness. The striped woman bent sideways and with her right hand snatched a handful of the seated old woman's jumper and jerked her to her feet. With her left hand she grabbed the outgoing patient by a sleeve, and with a practised flicking motion, she crossed her arms and spun the old woman tottering into the doctor's waiting arms, past the outgoing patient who was sent reeling into the centre of the room, where she was saved from falling over the coffee table by the swift action of the ambulance driver. I'd never seen anything like it. And no, I am not making it up.

Slamming the door behind the doctor and his patient, she snapped at the pink-suited lady to follow her. Then she noticed me sitting in the corner, and froze in mid-stride. "Who

96

are you? What are you doing in here?" she shouted indignantly. "You must leave." She waved her hand towards the door. While my mouth opened and closed silently like a goldfish as I tried to reply, the ambulance driver explained why I was there.

"She has no right to be in the waiting room! She cannot sit in here. She should not be in here without an appointment. Go into my office," she barked at me. She glared at the pink-suited patient. "And you, Madame."

In her office she slammed down into her chair and shoved a heap of papers around her desk, not bothering to look up when she asked what I wanted. I took off my sunglasses, and showed her my eyes, saying that I had hoped the doctor would be able to spare just five minutes to prescribe some sort of treatment to stop the flow.

"Just wash them with water. They'll be fine. You don't need to see him. Doctor is far too busy."

"I'd be very happy to wait until he's seen his last patient," I offered. "I don't expect a lengthy consultation, but he may be able to give me a prescription that would help temporarily."

"Impossible! Quite impossible. You must have an appointment. There are no appointments free for the next two weeks."

"What about going to the hospital?" the pink-suited patient suggested. "Her eyes do look terribly sore. Perhaps she should go to the Emergency department?"

"Waste of time. Far too busy there. She'll just have to keep putting water in her eyes."

I knew when I was defeated. Giving her the most withering look I could manage, I said "*Au revoir*" to the other lady, who followed me out into the passage. She said: "Madame, you could try the pharmacy. Maybe they can help you," and gave me an encouraging little pat on the hand.

After the rudeness of the stripey-dressed woman, and her assertion that the local hospital didn't have any time for people like myself, my confidence in the medical profession in this town was low. I was quite reluctant to ask for any help from the pharmacy. Terry pushed me through the door. With no expectations I went in and showed my eyes to a petite lady behind the counter, who drew in her breath and said that I should see a doctor immediately. Two women next to me at the counter and the pharmacist all agreed that somebody must do something without any more delay. There was, said one of the customers, an eye specialist nearby.

"I know," I replied. "But he's guarded by a dragon, and I can't get past it."

"Yes," agreed the other customer, chuckling. "We know all about her."

After making a number of phone calls, the petite lady directed us to a surgery about 100 metres down the road. She brushed aside my thanks, and refused take any payment for the calls.

The doctor, a kindly man in a knitted waistcoat, diagnosed a severe case of conjunctivitis, and prescribed two different types of eye-drops. I wondered why fate had felt it necessary to send me conjunctivitis at this particular time in my life, when I had never had it before.

Châlons-en-Champagne has several beautiful parks, and for our picnic lunch we chose the pretty Parc du Jard, with its magnificent mature trees and elegant statues of nearly-naked ladies representing the four seasons. Sitting opposite us, on a wooden bench, a stylish lady was nonchalantly tweezing hairs out of her legs. Although I love doing that, I hadn't ever considered doing it in a public place.

I had a brief but very intense love affair with an English bulldog who was sitting with his owner, avidly watching people eating their lunch. It was love at first sight – *un coup de foudre*. He writhed about on his fat back and offered me his tummy to scratch (the dog, not the owner), then he rolled over and put his front legs on my shoulders, whispering and snuffling asthmatically in my ear that he loved me. I could have very happily spent the rest of the day sitting on the grass with him, but Terry, who never stays in one place more than a few minutes if he can help it, was fidgeting and wanting to move on. We went for a glass of wine in the square in front of the rather splendid Town Hall, and then to visit the Gothic church of Notre Dame en Vaux. Terry stayed outside with the bikes – we were still concerned about leaving them unattended.

I pushed open the old door. Several years imprisoned in a Roman Catholic boarding school had left me with an enduring aversion to churches. It had taken decades for me to be able to walk into one without associating it with pain, punishment, sin and everlasting damnation, and even after all these years I still found it an uncomfortable experience. From the long hours of enforced daily worship, knee bones pressed painfully against cold stones, shivering at 6.00 am Mass on freezing winter mornings, or the torture of keepings arms raised in protracted prayer for the Stations of the Cross, I felt that I had earned not only eternal redemption and a place in the front row in Paradise, but also a dispensation from having to endure any more religious activities in dark, damp, musty old buildings. Still, as the church is so much a focal point of French towns, it seemed a shame not to at least have a quick peek.

Notre Dame en Vaux is really very lovely. The stained glass windows threw shafts of dappled colours into puddles on the floor; a magnificent vaulted ceiling surmounts three tiers of arches stacked upon each other like a wedding cake. There was not another soul there. I stood in the warm beam of the rainbow colours with my eyes closed listening to the silence and feeling the atmosphere. For the first time that I could recall I felt comfortable and safe in a church - like a human being rather than a sinner. Despite its towering Gothic construction, this church did not seem to me at all sinister or oppressive, but peaceful and rather cosy. If Terry hadn't been waiting with the bicycles I would have been comfortable sitting in there for a couple of hours. That was certainly a new and very unexpected experience for me. Untouched by religion, but moved by the beauty and peace of the building.

When I rejoined Terry, he was watching a young pigeon

huddled beside one of the buttresses. It was too young to fly, and looked at us hopefully, but there was nothing we could do except trust that its mother, who was watching from a nearby tree, would tend to it until it could manage to fend for itself, and that Notre Dame would take good care of it.

The staff at the campsite were very pleasant, and the sanitary facilities, the yardstick by which I rated the places we stayed, were impeccable. Beside the large lake families of ducks swam around in circles, and grey geese patrolled the lawns. Dozens of grubby-looking goslings, still wearing their adolescent fuzzy plumage, cropped at the daisies under the protective eyes of their parents, who hissed and stuck out their tongues if they thought we were getting too close to their offspring. After a long, refreshing shower we lay on the grass, reading, and both fell asleep in the sun. Later, we were woken by a persistent croaking. A pair of pretty mallard ducks was next to the tent, marching backwards and forwards, and poking their heads through the flaps, plainly expecting to be fed. They enjoyed the croissants we gave them, and when they had reluctantly accepted that there was nothing else on offer they waddled away to a nearby caravan to try their luck there. Next morning, they woke us up quite early, trying to burrow through the fabric of the tent in search of breakfast.

Whilst we'd enjoyed our relaxing interlude in Châlons and found the Châlonnais friendly and helpful - apart from the ophthalmologist's secretary - the royal escapees were less fortunate.

By the time they arrived from Etoges, although several hours behind schedule they must nevertheless have been confident that they were winning their game. They had covered more than half the distance between Paris and their destination of Montmédy, where loyalist supporters awaited them. But luck was running against them and at Châlons their situation began deteriorating inexorably.

When they stopped to change horses the splendid carriage and smartly-liveried servants naturally attracted interest. Spectators were surprised that the passengers did not climb out to relax, as people normally did, especially on a roasting summer day. Word buzzed through Châlons that the King and Queen had just passed through, heading eastwards. Although no attempt was made to stop them, they had certainly been recognised.

Continuing on their way, and expecting soon to be met by a military escort, by the time they reached Sainte Mènehould, the loyal dragoons who had been waiting for them had given up, and drunk themselves silly. The vigilant and very Republican local postmaster, M. Drouet, watching the great carriage and noting the excessively deferential behaviour of the driver towards the passengers, guessed their identities. He galloped ahead to Varennes, where he alerted the citizenry that the royals were trying to flee the country. By the time the carriage arrived at Varennes, the roads were barricaded and, tantalisingly close to safety, the refugees were captured. Their dream of freedom was over, and their worst nightmares were just about to begin.

The royal family spent the night in the grocery shop of the aptly-named M. Sauce. Louis did almost nothing to help himself and his family, accepting his situation stoically, unable to make up his mind, or uninterested enough to take a possible escape route proposed by the Duc de Choisel. He did at least have the presence of mind to ask for a bottle of wine and some bread and cheese. He was not a man to let adversity spoil his appetite.

Surrounded by a hostile mob of several thousand people, the next morning the prisoners and their captors set off back to Paris. Every attempt by members of the party to buy more time in the hope of a last-minute rescue failed, and the carriage turned back towards the west. The cavalry that could have rescued them arrived just half an hour after they left Varennes. Once again, time had conspired against them. A royal supporter who approached the carriage was shot and hacked to death by the crowd, his severed head waved aloft on a pike.

After having been ignominiously chased out of Sainte

101

Ménehould, the captured royals "shaken, exhausted, broken" found themselves back in Châlons, still a solidly royalist town, where they were greeted by the mayor, and wined and dined in fitting style. However, the vicious crowd that had accompanied them from Varennes recruited others, and the next morning they interrupted Louis while he was at Mass. Screaming threats and insults, they forced the family to leave in haste. They set off on their way back to Paris.

Our next stop was Reims.

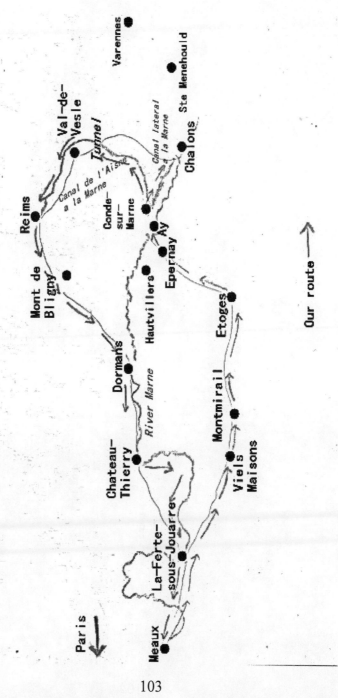

Varennes

Ste Menehould

Chalons

Canal lateral a la Marne

Val-de-Vesle

Tunnel

Conde-sur-Marne

Ay

Canal de l'Aisne a la Marne

Epernay

Reims

Hautvillers

Mont de Bligny

Etoges

Dormans

River Marne

Montmirail

Chateau-Thierry

Viels Maisons

La-Ferte-sous-Jouarre

Paris

Meaux

Our route ⟶

103

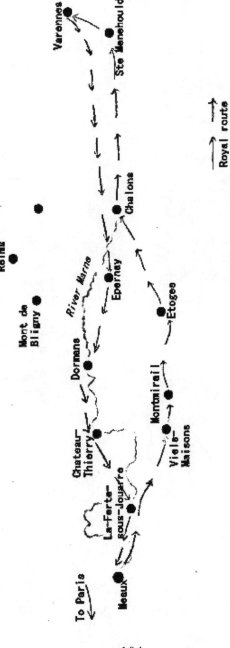

Varennes

Ste Menehould

Royal route

Reims

Mont de
Bligny

River Marne

Epernay

Chalons

Etoges

Dormans

Chateau-
Thierry

Montmirail

Vieis-
Maisons

La-Ferte-
sous-Jouarre

To Paris

Meaux

CHAPTER NINE
Tunnel Trauma, Nocturnal Noise

"Go placidly amid the noise and haste, and remember what
peace there may be in silence."
Max Ehrman: Desiderata

ORIGINALLY we had planned to stay a second day in Châlons, and cycle directly from there to Reims, a distance of nearly fifty kilometres, but because of the extreme heat we changed our plans and decided to head instead to Val de Vesle about twenty kilometres south-west of Reims to spend the night there. Terry planned the route and we picked up, at the small town of Condé-sur-Marne, just west of Châlons-en-Champagne, the canal de l'Aisne à la Marne.

Canals are very wonderful. Wild creatures live in and beside them; interesting craft sail upon them; there is no traffic beside them, and they are normally flat and usually shaded by trees, which suited me very nicely. I had been gradually training Terry to slow his pace, but as somebody who is by nature always moving at high speed, it had taken some time for him to accept that we were not involved in a race, either with each other, or with anybody else. There was no need to hurry. Indeed there was no purpose in hurrying. This was a holiday, not a contest to see how fast we could finish it. I could not maintain thirty kilometres an hour, and I didn't want to anyway. Somewhere between fifteen and twenty was comfortable for me, and meant that we could hold a conversation as we went along. Sometimes he forgot and speeded up and cycled far ahead, only slowing down when he realised he was talking to himself.

The towpath was shady and cool. A pair of herons kept flying twenty metres in front of us, landing, and then taking off as we closed on them, for about fifteen minutes. It was as if, in their rather solemn way, they were playing with us. At a

105

lock we stopped to talk to the crew of a 10-metre Danish yacht with her mast down, waiting for the water to rise. They had spent the past month motoring here from Denmark. Like us, they had been very disappointed in the weather until the previous day, and while it had been bad enough for us in the tent, in a small boat in the water it must have been thoroughly miserable. Still, their Viking blood probably helped.

We were pedalling along smoothly and effortlessly when the towpath began to deteriorate. Its smoothness became bumpy. Stones jutted up; ruts developed, then potholes. There were rocky patches, and sandy patches. It did not have the appearance of a path that was very much used. In fact it no longer had a path-like appearance at all. Unlike Terry's mountain bike, my machine is not designed for bumping around on rough surfaces. It does not have that kind of suspension. Each time we struck a rut or a bump the whole bike jolted and shuddered; I was bucked out of the saddle, and my feet flew off the pedals.

"Terry, this doesn't look right to me."

"Come on," he called. "Just follow me. It's fine."

The red panniers leapt wildly up and down as he bounced ahead, and I knew quite well that it wasn't fine at all, and that it was almost certain to get worse, which it did.

We shortly arrived at a 3-metre high chain link fence blocking our route. A sign on the fence said: "NO ENTRY."

Terry pushed open a door in the fence.

"I really don't think we should …."

But he was already wheeling his bike through.

To our left was a flight of high stone steps, some 30 of them, rising at an angle of about 45°. To our right was the canal. Between them, the entrance to a tunnel, which also bore a "NO ENTRY" message. Over the bridge, a man looked down on us from an office.

"Terry," I said, very firmly. "I am not going into that tunnel."

"Let me go ahead and have a look," he said.

While he did so, I tried to think of any way we could somehow heave the bikes up the steps, and later wheel them down the other side, without killing ourselves. I couldn't.

"It's not very long, and you can see the light at the other end," Terry called. "Just have a look."

Peering into the tunnel I estimated that the distance to the daylight visible at the other end was 200 metres, or 300 at most.

With very great reluctance, but faced with the alternative of having to backtrack all the way to Condé-sur-Marne and find a different route, I followed Terry through the tunnel's entrance. I would scuttle quickly through, and we'd be out at the other end in a few minutes.

Between the arched wall of the tunnel and the water was a one-metre-wide path. This path was blocked by a heavy wooden platform about four metres long, on small metal wheels, sitting on a narrow iron railway track. I've no idea what it originally transported, but it was in our way and we somehow had to get past it. While I braced the platform to stop it rolling away Terry heaved the bikes onto, over and off it, and then we began making our way towards the distant light. In places the path was gritty and filled our trainers with sharp little stones. In other places it was muddy and slippery, and in those places that were neither gritty nor muddy, it was cobbled and bumpy. There were the metal rails to contend with, too. We pushed for several minutes, as the light at the far end grew no nearer, and the light from the entrance grew dimmer, until we were in near darkness. One metre isn't much width for a plump person and a heavy-laden bike, and frequently the pedals struck against my leg. The tunnel eerily echoed my curses. We lit the lamps on our handlebars; by their weak glimmer I marvelled at the construction of the tunnel; the way every brick fitted perfectly into its neighbours in an elegant arch, and how it was somehow supporting a heavy road above it with all its traffic. Then I started to wonder how long it had been there, and how long tunnels generally lasted before they might show signs of collapse; and while thinking about time in general, I thought about how long we had been trudging, and how the tunnel's end seemed

107

much further than I had expected, and how long this tunnel could possibly be. It was starting to make me feel angry for being so long.

"Isn't this great!" called Terry. "Imagine during the war – there must have been all sorts of things going on in here." He kept stopping to peer into niches cut at intervals into the wall.

"Keep going," I urged him. "Stop stopping."

Apart from the rattling of the bikes, it was weirdly quiet. Still the light at the end was barely larger than the pinprick it had been when we set out so long ago. It was cold, and damp, and dark and spooky. What if there were giant eels, or huge slimy things that lived in the waters, which might reach their tentacles up over the edge of the path and wind around our ankles to pull us in? Then an even more alarming thought – what if there was a portcullis at the end of the tunnel? What if it slammed down just as we reached it? There was no room to turn around on the path; we'd be trapped. And then – what if there had been a matching portcullis at the entrance? What if the man in the office had seen us ignoring the two "NO ENTRY" signs, and was going to teach us a lesson and imprison us in the tunnel? Even in the cold I began to sweat, and snapped at Terry to get a move on.

Suddenly the previously still waters began slapping and slurping against the side of the path. Something was moving. When the whole tunnel was unexpectedly flooded with light, my tattered nerves gave way, and I screamed. Terry jumped. We felt like characters from a James Bond film, trapped in the glare by the forces of SMERSH or SPECTRE. A loud purring noise came from behind, and looking round we saw a very large motor cruiser gliding towards us. The width of the boat spanned the canal, and the pilot's head almost touched the ceiling of the tunnel. He seemed to be laughing as he waved to us, no doubt thinking: "English, obviously. Crazy!"

He floated off towards the distant speck of light, momentarily obscured it, and then as suddenly and unexpectedly as they had come on, the lights went off, and we were plunged into complete blackness.

It took Terry a moment to find his flashlight, while I froze, afraid to move forward. We'd been in the tunnel 40 minutes, and I was steaming with fury and shivering with fear; it seemed we were never going to reach the end. Blood tickled my leg from several abrasions caused by the pedals, and trickled into my trainers to join the grit, sand and mud they had been collecting. A new thought struck me: what if, when we reached the end, there was no way forward? Why would there be – it was a no entry place. There must be a reason for that. What would we do? Whatever it was, I knew I was not going back. I'd rather abandon the bike and swim to the other side.

By the time we finally reached daylight, we'd been plodding through the tunnel for seventy minutes. Seventy minutes of ankle-cracking, footsore, fearful tunnel-trekking. On the opposite bank two old boys were fishing; they gave us no more than a cursory glance. Ahead, on our side of the canal, the rail tracks continued for about fifteen metres, and then disappeared into a head-high thicket of brambles and stinging nettles. There was no sign of a path.

I snatched the map from Terry, and traced our route with my finger. The Mont-de-Billy tunnel is 2,300 metres long.

"You knew, didn't you? You bloody well knew!"

He had the grace to look embarrassed.

"Yes, but it did save us a long, hot and boring ride on the road. And anyway, you did it. What are you worrying about?"

"What I'm worrying about is the fact that having arrived here, there's nowhere to go!"

That wasn't quite true – there was a similar flight of stone steps to the one at the other end of the tunnel, equally insurmountable with bikes.

"You brought us here, now you find a way out," I snarled.

Undaunted, he stamped down a rough path through the undergrowth, and after about fifty metres we found our way up a bank and onto a woodland track which led back to the canal a while later. Although completely overgrown and bumpy, we managed somehow to ride on the track, even if the very long grass sometimes tangled itself in the spokes and brought the bikes to a halt. We met a family of black swans, two parents and three cygnets, a friendly little bunch, obviously well used to humans. They cheeped softly and clambered out of the water to enjoy a handful of crumbs and then posed obligingly to have their photos taken.

Because of our unplanned detour through the woods, we had no idea where we were. There were no distinguishing features, just trees, grass and the canal. It was very hot, so we were pleased and relieved when we arrived at a bridge bearing the sign "Camping 400m."

It is no reflection on the delightful small town of Val de Vesle that some of France's most lurid crimes and murders took place in the immediate vicinity. Notorious serial killer Pierre Chanal, an adjutant at Mourmelon military barracks, eleven kilometres away, was suspected of the sadistic murders of the eight young conscripts from the barracks, between 1980 and 1987, who became known as "The Missing of Mourmelon." The scandalous ineptitude of the authorities in their handling of the case, and the fact that Chanal was able, in 2003 while on trial in Reims, to commit suicide in his cell and thus thwart justice, outraged the public and in particular the families of his supposed victims, and made the case a *cause célèbre*.

In 2008, the "Ogre of Ardennes," Michel Fourniret was brought to trial, and confessed to seven murders. He and his accomplice wife were both given life sentences. One of his victims was a 20-year-old girl whose body was found, coincidentally, at Mourmelon barracks in 1987.

In 1989 the body of a 30-year-old woman was found at Villers-Allerand, sixteen kilometres west of Val-de-Vesle. She had been strangled and beaten to death by homeless sociopath Francis Heaulme, suspected of killing at least 40 people. He is currently serving several consecutive life sentences, plus an extra 30 years.

The 1980s seemed to have been a busy time for homicidal maniacs in the area.

Now the fact that all these unhappy events occurred within just a few kilometres of Val-de-Vesle should not deter those looking for an excellent campsite with beautiful mature trees and a really luxurious sanitary block; and as far as I know, it's the nearest campsite to Reims. The showers are squeaky-clean and so spacious you could turn cartwheels in them if that's what you feel like doing. I just wanted to stand under a stream of hot water and wash away the dust of the day and the memory of the tunnel. That is what I was doing when just outside the door I heard an urgent, exasperated male voice and a quivering female one. The man was definitely annoyed, and the woman plainly distressed. Their discussion went on for several minutes. I dried and dressed, and poked my head around the door to ask if they needed help. The man leapt towards the exit as if he'd been scalded, stammering that he was only trying to help his wife understand the showers. She thought they were lavatories. I said that I'd look after her, and he shot out of the door, leaving a poor old lady gazing at me for reassurance, like a baby bird asking for food.

"I don't know how they work. Are they for washing, or are they some sort of lavatory?" she asked. "There aren't any taps."

I took her in to the shower for handicapped people, where there was a safety rail that she could hold while she showered, and explained how to lock the door, where to hang her clothes, and how to push the button that would turn on the water.

"But when you push it the first time, wait for a moment because the water may be a bit chilly when it first comes out."

"Where are the taps?" she asked.

"The button is instead of the taps."

She wasn't convinced.

"It's such a long time since we came to France. They used to have taps. I don't suppose they have a bath here, do they?"

"No, I don't think so," I said. "But the showers really are easy. Just push the button, and when the water stops running you push again, and more water comes out. As much as you want. And hold the rail if you need to."

111

She looked doubtful.

Did she think she could manage?

Yes, she said, rather uncertainly.

"I'll be outside. If you need any help, you can call me."

While I applied eye-drops and cleaned my teeth, I could hear her talking to herself, but no water running, so I tapped on the door and asked if she was managing.

"I'm fine, dear, thank you. Don't worry about me."

Should I have offered to stay in the shower with her? Would she have been grateful, or offended? Whether she ever did succeed, I'll never know, but I felt so sorry for this old lady who was confused by a shower with no taps. I thought how difficult it must be for older people to keep up with the amazing acceleration in design and technology that has made something as simple as having a shower turn into a struggle. I hope it won't happen to me.

A few kilometres west of Val de Vesle is the small town of Verzy, and once we'd freshened up we thought we'd cycle there to have a look at the strange, twisted little beech trees that grow in the forest, the *"faux de Verzy,"* and to have our evening meal.

In whichever direction we looked, there were champagne vineyards stretching to the horizon. Nothing but a vast, tranquil sea of vines. Oh, and arising from this ocean, a lighthouse, built at the beginning of the 20th century to advertise one of the local champagne producers. For a few years it was a place where local people came to eat and drink, and the children to play. When WWI broke out it was requisitioned by the military and used as an observation post, and after the war it fell into disuse until quite recently, when it was converted into a wine museum.

On the way to Verzy we had a rather surreal experience. There was a very long, smooth road with a slight downhill gradient but, oddly, we had to pedal hard to make headway, when logically we should have been able to cruise. The temperature was 38°C at 7.00 pm, causing the sticky tarmac surface to snatch at our tyres. Even Terry was feeling the heat.

112

When we arrived in the town and discovered that the mutant trees were another kilometre further on, up a very steep hill, we felt we could live without seeing them, and were content to simply sit in a bar instead, drinking shandy. Only one restaurant was open, and it didn't look like the kind of establishment where sweaty cyclists would be very welcome or feel comfortable. Apart from that, the menu was all meat apart from the lobster menu – three courses all made out of lobster and priced accordingly. Not for us, sadly.

So we bid farewell to Verzy without having accomplished either of our goals, and cycled back to Val de Vesle. On the way we passed a field of horses, reminding me sadly that our lovely old mare, Leila, had died just one month previously, at the great age of 40.

Back in Val de Vesle we stood outside a vine-swathed restaurant debating what we would choose from the enticing menu, when an open-top sports car drew up noisily. An English gentleman climbed out, shouting to his companion that this was the place with such an excellent reputation and he'd give the menu a quick snifty. We moved aside for him, and he read it out loud, smacking his lips and saying "Mm, mmm," turning to call out some of the dishes to the lady in the car.

"Damn fine food, so I'm told," he said.

"Looks pretty good," said Terry. We'd had nothing to eat since we left Châlons ten hours earlier.

A lady came out of the main door to the restaurant, and looked at us in surprise.

"*Mais c'est fermé ce soir,*" she trilled.

"Eh? What's that?" asked the lip-smacking man.

"Apparently they're closed tonight," I replied.

"Bugger! Double bugger!" he said. That summed up our feelings perfectly. We had no food with us, there were no other restaurants in Val de Vesle, and it was 8.15 pm. With a car it was still feasible to find somewhere open, but on bikes it looked as if we were in for an enforced fast. The Englishman and his companion roared away with a cheerful wave, and we rather despondently turned towards the campsite. Terry spotted a young man carrying a large, flat carton. "Pizza?" he asked. "Oui," replied the young man, pointing to a lane leading to a small square where a van was parked. We were saved.

During the night I was woken up by a strange noise, a harsh crackling sound like a crisp packet being rhythmically crumpled up. At first I thought it might be a hedgehog, and then perhaps a fox, or a rat. It sounded very close, and went on for what seemed like hours, while I lay trying to ignore it and feeling more and more irritable. Surely Terry couldn't be sleeping through this racket? I nudged him.

"Are you awake?"

"Yes."

"Can you hear that peculiar noise? It's been going on for hours. What do you think it can be? It's driving me mad."

"It's me. I'm fiddling with my wallet. Opening and closing the Velcro fastener."

"You must be disturbing everybody around us. Why on earth are you fiddling with the Velcro on your wallet, in the middle of the night?"

"I don't know."

I took the wallet away from him and put it under my pillow.

The eyedrops were not helping. From the neck up I still resembled a mottled crimson rugby ball with purple hair. I couldn't possibly have looked any worse unless I had a giant cold sore on my nose.

CHAPTER TEN
A Lame Duck and a Second Epiphany

"Anything may happen in France."
François de la Rochefoucauld

THE next morning I woke up with a huge cold sore on my nose. Could things possibly get any worse? I freely confess to having more faults than most – as the kindly nuns used to remind me at every opportunity during my school days – but vanity has never been one of them. However, I felt very self-conscious knowing that I looked such a frightful mess, and began to resent my own face for the way it was letting me down.

Once every year, Reims holds a spectacular two-day folklore festival and a great pageant in honour of Joan of Arc, and I'd arranged our itinerary to be there for this special event. As there were no campsites in the city, and I had heard that it might be difficult to find hotel accommodation due to the great number of visitors coming from all over the world for the spectacle, I had panicked and booked the first available room I could find on the Internet. Subsequently, reading reviews of the hotel, I regretted my choice, because many people who had stayed there didn't have a good word to say for the place. Noisy, cramped and rude staff were just some of the complaints. I had e-mailed them several weeks before to ask about overnight storage for our bikes, but had never received a reply, and I was worried that we wouldn't be able to find anywhere safe to leave them. Not wanting to alarm Terry, I had kept all this to myself, but privately I wondered what I had let us in for.

In sizzling heat we left Val de Vesle. We passed the airfield at Prunay where we had landed twenty years previously, during a light aircraft rally with the Beagle Pup and Bulldog Club in Terry's little Beagle Pup aircraft. At the *grand cru*

115

village of Sillery, from whose wine the ambrosial dessert called syllabub was born, we sipped a prosaic chilled cider, and then picked up the Canal de l'Aisne. After a peaceful and uneventful ride, we arrived at mid-morning almost in the very heart of Reims. The only problem was that we arrived on the opposite bank of the canal from the town. Over a high metal bridge a very thin, tanned man who looked about eighty was carrying his bike on his shoulder. He trotted nimbly down the forty or so metal steps.

When I asked him where we could cross the canal, he turned and pointed up the same steps. It was simple – just carry the bikes up, over and down the other side, and we would be right in the centre of town. I pointed to our bikes, and invited him to try to lift mine. With a grimace he raised the front wheel about 10 centimetres off the ground. He pointed to a road a few hundred metres away, pirouetted gracefully onto his machine and purred away.

The road he had indicated seemed to be the main artery leading into the town, and it was heaving with traffic. It took a few exciting minutes to navigate our way into a smaller minor road, and then we found ourselves right outside the door of the hotel, a narrow orifice clamped between two shoe shops in a shopping arcade.

"Funny sort of hotel," remarked Terry.

"No, I'm sure it will be fine. And such a great location right here in the centre of town," I said, more positively than I was feeling. "I'll go and check in and find out where we can put the bikes."

There was only just room in the tiny ground-floor lobby for a single armchair, a staircase and a lift door. On the first floor, a beautiful black girl stood at the reception desk. A youth sprawled out on a settee, playing a computer game. Somebody else was laughing, out of sight. Yes, reception said, she had a record of our booking. Our room was ready.

"Do you have somewhere we can leave our bikes overnight, or do you know anywhere we can lock them up? We can't leave them out on the street."

She had a quick conversation with another girl. It was no problem: we could put the bicycles in one of the empty bedrooms, and there wouldn't be any charge. It seemed quite normal to them that bicycles should be brought up into the rooms, and it would suit us very well.

The receptionist took me up to see whether I was happy with our bedroom. On the way, she told me that she came from the Congo, that she was studying hotel management, and that although she liked France well enough, where she really wanted to be was in the United States, where she would be going next month to continue her training.

I asked her if she didn't feel homesick sometimes, and her eyes turned soft and dreamy, like her voice. "Yes, I love my job but I miss my family, and I miss the Congo. But when I have finished my training, one day I'll be able to go back and work in a hotel there."

Our room wasn't luxurious. It was quite small and basic. The furniture wasn't antique. There was no wardrobe, just a rail with a few coat hangers. The view from the window was of the glass roof of the shopping arcade. But it was clean, the bed was firm and comfortable, the location was ideal, and the staff couldn't have been more helpful. I am fairly easily pleased: a night sleeping on a proper bed, and being able to soak in a bath, were all I wanted. Apart from a new face. And body.

Somehow we were going to have to get the bikes upstairs and into their bedroom. Outside in the arcade we stripped off all the attachments and baggage, and heaved and twisted the machines into many kinds of unusual configurations to squeeze them in through the narrow glass doors, which were further narrowed by a thick vertical pole between them. Terry's lightweight aluminium mountain bike was relatively easy to manhandle into the lobby, but getting it into a tiny little lift, with himself, was rather a challenge. We could squash 98% of the bike in, but there was always a small piece that wouldn't quite fit, making it impossible to close the lift doors. Eventually, with the handlebars draped over his shoulders and the pedals jammed against his legs, Terry succeeded and arrived on the first floor, and we wheeled the bike through a tight corridor and into a bedroom that was almost entirely filled with a double bed. Somehow he managed to fit the bike in. How, though, I was wondering, could he possibly find room for my far larger, and much heavier bike, let alone bring it up to the first floor. It would never fit in the lift, and neither could it come up the stairs, which were steep and narrow with a sharp turn.

It looked as if the only way we'd be able to get the thing inside was by taking it entirely to pieces, or by smashing down the doors. I began wringing my hands and tutting.

"Why don't you go and do something useful," Terry suggested. "You could wash our clothes instead of standing there moaning."

So that's what I did, in the bath, bashing and thrashing and wringing and rinsing until the whole room was steamed up and filled with wet clothing, which I hung out of the windows, and draped over the door handles and anywhere else I could find. Twenty minutes had passed, and there was no sign of Terry, so I was sure that he was either having to dismantle the bike so he could get it in the lift, or he had found somewhere else to put it.

It was another fifteen minutes before he arrived, and I said cautiously: "Did you manage to sort it out? Did you get it in the lift?"

"Of course I did. They're both in the bedroom."

I should have had more faith. It constantly surprises me, although it shouldn't any more, how he can achieve things that most people regard as impossible. In fact the more difficult something is, the more determined he is to succeed. I'll never know how he fitted that machine into the tiny lift.

Once we'd soaked in a soapy bath, we went out sightseeing. It felt strange to be travelling around on feet instead of wheels, and while Terry said he felt he could happily live on a bicycle, I much preferred walking and was looking forward to the prospect of having a rest from pedalling.

We sat over lunch in a square just around the corner from our hotel, listening to an Italian brass band tuning up, and then playing stirring tunes *con molto brio*. A bearded young man and his brown mongrel dog came and sat at the table adjacent to us. The young man had some slight mental disability, and he wanted to talk to us. Because of his speech impediment, we had great difficulty understanding most of what he was saying, but very happily he put this down to our foreign stupidity and was not at all embarrassed. He stood up, and said to the dog, "Wait here, next to the lady, until I come back. Don't move." Giving us a meaningful look that said, "Just you watch how my dog understands me," he disappeared, returned after five minutes, walked to the bar and stayed there talking to the barmen, and then went away into the gents. All that time, his little brown dog didn't move an eyelash. It sat like a rock, absolutely motionless, just as its master had told it. I called it, clicked my fingers, offered it a chunk of baguette, but it wouldn't even turn its head until its owner came back and gave it permission. When we had finished our lunch and stood up to leave, he reached out and shook my hand, saying something that I couldn't make out. Only later it occurred to me that he maybe felt he had found a kindred spirit.

Reims is a reassuringly solid sort of town, of substantial three-storey buildings with slate roofs, sufficient chic shops to cater for the most exacting tastes, and generously wide streets that were submerged beneath a sea of weekend visitors - Japanese, Italian, American and others speaking in tongues I did not recognise.

The air was pungent with grilled meats, wood smoke, charcoal, toffee apples, candy-floss, perspiration, leather, and gunpowder from battle re-enactments. Metal grated against metal as soldiers in chain mail fought with broad swords; canon and musket fire resounded, and trumpet blasts announced the passage of royalty resplendent in silk and velvet.

It was impossible not to be excited and carried away by the

cacophony of sounds, the cocktail of smells and the panorama of sights. Stalls offered leatherware and ornaments, foods, jewellery, ceramics, clothing, souvenirs and gifts. Men in lederhosen and ladies in dirndl (actually I don't know if that's what it was, I just wanted to use the word, never having had an opportunity to do so before,) wove themselves around a pole, holding ribbons. Children queued for the chance of an archery lesson; vultures, falcons and owls stood patiently on wooden blocks in a square, staring inscrutably at the crowds watching them; a lady selling large metallic balloons in the shapes of birds and animals looked in danger of being lifted by them into the skies. Bejewelled nobles in sumptuous robes and floppy headwear strolled around, nodding regally to the hoi polloi. A ragged wretch begged for mercy as he was hauled away in a metal cage to be executed. Plump clergymen, knights clanking around in full suits of armour, peasants in rough woollen tunics, lepers ringing bells, and jesters with jingly hats mingled with the 21st century crowd.

A handful of medieval buildings remain in Reims, and a few vestiges of the Roman occupation still stand, but in the main the architecture is predominantly early 20th century, a consequence of the city having to be almost entirely rebuilt after WWI. Over the four years of the war, the Germans slowly and systematically destroyed the cathedral with their heavy artillery.

It was an act of vandalism that shocked the world: the deliberate destruction of one of Europe's greatest architectural jewels and France's most sacred church. If it was a tactic designed to crush the morale of the Remois, it failed. The townspeople continued going about their daily lives with determination and good humour. I remembered reading somewhere that out of 40,000 houses only 40 remained when hostilities ended, and the champagne house of Pommery was hit by 200,000 shells. When the war ended, thousands of German prisoners were put to work clearing the rubble and rebuilding the city for its citizens.

During the Second World War Reims was targeted again by

the enemy, although the cathedral was spared. And the city had its revenge when it witnessed the signing of the German capitulation at 02.41 hours on 7th May 1945, behind the railway station in the building that had served as the Headquarters of the Allied Expeditionary Force.

We weaved our way through the mob towards the cathedral, and walked down the wide, tree-lined Rue Libergier for several hundred metres, to approach the great church as the French kings would have done on their way to their consecrations, and see it through their eyes. For thirteen hundred years, nearly every French monarch had been crowned there. I tried to imagine the emotions, scenes and sounds that this street had witnessed over the centuries: jostling, cheering crowds, soldiers and courtiers and horses surging around. Surely everybody must have been be stunned then, and must still be stunned today, at the first sight of this beautiful, magnificent church, whose stonework truly deserves the description of "stone lace." The New York Times carried an article in 1916 describing the ruined church as beyond restoration after the damage inflicted by the Germans. Happily, the reporter was quite wrong; although it took over four decades, with generous donations from the Rockefeller family the cathedral rose again to its original glory.

Notre Dame of Reims is famous for its historical significance, beauty and for the jolly, beaming smile on the face of the curly-headed angel at the door of the cathedral, which made me want to hug it. This is the funniest angel I've ever seen and it's hard to believe that during WWI, the Germans shot its head off. Just like the Mona Lisa, the reason for the angel's enigmatic smile has intrigued people over the ages. I'm pretty sure that I have found the answer. If you look, you'll notice that with one hand it is pulling its cloak across its tummy. Poking out of the cloak is the stump of its other arm, which has no hand and looks like the barrel of a large calibre gun. The angel is clearly saying "Stick 'em up!" And that's why it's laughing.

Terry wandered off with his camera, while I stood gazing

around, and thinking of the sights and sounds these stones had soaked up in their long history: choirs and sermons; chanting and hymns; the voices of bishops, and of the kings of France making their vows; cheers and jeers; and the roar of gunfire and crackle of flames. The walls were home to so many ghosts, and what emotions must lie within them: pride, joy, jealousy, sorrow, triumph, defeat, love and hate.

During the ceremony of the *sacre du roi* – the consecration of the king – kings swore their allegiance firstly to the Christian church, and secondly to the kingdom of France. They were regarded not only as monarchs, but also as gods, which gave them supreme power over their subjects. The cathedral is said to be built upon the site where Clovis, first king of a unified France, converted to Catholicism in the fifth century, following a victory in battle that he believed was due to Christ's help. Becoming a Catholic Christian was a clever political move, strengthening his ties with Catholic Rome and winning him powerful allies. He was anointed with a magical holy oil from an ampoule supposedly delivered by a dove directly from Heaven, which was safeguarded for centuries.

The miraculous qualities attributed to the holy oil were not sufficiently powerful to protect the Sainte Ampoule from the fury of the Revolution, when the flask was broken. However, some of the contents and fragments were apparently saved, and the repaired ampoule lives on in the cathedral.

Tomorrow the date would be Sunday June 11th, the date on which Louis XVI was blessed in 1775, by the grace of God, most Christian King of France. The Gazette of France reported his arrival in Reims on 9th June, in a ceremonial coach.

"After the Duke of Bourbon, Governor of Champagne, gave him the keys of the city, the King entered Reims escorted by the troops of the royal household and made his way through a people intoxicated with joy - which did not decrease but rather intensified as the procession moved along. The next day, the King listened to the first Vespers in the Cathedral, and on Sunday, June 11th, around seven o'clock, His Majesty - with the greatest pomp - went back to the same Church and was crowned in the usual ways."

The consecration ceremony was a lengthy one, with many changes of clothing, much anointing, plenty of praying and speeches, Mass and rituals involving various regalia. I thought it quite likely that at the time of his consecration, Louis would have been more interested in what he'd be having for dinner than in the ceremonial. Queen consorts attended the ceremony purely as spectators, so Marie-Antoinette had no role to play, but wrote to her mother saying that she'd been moved to tears by the acclamation of the crowds, who had forgotten for a while the national shortage of bread and rejoiced at the sight of their new sovereigns. The people of France, with all their problems, had been able to put aside their miseries and show their pleasure. This would make her, and the King, work ever harder to bring them happiness, and, if she should live to be a hundred, she would never forget the day of her husband's consecration.

Reims was one of very few places we visited where the royals had not passed during their flight. Ironically, they had avoided the city because Louis feared that he might be recognised by the subjects who had welcomed him so warmly sixteen years previously. Their route had taken them instead to Châlons, where he was recognised anyway.

After the Revolution, with the French monarchy temporarily restored, Charles X, Louis XVI's brother, was the last French monarch to be consecrated in Reims. Watching that ceremony and accompanying jubilation, Chateaubriand wondered whether Charles remembered that the sacred oil hadn't done much to protect his brother from the disapproval of the people. It wouldn't do much for Charles, either. Five years later he'd be fleeing for his life, to the safety of England.

As I walked around there was muted, or occasionally loud speech in a dozen languages, the fall of hundreds of footsteps, and the click and flash of cameras. A small child crawled around on the floor in the aisle; the ubiquitous Japanese tourists listened intently to their guide; a group of handicapped people rolled along the aisles in wheelchairs; a

123

band of schoolchildren craned their heads to follow a teacher's hand pointing to the vaulted ceiling 100 feet above them.

Just as it had in Châlons, the afternoon sunlight projected rainbow patterns from the stained glass onto the flagged floor. The oddest thing happened: I found I was crying. Not the irritating drips from my afflicted eyes, but from somewhere deep down inside hot, heavy tears welled up and flooded down my cheeks, and then sobs began climbing into my throat, and heaving my shoulders, and it felt as if at any moment I might break into a noisy and embarrassing display. I went and stood in a dark corner and stared into the shadows until I had recovered my habitual sang froid, and wondered what had caused this very unusual emotion. I wished I had a tissue as my nose came out in sympathy with my eyes. I've visited many historic buildings in various countries, but they have mostly left me unmoved. Here in Reims something had happened, which I could not explain. It was a deeply spiritual experience that did not have anything to do with Christianity. I did not want to take Holy Orders, or read the bible from start to finish, nor go to Mass, or indeed to any church service. But standing there had touched something right in the depth of my soul, and it left me feeling both euphoric and mystified. I wiped my arms over my wet face, and went outside to find Terry.

Like Epernay, beneath the streets of Reims lies a network of crayères – deep subterranean pits left by the Romans quarrying limestone. The constant damp and cool atmosphere provides a perfect storage environment for the bottles of the great champagne houses of Reims - Krug, Veuve-Clicquot, Tattinger and Mumm, but it was slightly disconcerting to know that much of the city was standing on top of a honeycomb of caves and tunnels.

After we had walked around in the heat for several hours, my feet had grown three sizes larger than my trainers. Back at our hotel I settled down in the bath for a second long soak. When you have missed the luxury of lying full length in warm water for so long, you must snatch every opportunity that comes your way.

I emerged from the bath with an even redder face, frizzed up purplish hair, and huge feet that looked as if they belonged to somebody else. I put the cycling helmet on for half an hour to squash the hair flat, and jammed on my trainers with the laces undone and my toes tightly curled. Looking at my reflection in the mirror, I felt like hurling myself from the window.

There were two things I needed: some green face powder to camouflage the red, and a pair of shoes that could accommodate my feet. It was after 5.30 pm, and the shops were preparing to close. Sales assistants looked at me with open ridicule when I asked for green face powder; clearly Remoise ladies never had red faces. I had to settle for a thick foundation instead. There were probably more shoe shops in the city than any other kind of shop, but they were all very expensive and I didn't plan on spending a fortune on a pair of size 8 shoes that I would only wear once. By 6.30 pm desperation had set in, and I was reduced to buying the ugliest footwear I'd ever seen. They were that type of sandal with very flat, thick soles, two Velcro fastening straps over the foot, and a similar one round the heel. Globetrotters wear this style of footwear, and on long slim legs and slender feet with a healthy tan they can look attractive, on a beach or trekking across deserts. Teamed with sunburned legs and inflated feet, they were indescribable. Every strap was cumbersome; they were filled in at the outer edges so that from the outer sides they looked like a peep-toed shoe, and from the inner sides like a sandal; and they were grey. Terry remarked that they looked like correctional footwear. But they were cheap, and they were blissfully comfortable. They were also our final option, so we bought them, and went back to the hotel to dress for dinner.

The little black chiffon skirt and top did not go well with the sandals and the strange flattened hair. I remember a children's game that was made of cards, with people on them. The cards came in three parts – head, body and legs. You had to try and make as many whole people as possible from the different parts. My top section was made up of the black and diamanté baseball cap covering my hair and the giant sunglasses half of my face – Mrs Beckham. The mid-section was in the snug-fitting skirt and top – Mrs. Podge, and the lower section showed the white legs and swollen feet in the frightful shoes – Miss Splott.

I had already remarked to Terry that the ladies of Reims are the most slender, long-waisted and chic females I have seen anywhere. Nobody seemed to be over a size 8. Except me.

Off we went into the night, out into the elegant streets. Everybody seemed dressed to the nines, befitting a night out in this sophisticated city. I was so embarrassed by the bizarre footwear that I adopted a strange gait, swinging and dragging my feet haphazardly, pretending to be afflicted by some physical infirmity. People smiled sympathetically and moved aside on the pavement to let us pass.

After trying for half an hour, in vain, to find a restaurant that was not full to capacity, we arrived at Le Bistro du Boucher, which despite its name had a comprehensive menu of fish and vegetarian dishes. It was full, and the manager was sorry but he didn't think a table was likely to become available very soon. I shuffled my feet, and he glanced down, took in the swelling, and the grey straps, and held up an index finger. "*Une minute,*" he said, signall ing a waiter and saying something in his ear. A moment later the waiter came back and set up a small table on the pavement, and tenderly ushered me into a chair.

I had momentary pangs of guilt as other people were turned away, especially as the food was really excellent – almost as good as the meal we'd had at the château, but half the price. I felt in need of something very comforting, and chose to finish off our meal with the "*baba au rhum avec sa petite bouteille de rhum ambré.*" The baba arrived swimming in rum, and accompanied by a full 75 cl. bottle of more rum, which our waiter recommended I should use generously. For service, quality and value for money, we'd recommend this restaurant

126

very highly. We had each already drunk a complimentary kir Royale, and shared a bottle of rosé, and by the time we left the restaurant I no longer cared what I looked like. Somehow it really didn't seem important any more.

In fact it didn't matter at all, because it was dark by now. Crowds were heading towards a platform in front of the town hall. A group of lively ladies in swirling multi-coloured dresses danced around stamping their feet, snapping their skirts and clicking castanets, while their menfolk made yodelling noises. We bought a drink of something called "witches' brew," which was pleasant in a strange way, and a glass of red wine served by a bad-tempered man who slapped our glasses down on the table so hard that half of the wine slopped out. No bad thing – it was sour. The atmosphere zinged with excitement. Tiny little tots long past their bedtime sat perched on the shoulders of their fathers, clapping happily and singing to the music. We resisted the temptation to buy an heraldic shield, toy animals made out of rabbit skins, hand-spun woollen garments, replica swords, balloons, jars of honey, or ceramic pots with our names painted on. A South American group in beautiful costumes, who sang plaintively and made haunting music with strange wooden instruments, replaced the twirling ladies. It was long after midnight when we wandered back to our hotel through the hot, dark night in a town filled with music and laughter and the clinking of glasses and cutlery.

Despite all the dreadful reviews I'd read about our hotel, we enjoyed a peaceful and comfortable night. Once we briefly heard a baby cry, but only for a couple of minutes. Maybe we are too easily pleased, but we found nothing at all to complain about.

While Terry magically extracted the bikes from their bedroom and manhandled them into the tiny lift and out onto the street next morning, I sat in the hotel lobby watching a succession of elegant, arm-linked old ladies, perfectly coiffed, dressed and shod crossing the square on their slow way to morning Mass.

127

Outside a small café we munched on crusty baguettes stuffed with Camembert, while dozens of squealing swifts swooped overhead, and the streets filled with people heading to the medieval market. Children in buggies, on shoulders, on tricycles or attached to a parent's hand all wore hats and sunglasses, even tiny babies dangling from sacks around their mothers' necks. One small boy was channelling all his energy and vocal range into a monumental tantrum, flinging himself down in the gutter, kicking his feet up and down and screaming with pure rage, while his poor mother and father tried unsuccessfully to reason with him. As we moved away we heard the thump of a hand contacting a backside, followed by furious roars and bellows, and then a miraculous silence. The next time we saw them the child was hand in hand with his parents and laughing.

We watched stirring re-enactments of jousts, sieges and executions, and a realistic sword fight between two grunting, armoured men swiping and bashing at each other with broadswords as if they really meant it. The main event of the day, the grand parade, would begin at 3.30 pm, and with a long ride ahead of us we planned to watch for just half an hour. Down the road from the basilica of St Rémi, where the procession would begin, we found a vantage point in a street that was almost empty apart from a few people setting up folding chairs and a group of police winching onto trailers cars that had ignored "no parking" notices. On the bridge we could see horses tossing their heads and stamping in the heat, milling crowds of people in costumes, and vintage vehicles forming into a queue.

On the pavement in front of us somebody dropped a lump of masticated chewing gum, and I watched in fascination as it was trodden on by a succession of people and trailed in long, long threads to their shoes. It was quite extraordinary how far one small piece of gum could travel. The street started to fill until it was packed three-deep. Residents came out from behind shutters to look down from their balconies. A girl cycled backwards and forwards distributing leaflets from the saddle of her two-metre tall unicycle. It was as much as I could do to ride my bike with two wheels and both hands; how on earth did she manage up there, without any handlebars?

When promptly at 3.30 pm, leading the parade, the Kent Police Band marched into sight, the band leader, drummers and standard bearers in full uniform, the brass in their shirt sleeves, it brought a lump to my throat and a few extra tears to my eyes.

Morris Men followed, and for the next hour groups from Europe, Asia, Africa and the Americas marched and danced and sang their way past us, stopping happily to be photographed. The simple coloured cloths and animal hides worn by the South African cultural group were suited to the scorching afternoon temperature, but many others, like the Paraguayan ladies dancing with brown teapots balanced on their heads, wearing thick layered skirts or dresses, woollen stockings and heavy headdresses must have felt impossibly hot.

After the groups had passed, a brief interval followed; the crowd moved uncertainly. Then a deep drum roll sounded, followed by a solemn drum beat heralding the Archbishop of Reims, majestic in his Sunday best, followed by lords and ladies in vibrant jewel-coloured satins, heavy velvet robes and furs, wimples and veils, and droopy hats. Young page-boys in blue tabards and thick, wrinkled white stockings, and little maids in full-length robes with circlets of flowers in their hair were visibly wilting in the heat but stoically marching onwards. An earnest, bespectacled small page-boy carried the coronation crown on a cushion in his white-gloved hands. All these people were members of historical societies and re-enactment groups; the quality of their costumes was outstanding. Trumpeters from the Conservatoire of Reims, dressed in turquoise and scarlet, led the star of the pageant, Joan of Arc, The Maid of Orleans, mounted on horseback, carrying her standard, and escorting Charles VII to his consecration.

It was almost 600 years since Joan of Arc had brought Charles VII to Reims cathedral to assume the crown and turn the tide of the Hundred Years War against perfidious Albion and its Burgundian ally in favour of France. When, within a few months, Joan was captured by Burgundy, sold to the English and roasted in Rouen, Charles did nothing to help her. Put not your trust in Princes ......

As the nobility turned the corner out of view, they were followed by rough peasants in animals skins; a juggler dressed all in black, throwing knives – the crowd gasped when one flew out of control and clattered to the ground; some plump bourgeoisie; yeomanry, and soldiers dragging canons.

A five-minute lull followed. It seemed to be all over, and again the crowd moved hesitantly. We were preparing to cycle away, when a Dutch band, magnificent in black and scarlet, with cockaded helmets came into view, followed by the Court of Roland – the mounted knights in chain mail and tunics, beating leopard-skin kettle drums and clashing cymbals. A brown bear glared at the crowd from a rustic cage towed by a team of five heavy horses, and an anxious lady ran down the street, urging everybody to stand well back – the horses were dangerous, we may be crushed. Nobody cared; we all wanted to be as close as we could to the characters and creatures passing by. For those few moments we were transported to the Middle Ages.

"Well, that's it. Time to go," said Terry, putting away his camera. But, just as we thought we really had seen everything, who should appear but Marianne herself, symbol of the French Republic, leading the French postal services. They were represented by a romantic old diligence of the *Messageries Générales*, followed by the Russian Czar's Courier, a troika drawn by three superb white horses abreast and laden with heavy wooden trunks and boxes. Bringing up the rear were the riders and stagecoach of Wells Fargo.

From the world of entertainment came cheerful girls in taffeta dresses with leg-of-mutton sleeves and pert, ribboned hats; a music-hall singer went past on a float, singing one of my favourite old-time songs "*On n'a pas tous les jours vingt ans,*" a beautiful little story about a young Parisian seamstress celebrating her 20th birthday. She and her workmates are enjoying biscuits and a little drop of port in the workroom, when the boss gives the girls the day off work, and in fine spring weather they go out to a little place in the country, beside the river, to lunch, and later dance to a gramophone with their beaux. After all, says the chorus, it's not every day that you're twenty! It's a special day that only comes once in your life, so you must make the most of it and enjoy it to the full. Sung nasally, to an accompanying accordion, it's a French classic from the 1930s.

Glowing in a bright red sparkling suit, with his famous blonde hair, the mega-iconic Claude François - or rather an impersonator - glided past on a moving stage singing, inevitably, "*Comme D'Habitude*"– his legendary composition of unrequited love that would morph into "My Way" and become one of the greatest international hits of all time. He, poor man, met a premature and very horrid death when he decided to change a light bulb while standing in a bath. Don't do that.

After a fleet of immaculately restored vintage cars came Charlie Chaplin, directing a film from a truck. Then Elvis in his bejewelled, skin-tight white suit waving to the crowd from an outrageously long American convertible. Finally, the very end, the very last celebrity, sitting high on the cream leather upholstery of a chauffeur-driven maroon 1970's Rolls Royce Corniche, the beautiful, the adorable, the sexy, the one and only – Marilyn Monroe, with her glorious blonde hair, scarlet lipstick, wearing her famous white dress, displaying her famous cleavage, and seductively blowing kisses from behind a fan.

All afternoon the parade had travelled through the streets to continuous cheers and applause that could be heard far into the distance. It had been an unmissable event, faultlessly organised and a joy to witness the enthusiasm of both the participants and the spectators, and we were particularly impressed by the impeccable behaviour of the small children

131

and horses for whom the crowds and the intense heat must have been a real ordeal.

Two hours later than intended, we prepared to set off for our next destination, Dormans, forty kilometres away by the shortest route. A small crowd had collected around my bike, and we asked them which direction we should take out of town to put us en route for Dormans. Faces lit up with glee.

"You're going to Dormans? Tonight? Now?"

"Yes."

Our new friends smiled knowingly at each other, and a little jingly bell went off in my head. What did they know that we didn't? Had there been an outbreak of bubonic plague in Dormans? A nuclear strike? An earthquake? We hadn't seen any news of the world outside our own for nearly a fortnight.

"Is there something bad in Dormans?" I asked.

Everybody laughed. "No – not at all! It's just getting there that's the problem!"

Had the road melted in the heat? Was it blocked by a dreadful accident?

"*C'est la Montagne de Reims*. It's uphill all the way! Very hard!"

"Ah," I replied confidently, "but I have my electric bike, and my husband has electric legs!"

They all laughed again, and somebody said: "I hope they last! Good luck."

Everyone had a different idea as to which was the best route; they all spoke simultaneously and within a minute were arguing amongst themselves. A luxuriant, beautifully groomed grey moustache with a rotund gentleman attached to it called for order, and outlined his idea of the simplest route. The rest of the audience conferred briefly, nodding and murmuring, before agreeing with him, and reassuring us that we could rely upon his directions absolutely.

"*Bon courage*," they all said, shaking our hands.

"*Vive la France!*" we called.

"*Allez les rosbifs!*" they shouted back.

132

CHAPTER ELEVEN
No more champagne

"Anyone who has ever looked into the glazed eyes of a soldier dying on the battlefield will think hard before starting a war."
Otto von Bismarck

"There's no such thing as a crowded battlefield. Battlefields are lonely places."
Alfred M Gray

WE pedalled hard in the direction we thought the moustache had given us. After we'd been cycling for twenty minutes up an incline, and covered six kilometres, we had still seen no sign to Dormans. I pulled up and said to Terry: "Are you sure we're going the right way?"

"Not really," he answered. "I thought you had understood the route."

"So did I, but I'm beginning to wonder."

We went in to a filling station and asked the cashier if Dormans lay ahead of us.

No, we were going in the opposite direction, he said. We were several kilometres north-east of Reims, when we should be heading south-west. What we needed to do was to follow the road for about four kilometres back the way we had come, and turn left at the junction signposted to Soissons. Then we'd see the signs to Dormans. "But," he added cheerfully, "it's a very hard ride. I'm a cyclist myself, and I can tell you it's hard. It's uphill all the way!" I had noticed that people always showed a gentle schadenfreude if they were able to advise that the road ahead was going to be particularly arduous. There was no malice in it, though; in fact we accepted it as a sign of camaraderie.

We backtracked until we found the Dormans sign, and

133

started the most gruelling ride we had so far experienced. Maybe "proper" cyclists will scorn our efforts. Frequently, as we pushed and puffed up hills, scrawny people sped past effortlessly, on racing bikes with no appurtenances, yodelling or whirling their arms in the air. But as amateurs we thought we were making a fairly doughty stab at the challenge of cycling in this demanding part of the world with our heavy loads and in the intense heat.

I had imagined the Montagne de Reims as no more than a slight bump on an otherwise flat plain. But no, when you cycle upon and around it, it is worthy of its title. Like a stack of pancakes, the mountain is made up of layers of chalk, clay, silt and fossilised marine skeletons, formed 90 million years ago and left behind when the Paris basin subsided 70 million years later, when the seas that covered the area retreated. Beneath the plateau, an area of dense forests of pine and broad-leafed trees, the sides of the mountain are home to vineyards that benefit from sunshine and the porous soil that retains moisture and aids drainage.

Terry has muscles of steel and sufficient energy to fuel an aircraft carrier; I have muscles of dough and the energy level of a sloth. Once again we were facing a killing slog. I could see Terry's legs moving fast, and his bicycle moving slowly, and pedal as I might, and even in my lowest gear, and with a fully charged battery, I could not make any further headway up the road. My leg muscles were shaking like jellies in an earthquake, and sweat poured down my face, down my torso, and down my legs into the hideous sandals. I could hear the too-fast pounding of my heart, and I thought, "Oh crikey, I'm going into cardiac arrest."

For a moment the world went black. Maybe it was the thought, or maybe my reserves really were all used up, because with a graceless sideways movement, I toppled off the bike onto the verge, having had just sufficient foresight to make sure I was near enough to do so, and not onto the melting tarmac.

Being almost stationary when I went over, I was quite

unhurt, despite landing on sunburnt grass that was stiff and spiky, the ground as hard as stone, and part of the handlebar digging into my ribs. It felt wonderful, euphoric, to be still, not to be pedalling. I felt I could curl up into a ball like a hedgehog and lie there for hours, quite happily. Terry had been some way ahead, and turning back to see me lying beside the road, ran back down. I called out: "I'm OK. I'm fine."

We sat on the roadside trying to restore our energy, and once he had done so Terry cycled my machine up to the summit of the hill, then came back for his. I tottered slowly up the last few hundred metres to the cool and peaceful Italian cemetery on the crest of the Mont de Bligny.

Even on a brilliant day this is a mournful place, with its sad cypress trees casting their shadows across a sea of more than 3,000 stark white crosses representing the Italians who had died here during the so-called Great War. Among them lie two of Garibaldi's grandsons, members of the regiment that bears his name, who fought as volunteers with the French Foreign Legion until Italy officially entered the war, as an ally of France, in 1915. On the opposite side of the road to the cemetery, like the backdrop for a tragic opera, is a poignant monument: a Roman road bordered by cypress trees, leading to a symbolic broken Roman column.

It was tempting to sit all night on this lonely hilltop in the sombre shade. Once more in the saddle, we were soon flying downhill, past the smaller British cemetery at the bottom of the hill, just outside the village of Chambrecy. Our speed generated a welcome cooling breeze that refreshed the spirit and drove us on to our destination, the slumbering little town of Dormans.

From here onwards through the Marne valley, for the most part the landscape would be remarkable for its battlefields rather than its vineyards.

The campsite at Dormans is beautifully situated on the banks of the Marne river, facing the town and looking up at the church, beside the bridge that for centuries has been a

135

strategic site with a recurrent history of death and rebirth. The first wooden bridge was destroyed during the Wars of Religion to hinder the Protestant troops before the Battle of Dormans. The replacement was destroyed in 1918, rebuilt, destroyed in 1940, and replaced with a wooden passageway, until the current robust new suspension bridge was built in 1951.

As we arrived at the site, a couple of hours before the advertised closing time, the *gardienne* was locking up; she hesitated fractionally, before driving away and leaving us to sort ourselves out. That meant that we didn't have any access to electricity, and the battery of my bike was completely depleted after today's efforts, so the indefatigable Terry went off to find a kind soul to recharge it.

The campsite was almost full to capacity, and amongst the camping cars and tents there were also many static caravans with built-on extensions, awnings and patios, flowery gardens, ponds and shrubs, stone animals and gnomes, owned by town dwellers who came here for weekends. A group of twenty weekend regulars were enjoying an al fresco supper together at a long trestle table.

Terry set up the tent while I crumpled gratefully onto the cool grass, then we went to shower. Although the showers were primitive, the water was hot and welcoming on weary bodies, and afterwards we sat in the balmy evening air listening to the noises of the night. We had noticed that the very last sound before darkness fell was always the song of a blackbird. The other birds gradually fizzled out, but the blackbird sang on, and it was to its beautiful notes that we fell asleep most nights.

It was a peaceful Monday morning in Dormans, a small town of 3,000 inhabitants, whose largest employer is the manufacturer of the labels for the ubiquitous *Vache Qui Rit* (Laughing Cow) processed cheese. Chatting ladies stood in the sunshine with shopping baskets over their arms, while their menfolk sat at pavement tables reading *L'Equipe* or murmuring to each other over cups of coffee or little glasses of *rouge*. In the bar everybody smiled and wished us good day, and the lady who served our croissants in the bakery remarked that it was going to be another very hot day, and asked whether we planned to visit the memorial? I replied that we certainly did; we had heard a great deal about it.

"Ah yes. It makes you think. It really makes you think," she said, handing over the croissants and a few coins in change.

A lady beside me nodded wisely: "Everybody should see the memorial. Then there wouldn't be any more wars."

The Tourist Office in Dormans is rather grandly situated in a handsome symmetrical château with a witches' hat turret at each side, in a verdant park at the end of a sweeping tree-lined drive. While I went in to find out what I could about Dormans, Terry entertained himself watching the frogs leaping in the pond on the front lawn, and trying to capture on film a snake lacing its way silently through the plants at the water's edge.

We've visited a great number of tourist offices in France. Many have been helpful and have gone out of their way to give us information; some have been helpful within their limits; and one or two have been politely disinterested and have merely pointed to stacks of brochures in answer to requests for information. But I had never met a girl like the one in the Tourist Office of Dormans. She bubbled with enthusiasm for her work. She was proud of Dormans and happy to talk about the town and its history for as long as I was happy to listen. I always find it such a pleasure to meet somebody who doesn't just do their job, but loves it. She walked up and down the racks of brochures, plucking out any that she thought would be of interest, and remembering a leaflet that was in a drawer somewhere. She searched until she found it, waving it triumphantly. Soon I had a healthy fistful of paper containing all the information anybody could possibly want to know about the town.

Only one thing was missing: the royal captives had stopped there on their way back to Paris, but there was no mention of where they had stayed in any of the leaflets or brochures. I asked about this, and her face lit up.

"Yes! That's right – they did come to Dormans, and they spent the night in a hotel here."

"Is it possible to visit the hotel – to see where they actually stayed?"

She grimaced. "Unfortunately, it's a private house now. But I can tell you," she smiled, "that it is the house just up the road from the Post Office. At least you can see the outside."

We went later to look at it, an unremarkable building bearing a very discreet plaque that reads:

"Dans cet immeuble alors Hotel du Louvre le 21 Juin 1791 Louis XVI et la Famille Royale ont séjourné après leur arrestation à Varennes." (In this building, known at the time as the Hotel du Louvre, Louis XVI and the royal family stayed after their capture at Varennes.)

With the Royal family back in the hands of their captors, their lives returned to the public domain, and we were able to find more information about them and their ongoing trials.

After they had been chased out of Châlons, their next stop was at Epernay, where they received a most hostile reception. The mayor told Louis that he should think himself lucky that the town had allowed a fugitive King entry. Marie-Thérèse, the thirteen-year-old daughter of Marie-Antoinette and Louis, remembered the occasion in her memoirs:

"We reached Epernay at three in the afternoon. It was there that my father ran the greatest danger of the whole journey. Imagine the courtyard of the hotel where we were to get out filled with angry people armed with pikes, who surrounded the carriage in such crowds that it could not enter the courtyard. We were therefore absolutely obliged to leave it outside and cross that courtyard on foot amid the hoots of these people who said openly they wished to kill us. Of all the awful moments I have known, this was one of those which struck me most, and the horrible impression of it will never leave me.

Entering the house at last, they made us eat a miserable meal. In spite of all the threats of the ferocious populace to massacre every one, they did not go farther and we started from Epernay about six in the evening."

The weather then, as now, was very hot, and the dry roads were stirred into a dust bath by the marching mob. Inside their carriage, the captives were tired, travel-stained, dishevelled. It must have been particularly frightening and physically hard on a little six-year-old boy who had been brought up in comfort.

Just to the east of Dormans the cavalcade's progress was temporarily halted by the arrival of three members of the National Assembly, who had come to escort them back to Paris and ensure their safety. The three men squeezed themselves into the carriage, where the occupants found themselves jammed uncomfortably against each other. The Queen impressed the new arrivals by asking for a guarantee for the safety, not of herself and her family, but for the members of their retinue.

Louis had recorded in his diary events since their departure from Varennes as prisoners:

"Wednesday 22, left Varennes at five or six in the morning, had *déjeuner* at Sainte-Ménehould, arrive at ten in the evening at Châlons, supped there and slept at the old Intendant's office.

"Thursday 23, at half past eleven they interrupted Mass in order to hurry our departure; partook of déjeuner at Châlons, dined at Epernay, found the Commissioners of the Assembly near Port-à-Binson; arrived at eleven o'clock at Dormans, and supped there; slept three hours in an armchair."

Their plight had not affected the King's appetite.

Marie-Thérèse wrote:

"We reached Dormans in the evening, and slept at a little inn. The deputies were lodged side by side with us. Our windows looked on the street, which all night long was filled with the populace shouting, and wanting us to go on in the middle of the night; but the deputies no doubt wanted to rest themselves, and so we stayed. My brother was ill all night and almost had delirium, so shocked was he by the dreadful

139

things he had seen on the preceding day." [6]

As we were unable to visit the inn where they had spent the night, was it possible to have a look around the château, I asked. The girl pulled a face again, and said apologetically that the château isn't open to the public. It belongs to the town now, and is only used as municipal offices and for meetings. There is nothing really to see, no furniture left there. But, she brightened up, the memorial was superb, we would find that very interesting, although it wouldn't be open until 2.30, when the voluntary staff arrived. She came out to see my bike, which was surrounded by a group of admirers trying to work out what exactly it did, and exactly how it did so, although none could be persuaded to have a ride.

The pond snake was elusive. For many minutes of tip-toeing around and peering intently, the most we saw was a glimpse of sinuous tail sliding from the bank into the reeds. With four hours to kill before the memorial would open, we bought a picnic lunch and went to sit at one of the rustic tables and benches in the park, beneath a clump of towering trees. We shared our food with a few wild birds that hopped around our feet and darted onto the table, snatching up morsels and flying away with them. It was a welcome change to have an opportunity for few hours of inactivity, which we put to good use by reading all about the history of Dormans, its château, and the memorial we were going to visit.

We learned that Dormans had been a theatre for battles during not only WWI but also the Hundred Years War and the War of Religion. It was during the War of Religion that Henri, Duc of Guise took a bullet in the face at Dormans. He's one piece in an interesting little historical jigsaw. His father, François, uncle to Mary Queen of Scots, had seven children, of whom Henri was the eldest. François was nicknamed "Le Balafré," meaning "Scarface," as a result of a terrible wound inflicted during battle when a lance pierced his face beneath the left eye, passed through his nose and emerged on the right between his neck and ear. He made an astonishing recovery,

---

6   Royal Memoirs of the French Revolution by the Duchess of Angoulême

only to be assassinated eighteen years later, shot by a Protestant fanatic. On his death his son Henri inherited the title of Duc de Guise. Henri fathered fourteen children, thus doubling his father's score, and like his father was known as *Le Balafré*, from the injury he sustained in Dormans. And just like his father, Henri also died at the hand of a Huguenot assassin. I love reading these fascinating snippets of history.

We also read that during the Wars of Religion, persecuted Huguenots had taken refuge and hidden out in deep cellars beneath Dormans. As it was illegal for them to be interred in sanctified ground, if they died their bodies had to be buried instead in local gardens. Ever since, gardeners turning over their vegetable patch or digging up their flowerbeds have occasionally unearthed skeletons. I decided not to buy any locally-grown fresh fruit or vegetables while we were in Dormans.

Just as we finished eating, the volunteers arrived to open up the church. Perched pugnaciously on top of a small hill, the Dormans memorial appears a chunky, grey stone and rather grim Gothic building. A number of turrets of differing designs and heights climb towards the central spire, giving the memorial an asymmetrical appearance. The exterior looked, to me, a little bizarre, as if assembled by a child who has put the pieces together in the wrong order. However, the arched, Romanesque main entrance is softer, more honey-coloured, as if it is saying: "Don't be put off by the foreboding exterior. Come inside and see."

The lower chapel and crypt is a place of soft shadows, muted sunlight and vaulted ceilings, in no way sinister, but immeasurably sad. On the pale stones of the walls the names of dead soldiers are engraved in blood red. As we stood there reading those names, I found that I was crying again. Recently I seemed to be spending a lot of time in tears for one reason of another. Seeing all those hundreds of names, of officers and men – four brothers in one case, and a prince, just tore into my heart. The walls seemed built of sighs, and the white stones wept unbearable grief.

Maréchal Foch was the prime mover behind the building of the memorial, ostensibly as a tribute to the 1.5 million French soldiers whom he sent to their death in the two infamous battles of the Marne – in 1914 and 1918. Every stone bearing the name of a dead soldier signifies that the man's family made a donation to the construction of the building. Donations from those families lucky enough not to have lost any loved ones are acknowledged by a blank stone. If the family of a dead soldier couldn't afford to buy a stone, or were all dead themselves, that soldier's name presumably didn't appear anywhere in the building. It would have made good sense for those soldiers to be "adopted" by the families who were spared, don't you think?

The upper chapel of the building is less sombre, with radiant stained glass windows, and symbolic statues and carvings. Four pillars show scenes depicting the historic invasions of France – by the Huns, the Saracens, the English and the Germans. Statues of saints bear the faces of people who were prominent figures in the war and in the construction of the monument – Albert 1st and Elizabeth of Belgium, Maréchal Foch, and the Duchess of l'Estissac, one of the major fundraisers for the monument. This floor is as much a museum as a chapel, with models of soldiers in different uniforms; weapons and assorted items recovered from the battlefields; an exhibition of paintings and some immensely evocative pencil sketches of wartime scenes; diaries, and old photographic postcards showing scenes of all the towns we had recently visited – Epernay, Châlons, Reims and Dormans. More than anything else we had seen, or would see, these postcards illustrated the reality of what the war had done to this part of France.

Where today the roads lead through beautiful, peaceful vineyards, to orderly villages and dignified towns with shops, churches and squares where the inhabitants stand and chat, in 1918 all that had ceased to exist. The postcards showed scenes that were nothing but skeletons of blackened timbers, and piles of rubble. During WWI 80% of Dormans was destroyed.

Most telling of all was a scene of the river beside which we were currently camped against a background of gentle slopes covered with vines. The postcards showed how this same place had looked in 1918: the river banks were piled high with the dead bodies of men and horses, and overturned gun carriages. Soldiers waded through the water, clambering over corpses. It was a scene of the most terrible destruction and horror, as far removed from today's sounds of laughter and birdsong as the sun and moon are distant from each other.

From a balcony on the first floor of the monument, we could look out onto the town below, and the hills behind, where the grapes that would make champagne were ripening in the sun.

The contrast between the two scenes is graphically, and poetically illustrated by a German officer, Lieutenant Kurt Hesse of the 5th Grenadier Regiment, who kept a wartime diary. Here is an entry from the end of May 1918:

"Slopes to the right and left are luxuriously covered with woods, orchards and vineyards; there are numerous villages, pastures full of cattle. When on the morning of May 31st I stood with my commander on the heights to the east of Château-Thierry - truly, a paradise lay before me, the sun smiled over it, a brisk wind blew across the valley. Here one breathed a different air; no war - peace."

And that was how it looked to us.

In dramatic contrast, as the German troops were annihilated and forced to retreat by the Americans, his diary entry for July 15th 1918 reads:

"I have never seen so many dead. I have never seen such a frightful spectacle of war."

18-year-old Californian Harry St Clare Wheeler enlisted in the US Navy in 1917. In January of 1919, he wrote to his sweetheart:

"You take a look at the battlefield where there were happy homes once and all you can see is ruined buildings and big shell holes all over the country. Everything is as still as night, not a sound. The smell of the battlefield will make you sick.

You see bodies of soldiers that were never buried and some that they do bury have only a thin layer of dirt thrown over them. You see lots of the Yankee boys who have fallen, probably places where they could not be seen easily, and are still laying with their clothes nearly rotted off of them. The Germans they don't bury very good. They just throw them in a shell hole, probably sprinkle some dirt on the top of them. So you can see how awful a place it is. As far as you can see is nothing but ruined country like this. I hope there is no other war like this." [7]

That is what we were looking at in those old black and white postcards, and it brought us the realisation of what an immense undertaking it had been to rebuild all those towns and villages. It must have seemed at the time an almost impossible task to transform this terrible devastation into a place where people could live again.

7   Reproduced with the very kind permission of Keith Wheeler, son of Henry St Clare Wheeler

Beneath the lower chapel the ossuary holds urns of ashes from deportees of WWII, coffins containing the bones of unidentified soldiers, and the death mask of Maréchal Foch. Outside a symbolic *lanterne de la mort* stands, beside a row of national flags of the French allies; the cloth hung limp and still in the heavy afternoon heat.

We walked back to our bikes in silence. My mind was confused between the beauty of the interior of the monument and the horror it represented, and I could neither reconcile them nor separate them. It was a strange feeling.

Cycling back to the campsite, we looked around with different eyes to those with which we had come here. Everywhere we passed, every centimetre blessed with the sunshine today had witnessed suffering beyond imagination during WWI, and only had time to recover before it had all began again twenty years later. Yet, within a decade the enemies would become allies, political and economic, if not personal, and what had it all achieved? What would all those dead soldiers think? It really made me think of the total futility of war and the pointless sacrifice of all those lives.

Paul Valéry defined war as "*La guerre, un massacre de gens qui ne se connaissent pas, au profit de gens qui se connaissent mais ne se massacrent pas.*" (War, a massacre of people who don't know each other, for the benefit of people who do know each other but don't kill each other.)

It was in a sombre mood that we folded the tent and packed our bikes, and prepared to move on to the next stop, Château-Thierry. As we cycled out of the campsite side by side, Terry asked what I had thought about the monument, and I replied that I thought it was beautiful, tragic and interesting, and a moving tribute to all the people who had died in the two wars.

"No, it isn't. It's a memorial to Maréchal Bloody Foch," he said angrily. "Like all these damned things, the names of the hundreds of thousands who died are lost in long lists, but it is the brandy-sipping, cigar-smoking generals with their big moustaches who, from behind the safety of mahogany desks sent these men to die, whose names remain in our minds, and who are glorified by statues and paintings." When I thought back, the Maréchal's arrogant moustached face did feature very prominently throughout the building – glaring from a bust, dignified in a death mask, and his name was all over the place. Hm. Terry, who is generally moderate in his opinions, feels very strongly on this subject, and would, given the opportunity, have the remains of all those medal-draped, swaggering generals who squandered the lives of young men and basked in the glory of their actions, dug up and burned.

There was no cycle path beside the river, so we had to take to the road for a ride dominated by the 39°C temperature and terrible hills. In the small villages we passed there was no sign of life from man or beast. The shutters were closed. No birds sang. There was no traffic. The bars were closed. Everybody and everything, it seemed, was sheltering from the infernal heat. There were no cyclists on the road. Except us. Terry had somehow jammed into the already over-filled panniers a couple of bottles of water to supplement the flasks clipped to our bike frames. Every two or three kilometres we stopped to drink, an unsatisfying and unpleasant experience because the water was warm, the sort of warmth you could comfortably bathe in. Although it was late afternoon the sun was still high, and the shadows short, and there was no shade anywhere.

We pedalled on, disturbing the silence with pants and grunts. Sweat ran in salty rivulets down my face, mingling with the eternal tears and stinging my sunburned skin. I had to keep reminding myself that we had set off on this adventure to enjoy ourselves, and my only consolation as I fought for breath and tried to find the energy to push the pedals round once more was that Terry too was wilting under the scorching sun. He was a kilometre ahead of me when I saw him dismount and wait for me to catch up. We didn't have sufficient breath to speak, just took a few mouthfuls of hot water, and swapped bikes for the push to the top of the hills. That was the pattern of our journey; the upside was that hills generally have two directions, and we had some fantastically fast downhill runs. Although it was only 20 or so kilometres to Château-Thierry (a name synonymous with the Marne, but in fact geographically located in the Aisne *département* of Picardy,) it took us over three hours to reach there.

As for Louis, Marie-Antoinette and their entourage, when they left Dormans and continued on their way back to Paris, the initial antagonism between the two parties in the coach mellowed. The young Dauphin helped to break the ice, and the occupants of the coach began to realize that they were all human beings. The King and Queen were not the arrogant, unapproachable monsters that the Revolutionary representatives had imagined. When the Dauphin announced his need to pass water, it was the King who undressed him and held the silver chamber pot in place. They were a family, and their children were just like anybody else's children. Marie Antoinette, who so loathed the Revolutionary movement and its supporters, found that her fellow passengers were not bloodthirsty monsters, but intelligent and educated men, and in fact "they were more conversable than the Count of Artois (Louis' younger brother) and his companions."

CHAPTER TWELVE
The Threshold of Hell

"Thru the night winds wet and dreary,
Word goes on to Château-Thierry,
Ghostly Phantoms hear the call,
Gather those who gave their all."

Phantoms, by Pvt L. C. McCollum – doughboy and poet

PREDICTABLY, Château-Thierry's campsite was as far away as it could possibly be, right on the other side of the town, tucked away behind a McDonald's featuring a giant plastic squirrel in the car park. Previously I had stayed at 128 campsites all over France, but never one where the office was secured with such a robust lock. Nor one where a menacing Rottweiler stood a couple of metres from the door with a look in its eyes that said: "Come on punks, make my day." The office itself, once we had breached its defences, was cool, modern and comfortable, with a giant bird's nest fern occupying all the available space except for where the desk was. There were photographs of Rottweilers on the walls.

The *gardienne* was a charming lady who would happily recharge my bicycle battery, if I would deliver it to her later that evening. I asked how she had encouraged her fern to such a vast size and magnificent condition. She shrugged; she thought it was probably the fact that it had so much light, and was happy in its location. She didn't know it was a fern – she thought it was a banana plant. When we left, she carefully locked the door behind her.

We found a shady place looking onto the river, and Terry hammered the tent pegs into the concrete-hard ground. The most level pitch we could find sloped at an angle of 25° no matter which way we looked at it. While he hammered I sat in my habitually useless way, wondering whether the three-metre high chain-link fence securing the perimeter of the campsite to repel invaders was really necessary. As well as the lopsided pitches and hard tussocks of thick frizzled grass all over the ground, the sanitary block was both utterly primitive and absolutely filthy. We were not surprised to be the only persons at the site. We squatted uncomfortably on our inflatable pillows, wishing there was something else to sit on – a fallen log, a rustic bench, a concrete ledge, anything on which we could relax for an hour. But there was nothing except the rock-hard earth punctuated with stubbly spikes of vegetation.

Shortly a camping car pulled up just across from where we were sitting. Two minutes after it arrived a big man came over to us carrying a couple of folding canvas chairs.

"What you two need," he smiled. "is to sit in a comfy chair. I used to do a lot of cycling myself, and I know exactly how you feel." He opened out the chairs and patted them. "Sit yourselves down."

Our new-found angel was a retired policeman, who had worked undercover in the Drug Squad, and he and his wife were touring France for several weeks. Not only did they lend us the chairs, they also gave us an English newspaper, and exchanged paperback books with us. There wasn't anything more we needed to enjoy ourselves for a couple of hours as we waited for the sun to fade. A shower would have been very welcome, but not in the unsanitary block. Instead we went into McDonalds and washed as thoroughly as it's possible to wash in a handbasin.

On the other side of the chain-link fence a succession of teenage girls walked backwards and forwards along the path beside the river, pushing baby buggies, carrying infants on their hips, and smoking. Behind us, from the road outside McDonalds, motorbikes and cars with ineffective exhausts roared and farted through the streets.

When we went off to find somewhere to eat, we discovered a strangely fractured town. It seemed to me to have no heart, but several disconnected limbs. Some parts were on one side of the river, and some parts on the other. I had expected a great deal of Château-Thierry, both because of its wartime history and as the birthplace of one of France's most revered writers, Jean de la Fontaine. Every French schoolchild can probably quote verbatim at least one of La Fontaine's fables. Surely we would find crafty foxes, industrious ants, feckless grasshoppers, silly sheep, wily wolves, torpid hares and harried tortoises on every street corner? In topiary, wrought iron, paintings, statues, flowerbeds? But if there were any they were hidden well away. We couldn't find any signs at all, apart from McDonald's giant squirrel, and I don't think that was related to La Fontaine in any way. We thought we might have discovered something when we came across the Jean de la Fontaine museum, tucked away discreetly. However a passing French pedestrian told us that it contained nothing of any interest at all and advised us not to waste our time visiting it. It isn't like a French town to miss any opportunity to attract and enchant visitors, but from what we saw, Château-Thierry had done so.

Another son of the town was the infamous and enigmatic Henri Déricourt, a pilot, and secret agent for the British Special Operations Executive 'Prosper' network during WWII. Déricourt was responsible for organising the flights in and out of France of SOE agents, but when the Gestapo captured the whole network he was suspected of having betrayed them to the Germans. After the war he was tried in France for treason, but acquitted due to lack of evidence. As well as being suspected of being a double agent, there were suggestions that Déricourt was also in the pay of the SIS.[8] Whether he was a traitor, nobody has yet been able to prove or disprove, and he remains a very controversial and unfathomable character. He supposedly and quite conveniently died in an air crash in Laos in 1962, although his body was never found. There was no memorial to him in Château-Thierry.

Because we burned a great deal of energy during the day, we always had enormous appetites, so the perpetual question

---

8   British Secret Intelligence Service, also known as MI6

in our minds, as each day began to fade, was always "What Are We Going To Eat Tonight?" We could find nowhere attractive or inviting to eat in the town, so opted for McDonalds, which although it didn't reach great epicurean heights, at least was clean, and provided those all-important spotless toilets and wash basins.

Later we cycled around looking for something to admire in Château-Thierry. Maybe it has never recovered from the centuries of fighting there; maybe we were looking in the wrong places; maybe it grew weary of rebuilding and simply gave up, or perhaps it had never been a place of great charm. It seemed as if no effort had been expended to welcome visitors, but rather as if the town would simply be grateful to be left alone.

Maybe they had never been very hospitable people. For the Royal captives, never knowing what kind of reception to expect from the towns where they stopped must have been nerve-wracking. Would it be respect and affection, as in Châlons, or hatred, insults and threatened violence as in Epernay? I thought how terrified they must have been, especially the children, each time the carriage halted. Château-Thierry offered them jeers and gibes, and demanded that the young Dauphin shout: "*Vive la nation!*" which shocked even the deputies of the National Assembly.

Over the centuries Château-Thierry had seen invasions by Vikings, Huns and the rotten English, as well as civil wars in the 16th and 17th centuries. Napoléon had given the Prussians and Russians a good bashing here in 1814. But its name is best known for the events of June 1918.

In May 1918 the Germans were once again advancing quickly towards Paris, and had taken Château-Thierry. The inhabitants were fleeing, taking with them the few possessions they could carry. In his wartime memoirs "Fighting the Flying Circus, 1919" American fighter ace Eddie Rickenbacker recalled events as he witnessed them in Paris.

He described the pitiful sight of exhausted, tattered and travel-stained refugees trudging along in their thousands in search of safety and succour in the capital. From the very old to the youngest children, all in a state of bewilderment and fear, and carrying with them a strange assortment of precious possessions, ranging from gardening tools to bird cages and umbrellas.

These people must have wondered what would become of them, and despaired of ever seeing their homes again.

But, just as the German tide had been turned back at Meaux in 1914 with the help of the Parisian taxis, it was about to be on the receiving end of another nasty surprise in Château-Thierry. The "doughboys" arrived from the United States.

Why the American Expeditionary Force troops were known by this strange term nobody seems to be able to explain. Originally "doughboy" referred only to the infantry. But as the war progressed the name was applied to all American servicemen, including, rather to their chagrin, the Marines. By the outbreak of WWII, the expression had been replaced by G.I. or simply "Yank."

If "doughboy" evokes an image of soft and wobbly lads it couldn't be more misleading. Those green American troops displayed outstanding heroism. Despite sustaining terrible casualties, for six weeks they fought around the town, and succeeded in destroying the German-held Marne salient – the triangle contained within Reims, Soissons and Château-Thierry. They forced the enemy to retreat. By the time the three-week long battle of Belleau Wood was over, having changed hands between the Germans and Americans six times, the German threat to Paris was ended. The doughboys had claimed their place in history.

Much has been written in American military history about Château-Thierry; but amongst all the battles and phantoms, romance had blossomed for some. The town's name is immortalised in a song written by Irving Berlin's brother-in-law in 1919. Part of it goes:

There's a girl in Château-Thierry
One September I'll remember,

Never to forget
Battle weary Château-Thierry,
That was where we met,
'Mong the ruins I still can see,
Suzette smiling out on me,
Somehow it just had to be;
This love that bids me tell you:
There's a girl in Château-Thierry,
A girl who waits for me.
There's a weary heart made cheery,
By love and victory.
And her buddy boy's devotion,
Burns a trail across the ocean,
To Château-Thierry, where she waits for me.

Words by E Ray Goetz - 1919

I wondered if any of those wartime romances had endured.

The rigid stubble pushing up under the inflatable mattress turned it into a bed of nails, and in conjunction with the heat transformed the tent into a torture chamber. After a supremely uncomfortable night we were keen to move on. We returned their chairs to our kind neighbours, then packed up and loaded our bikes and set off for our next stop. As we rode away from the campsite, on the other side of the fence the young girls were still walking up and down the riverside pushing their prams, and puffing on their cigarettes.

We debated whether we would visit the American Memorial, a few kilometres off our route, and up a hill. But the day was already hot, the memorial was up a hill, we had a very long ride ahead. And we were carrying too many sad memories from Dormans.

No more than a couple of kilometres from the town many beautiful, elegant houses sat in well-tended gardens beside the Marne. The air was rich with the fragrance of the velvety roses that flourish in the region. For half an hour or so we cycled along effortlessly on a neat path beside the opal green river.

When the houses and gardens ran out, the path

153

deteriorated into what appeared to be a long-disused tractor track. A narrow central raised strip covered with long, slithery grass separated deep, concrete-hard, parallel ruts. We couldn't cycle on the strip, because the edges were hidden by the grass, so we had instead to follow the ruts. Sometimes we passed a jogger gasping along the track, scowling because we protruded over the central path and forced them into a rut. I had noticed while walkers and other cyclists were friendly, joggers invariably looked grudging and slightly angry and never offered or returned greetings. I'm not surprised. I tried jogging once – I hated it.

We battered our way through the jungular undergrowth beside the river, bouncing over rocks and tussocks. It was extraordinarily hard work keeping the wheels in the ruts. My head ached from the fierceness of concentrating. My hands dripped perspiration, and slipped on the handles when I tried to change gear. The long grass poked through our wheel spokes, frequently tangling itself so thoroughly that the wheels were brought to a sudden halt. I was first to fall off. I had recognised that this was going to be inevitable before long. There was nothing I could do to prevent it happening - it was only a question of time. Momentarily I lost the rut; the wheel, enmeshed in the grass, bounced off a rock-hard tussock. The whole machine toppled sideways, its weight dragging me over with it. I suffered nothing worse than two deep scratches inside my leg, but Terry had to haul the loaded bike off me. I lay there pinned to the ground like an overturned tortoise, on the edge of hysteria, undecided as to whether to scream with laughter or weep with frustration.

Soon afterwards I heard a clatter and looked round to see that Terry had also crashed to the ground, but was bouncing back up again, uninjured. Cycling on this path was such a challenge that we found ourselves bursting into laughter every so often as we ducked beneath overhanging branches or brushed past brambles and nettles. Sometimes we caught across the field to our right brief glimpses of the road. With the heat-haze shimmering over it like smoke, and the awful hills growing out of it, we agreed that as gruelling as this terrain was, it was preferable to slogging along on melting tarmac and up perpendicular slopes. However, what we gained in exchange for avoiding the inclines was paid for in distance. The river here is very sinuous, looping through the countryside like a gigantic, benevolent green serpent, and our ride was long.

"Let's take a break," Terry suggested. We propped the bikes against a tree, mopped our faces, and sank down in the shade. The air hung heavily without the benefit of the meanest breeze.

It was so peaceful. The undergrowth lush, the air sweet and hot. There was not a rustle in the trees, not a tinkle from the water; not a bird, not an insect, not a footstep. No traffic noise. In the sunlight, in the shadow, in the sky, on the ground, all was eerily silent. I closed my eyes. Terry took a notepad from his pocket and started writing. A few minutes later, he handed it to me. "Read this," he said.

"Our wheel spokes swirled as we cycled through the silent pain, forgotten phantoms, in sunlight. The silent screams in the silent air, the silent dead, the silent soldiers, the silent roar of the silent guns."

"Think," he said, "of the ghosts surrounding us. Beneath the ground, and up in the skies. How many spirits linger, watching us as we move, but forever trapped here."

"I was thinking exactly the same," I said. "It's very strange, sitting here now. It's unnaturally silent, as if every living creature is holding its breath. Can you imagine what it must have been like here during the war?"

Even in our light-weight, high-tech cycling clothing today's heat was oppressive and sapped our energy. How must it have been for men in thick battle-dress and heavy boots, carrying loaded packs and cumbersome weapons, and fighting for their lives? What was it like in bitter winters when the churned mud froze into ruts that they had to negotiate, or in driving rain that saturated their clothing? The peaceful, safe countryside in which we were sitting had been utterly devastated by artillery, the trees broken down, the ground piled high with dead and wounded. That we were actually sitting on ground where countless men had suffered the most murderous warfare ever known, where they had died in their hundreds of thousands, was impossible to comprehend.

Dressed like the cast of a Gilbert and Sullivan operetta, sporting jaunty little caps, postbox red trousers and blue tailcoats embellished with shiny brass buttons, the poorly armed French infantry had made perfect targets. Resplendent in uniforms unchanged since the battle of Waterloo, the cavalry's shiny breastplates and plumed helmets were beautifully conspicuous. They fell like hay before a scythe, pushed forward by their generals whose orders were that the men must hold their ground at any cost. There would be no retreat. There would be no retreat. Guns ahead of them, picking them off, guns behind them to shoot any man who turned from battle.

From England came little boys who had lied about their age in order to enlist, seduced by misplaced idealism, the great lie *"Dulce et Decorum est Pro Patria Mori,"* [9] and visions of glory. When they cracked on the battlefield they received no mercy from their own: death by firing squad awaited them - even those still officially too young to have enlisted.

The 15,000 British officers, men from superior social backgrounds, who could sit well in the saddle and knew how to order from a menu, found that in this new and terrible warfare impeccable accents and *savoir faire* were no protection from enemy fire. Their numbers were whittled away until there were none left among their class to fill the spaces. So a new breed was born, the "temporary gentlemen" - promoted to officer status from the middle classes for the duration of the war. They were whittled away too, as were all colours, ages, sizes, creeds and classes trapped in the same nightmare. Their lives were coloured pins in the hands of politicians and military tacticians playing out their games.

In England, the public had no idea of the reality of what

---

9   It is sweet and right to die for your country

their armies were enduring. There was no sympathy for the shell-shocked. Wounded men were expected to be champing at the bit to return to the battlefield once they were mended. Featherbrained females carried in their reticules white feathers, symbols of cowardice, to hand to any able-bodied man not in uniform. It was a handy way to get rid of unwanted suitors, too.

The British high command had been unimpressed when the Maxim machine gun was demonstrated in 1885 – some officers regarded it as an ungentlemanly and unsporting weapon. The Germans had no such qualms, and by 1914 they were far better and more heavily equipped than the French and English. One machine gun could do the work of about 80 rifles. Day upon day men watched their comrades die in swathes, and waited for their turn to follow them.

Could we visualise the sights of dead and wounded, imagine the noises of whistling shells, rattling gunfire, bellowed orders, pants, groans, screams of pain? Could we share the terror of men in trenches being strafed from the air and attacked by the sinister new enemy, gas, invisible and silent, while they waited for the dreaded order to go over the top? Could we imagine wounded men and animals waiting for somebody to find them, to help them, to ease their pain? Could we feel any of the emotions that had swirled and festered along the banks of the Marne during those four mad years of WWI? Could we imagine the smells of sweat and dirt and human waste, or the feeling of rats running on our bodies while we tried to sleep in trenches filled with cold water?

Sitting in this silent sunshine, beside a tranquil river, no, of course we could not. It was entirely beyond the scope of our imagination. And yet, even it today's sunshine, you could feel in the air around you that the past lingered here. It was almost tangible.

There's a poem called "A Girl's Song" written by Katharine Tynan in 1918, and the first lines say:
"The Meuse and Marne have little waves;
The slender poplars o'er them lean.

One day they will forget the graves
That give the grass its living green."

Such prophetic words, because there is not one sign, no speck of evidence, of the horrors that had taken place on every inch of land around and beneath where we sat. Nature has erased them, replacing them with those tall poplars, thick hedges and lush undergrowth nourished by the contents of the soil beneath them. We continued sitting in silence, silent ourselves, thinking our own thoughts of the past, until the heat, the irritating flies and the hardness of the ground persuaded us to move on.

Despite our brief rest, we were very hot and very thirsty, so when a church spire peered out from the other side of a field of stubble Terry said: "Let's go and find a drink." The only way to reach the village was by dragging our bikes across the lumps and ridges of the field. Our shoes filled with thick dust, the stubble scratched our legs and clouds of midges danced around our faces. The only sign of life in the village was a faint clink from the bar. The church was locked, but we found a stone bench outside in the tiny sliver of shade provided by a thin and dusty tree. Terry bought us two ice-cold shandies that became stickily warm in the few seconds it took to drink them. Even the act of simply sitting was exhausting, so we plodded back to the river and continued our ride.

Lurking in the undergrowth beside the track we noticed very old milestones, their inscriptions worn away. I thought this path could well be a remnant of what had been the original road along which the royal prisoners travelled back to Paris. If we were riding in their wheel-tracks, they would have looked upon the same stretch of river and the same contours of the land.

The track continued to fight us every centimetre of the way. Nettles stretched out to swipe our legs, the grass clutched at the wheels and the ruts harboured hidden rocks. My bike bounced so violently that sometimes I was bucked from the saddle and my feet flew off the pedals. The machine was developing some alarming rattles. Eventually we had to admit that we were defeated by the struggle, and fearing that we would never reach our destination that night we took to the hills and heat of the road. Alternating between hard pushes up and fast, windblown runs down, we arrived in the village of Saâcy, the westernmost end of the Champagne area of the Marne valley. We slumped down to eat our lunch on a stone bench in a deserted street.

Like all the other towns and villages at this time of day, at this time of year, the inhabitants were cool and comfortable behind their shutters. Only mad English people were to be seen out. It was eerily still and quiet, like a Western film where the bandits are hiding out on the rooftops of the various buildings, waiting to ambush the sheriff. Or vice versa. All that was missing was a roll of tumbleweed and a creaking "Saloon" sign.

Leaning back to back, dozing, we were almost lifted off the seat by a sudden eruption of roaring, screaming and screeching noises. A fleet of miniature cars and scooters driven by yelling children came roaring into the streets. They careered around corners, bellowing, hooting and shouting, revving up at the "Stop" signs and smashing the previous silence into atoms. Noise whirled around us like exploding fireworks. Ten minutes of it was sufficient to propel us on our way, back into the furnace heat. We followed a path that seemed to point to the river, stopping to talk to a small herd of fallow deer lying in the dust beneath the trees behind a chain-link fence. Terry wanted to photograph them, and made clicking sounds with his tongue. With reproachful eyes they heaved themselves to their feet and came to the fence to see if we had anything of interest to offer them. Satisfied that we did not, they retired, making irritable burping noises, and folded themselves back down onto the ground. A walker told us we were heading for a dead end, and directed us back on to the main road. We pedalled increasingly slowly up the endless hills until, with great relief, we reached the shady campsite at La Ferté-sous-Jouarre. The *gardien* greeted us like long-lost and cherished family members, and not like the one-night-

159

standers we were.

The royal family, too, had been welcomed with respect and kindness by a large crowd in La Ferté-sous-Jouarre. They lodged in comfort at the house of the mayor, where the ever-courteous Louis invited the National Assembly members to dine with him, an offer they declined.

Terry suggested that while he set up the tent, I should go and cool down with a cold shower. Standing beneath a cascade of icy water seldom appeals to me, but on this unbearably hot afternoon, all red from the sun and my feet swollen from the heat, there was nothing that I could have wanted more. Humming a tuneless but happy little ditty, I set off with shampoo, soap, towel and a heart full of anticipation. It was one of those small ironies of life that the campsite here fulfilled my most important criterion - that the water is hot. Every shower gushed a fountain of abundant, almost-scalding water. No mixer taps, just a single showerhead activated by a push button to deliver hot water. I pondered whether if I pushed the button for long enough I could drain away all the hot water in the system, until it ran cold. This was not only a very selfish and antisocial idea, but also an ecologically-unfriendly one. Instead I stood beneath the hot water and tried to imagine that it was cold, not completely successfully. At least I came out feeling clean, with the sweat and dust washed off. In the meantime Terry had assembled the tent and unloaded the bikes. I made my nightly contribution towards our comfort – inflating the mattress, which merely required opening a valve and giving two small puffs.

Later we went to find something to eat. There were numerous pizza parlours, a few brasseries, and a Chinese restaurant. I was very peeved indeed that Terry vetoed it – he doesn't particularly like Chinese food. I refused to eat pizza yet again – we seemed to have had it most nights. Around and around we cycled, up and down, hither and thither, in company with scores of boy racers in old bangers with noisy exhausts, around the neat and otherwise peaceful town. We eventually found an excellent restaurant where we had a splendid meal at a most reasonable price. If you are ever in La Ferté-sous-Jouarre, we can recommend Le Chat Gourmand very highly indeed.

Our journey was almost over. Soon we would reach Paris, and after a couple of nights would cycle back to Versailles where our car awaited. I would miss the changing scenery, meeting new people, our daily challenges and discoveries. But I looked forward to our own bed, meals I could control, a hairdresser, and throwing away the horrible cycling shorts.

Because my eyes were still streaming relentlessly, all day long, Terry suggested I should wear goggles. I'd have to wear them over my glasses if I wanted to see anything. I tried to visualise how they would look with the Lycra stretched to the limit of its seams, the clumsy sandals, the crimson face and the diamanté baseball cap. I'd already reached my personal nadir in the worst-dressed-woman stakes. Lower I would not sink.

The distance to our hotel in the eastern suburbs of Paris was too far to cycle in one day. It looked as if we were doomed to another night at Trilport's noisy campsite. As we prepared to leave, the *gardien* and his wife came to see us off. She shook our hands, and he gave us both a bear hug. We asked if they knew of any alternatives to Trilport. "Yes! There's a magnificent site here," he said, pointing out a place called Jablines on our map.

At Trilport we stopped to picnic in a small park.

"*Bon appetit,*" said a couple of passing schoolgirls.

"*Bon appetit,*" said a group of four young black men.

"*Bon appetit,*" chanted a gang of small boys.

"*Bon appetit,*" said a young couple walking slowly with a very, very new baby hanging from a sling across its mother's chest.

A man in a suit marched past, swinging a briefcase. "*Bon appetit,*" he called.

We threw our crumbs to the birds, and set off for Jablines.

CHAPTER THIRTEEN
Being Difficult

*"Reasonable people adapt themselves to the world.
Unreasonable people attempt to adapt the world to
themselves. All progress, therefore, depends on unreasonable
people."*
George Bernard Shaw

AS we cycled away, the mobile phone rang, sending me instantly into panic mode. At home we had left behind two goats, two dogs, two cats, a parrot and four hens. The year before our current adventure, a couple had come to stay in our *gîte*. The husband was a quintessential English gentleman with curly hair, very direct eyes that had stolen the blue from the sea and the sky, and a soft soothing voice. His tiny, beautiful wife was a talented artist, strict vegetarian and passionate animal lover. When they were away from their home, they left out food and water for the shrew that lived in their kitchen. In return, the shrew left them offerings of small piles of peanuts – beneath cushions, under their pillows, or stuffed into their shoes. They were our kind of people.

They established an immediate rapport with all our animals, and when they left, said: "If you ever want us to house-sit for you, we'd be more than happy."

And so, two days before we set off to Versailles, they had installed themselves in our house and, surrounded by barking, mewing, clucking, chattering and bleating animals, waved us on our way.

Each time our mobile phone rang, I was certain that something was terribly wrong at home. I don't know why, because I'm very much an optimist. But whenever we're away from home I always anticipate that something dreadful will happen. Despite assurances from our house-sitters that all was well, the house was still standing and the animals were behaving, I could never shake off private doubts that they were heroically dealing with a never-ending stream of disasters that they weren't telling us about. So I worried anyway, irrationally, particularly since I knew that if anything did go wrong we could rely on them to put it right.

Terry spoke for a few minutes, and when he finished, I asked: "Did they sound happy? Was her voice normal? Why did you say 'Oh dear' when you were talking to her? What were you saying about Dobbie?"

"Everything is fine. The animals are all well. There are no problems, and nothing to worry about," he reassured me. I continued worrying.

After we left La Ferté-sous-Jouarre the comfortably dull weather of the morning turned into another excessively hot and sunny afternoon. The first time we had cycled through Meaux's chaotic traffic I thought it couldn't possible be worse. But I was wrong. This time utter bedlam ruled. It was 5.00 pm, people were leaving work, and the whole centre of the town was in the throes of major roadworks. Diversionary signs seemed to have been dropped into place haphazardly, sending the traffic round in circles. Everybody appeared to be in the wrong lane for where they wanted to go, and nobody wanted to give way to anybody because everyone was in a hurry. Drivers were using brute force to get to where they thought they wanted to be, forcing paths through the long queues. Klaxons roared non-stop. The noise was deafening. Cars reversed, hooted, tried to do U-turns. People waved their arms and shouted. Terry threaded his way through slowly, but I had to dismount and stagger between bumpers, finding myself stuck in the middle of several lanes just as the temporary lights changed and the cars surged forwards. People shouted at me and ordered me to get off the road. If only I could. If tears hadn't already been streaming down my face, they would have been by now. My ankles were black and blue from whacks delivered by the pedals. Trying to negotiate my way through the traffic, at the same time I had to keep sight of Terry. Hair-raising wasn't the word.

The royal family and their captors had stopped briefly in Meaux, and made a very early start on their way back to Paris. Marie-Thérèse wrote that they slept at the bishop's house "which was full of priests who had taken the oath, but otherwise civil enough; the bishop himself served us. They informed us that we must start the next day at five in the morning so as to reach Paris in good season." (During the Revolution, the clergy were required to swear an oath of allegiance to the new Constitution, or face expulsion from the church, or even execution. Those who swore the oath were no longer answerable to Rome.)

Once clear of the town centre we were buffeted by a constant stream of heavy traffic on the undulating road. Downhill, Terry was always much quicker than me with his lighter, faster bike but uphill I could usually catch and overtake him. For many kilometres this was the pattern as we alternately passed each other, laughing.

When I spotted the first sign for Jablines, Terry was a kilometre ahead of me. By the time I had reached the same spot, he had vanished, and it was here that the road split into two. Jablines, said the signs, was both straight on, and off to the right. I sailed on straight ahead, and heard a bellow from behind. When I pulled on to the side of the road and looked back, there was Terry, on the other side of a roundabout on the bridge over the road. To reach him I had to turn and go in the wrong direction against the traffic, on the wrong side, up the slip road and clockwise around the roundabout in the face of the oncoming vehicles. I climbed off and pushed the bike against an unbroken line of trucks, heavily laden with rocks, sand and gravel from the quarry next to the roundabout. As I did so I was directing very rude words at Terry, the trucks, and life in general.

In all the accounts I had read of people touring on bicycles, none of them mentioned having encountered the kinds of conditions that we were meeting. The worst that ever happened to them was a puncture or broken spoke. They breezed through traffic like Moses through the Red Sea, and

164

they could pedal effortlessly all day long, regardless of the terrain, in weather that was always perfect. Their eyes did not leak constantly, and they didn't suffer from swollen feet or sunburn. I couldn't recall ever reading about any of them having to shove their bikes in the wrong direction while surrounded by lumbering trucks driven by jeering Frenchmen.

These vehicles were driving in convoys in the same direction as we were going. A stream of empty trucks came from the opposite direction, returning to the quarry to refill. The road was not very wide, and the trucks were uncomfortably close to us. The road surface was lumpy and broken from the constant heavy traffic. Our bikes jolted into potholes, and the wheels skidded on layers of sand and shale. As it went past, one of the trucks hit a bump heavily and spewed a thick cloud of dust and grit which bounced onto the road and created a desert-storm effect, momentarily blinding motorists and us. For a few seconds I could see nothing, and panicked as I tried to wipe the dust from my glasses. Our bikes, faces and clothes were covered in a coarse yellow coating. So were the cars behind the truck. We all looked as if we had just driven through the Gobi desert on a windy day.

We thought we had missed a turning during the sandstorm, because we could find no signs for Jablines. So when another cyclist whooshed past we called out and asked him for directions. He signalled us to follow, and led us a few kilometres to the entrance to the leisure centre. He stuck his thumb in the air and yelled out that he wished us *bon après-midi*, and swooped back around on himself at racing speed, vanishing down the road.

The Jablines leisure complex stands in 400 hectares of wooded and beautifully landscaped gardens, with lakes for sailing, fishing and water sports. Horse-riding, archery, football, tennis and mini-golf are all available there, but it's also a perfect place to just sunbathe, picnic or watch the rest of the world playing. There are chalets for rental, mobile homes, camping car and tent pitches, several snack bars, and a self-service cafeteria. It's all immaculately maintained and well-organised, and offered a heavenly oasis of calm greenery after the beastliness of our ride that afternoon.

While Terry put up our tent, I stood under the shower watching rivulets of sepia-coloured water swirling away, and sweeping piles of wet sand and grit down the drain hole with my foot. At the basins, where I looked bleakly at my awful appearance, a Spanish family of mother and three haughty small girls, with little brown noses tilted at the ceiling, were having an hysterical screaming match about the ribbons in the girls' crow-black hair. Ines wanted the red ribbon that Julia had; Julia wasn't prepared to swap it for Ines' blue ribbon, and Isabel didn't want to wear one at all. Her mother was holding Isabel by her splendid long shiny hair and trying to wrap a yellow ribbon around it with one hand, while Isabel writhed and squirmed and Ines and Julia shouted at each other. None of them appeared to be aware of the growing crowd of spectators watching with amusement and/or horror, as the children yelled and hissed and stamped their feet and wagged their fingers. As their voices rose higher and higher in fury and indignation, their mother tried to make herself heard over them. It was a scene of such dramatic outrage that it made me think of a particularly violent opera, and wonder how they might behave in a real crisis.

The restaurants on site didn't serve evening meals, and the small shop was closed, but the ladies in the reception office said there were two good restaurants close by – a *couscouserie* in one direction, and a pizzeria in the opposite direction. Having already eaten sufficient pizzas to last a lifetime due to force majeure, I welcomed the prospect of a change. Terry, on the other hand, would live on pizza if he could. It took a mixture of encouragement, threat and tantrum on my part to get him to go to the couscous restaurant. Off we cycled, and here I am going to make a confession.

The *couscouserie* was about four kilometres away. We studied the menu in its glass box on the wall and it seemed rather expensive for what is, whichever way you look at it, in essence just a pile of semolina with some bits and pieces in it. At €22 a head for the vegetarian version, Terry balked, but I had set my heart on having a meal that was a little different. Remember, he'd already vetoed the Chinese restaurant in La Ferté-sous-Jouarre. I did agree that the couscous seemed grossly overpriced, but wondered whether it really mattered, just this once. I think if Terry liked couscous we'd probably have gone ahead despite the price. But he said he didn't. (He eats it happily at home, though.) By his body language and grunts I could see there was no point in forcing the issue. We skirmished for several minutes, and feeling very grumpy, I scrambled onto my bike.

"Right," I said ungraciously. "Let's go and get another bloody pizza."

Then, of course, Terry was immediately contrite and said that if I really wanted couscous, we would have it. But I wasn't going to be mollified, and pedalled away really fast so he that had to follow. We cycled several kilometres to the pizza place, which was in fact a French/Italian restaurant that looked very inviting. It had a varied and exciting menu, and was closed. I was delighted. That would teach him a lesson.

Terry was frustrated and shook and rapped at the door.

"Come on, we'll go back and have the couscous," he said. Now I played my trump card.

"I can't – my bike's almost out of power. It won't get there and back." I didn't think that was true. I could probably have made it with power to spare, but I was enjoying being awkward.

"Never mind, you go. There's no reason for us both to be hungry. I'll go back and wait for you in the tent, and you go and enjoy a meal," I said cheerily.

"Don't be so stupid. Of course I'm not going without you. But what are we going to eat?" he asked sadly.

"Well, I think there's a bit of cheese in one of the bags. You can have it. I've already eaten more than I should today."

"But you can't go all night with nothing to eat."

"I wouldn't have to, if we'd had the couscous," I said

triumphantly. "Don't worry, I'll get something to eat in the morning, when the shop opens." I wanted to make him feel as bad as I possibly could. I sometimes wish I wasn't so difficult.

We cycled back to the tent in silence, and I rummaged around in the panniers until I found a small cylinder of goat's cheese and a bottle of Baileys that I'd forgotten about.

"Here you are," I said, handing him the cheese and hanging on to the Baileys. "Eat up."

In his guilt Terry tried to force the cheese upon me, but I obstinately refused, quoting my high cholesterol level. Then I tipped everything out from the panniers and discovered tucked away in their depths a small packet of withered apricots and half a jar of tapenade that we must have bought so long ago that we had forgotten it. Apricots dipped in tapenade may sound weird, and it was, but the combination of sweet and salty was actually rather delicious. Washed down with half a bottle of Baileys it put me in sufficiently good humour to share my feast with poor Terry, who had finished his cheese and was looking longingly at my odd meal. We sat there in a very fine drizzle, dipping, chewing and swigging happily.

Some English people in a large tent nearby had a small boy called George, who would only do what he was told if his parents explained clearly why he should do so.

"George, come in the tent please."

"Why?"

"Because it is raining, George, and you will get wet, and if you get wet you may catch cold. If you get a cold, you may not be able to go back to Disneyland tomorrow. You don't want that to happen, do you?"

George mulled this over in his about-five-year-old head, and went back into the tent.

"George, come and let Mummy wipe your hands before we eat."

"Why?"

"Because you have been playing in the dirt, and you might have germs on your hands. If those germs get in your mouth, you may have a bad tummy, and then you won't be able to go to Disneyland tomorrow. You don't want that, do you?"

Silence.

"Sit down while you eat, George."

"Why?"

"Because Mummy and Daddy are sitting down. That's what people do when they are eating."

"But I don't want to sit down."

"Sit down, George, because if you don't sit down, then Alexandra won't sit down either, and you are her big brother and have to show her how to behave."

"There's a good boy."

Silence for a while.

"Bed time, George."

"Why?"

"Because it's time to go to sleep if you want to go to Disneyland tomorrow. If you don't go to bed, and go to sleep, you'll be too tired in the morning, and you don't want that, do you?"

A short silence.

"Good boy, George. Night night."

What very polite parents, I thought. I seem to remember that the standard reply to children's questions used to be: "Because I said so."

During the night heavy rain beat onto the tent. "Mm, isn't that a lovely sound?" I asked Terry.

"Hm."

The next morning was cool, and overcast. This suited me perfectly because my sunburn wouldn't get any worse. We stopped at a small roadside café for a coffee. Despite the cold weather we sat outside, just a few metres from the heavy traffic. Inside the choking air was thick and blue with cigarette smoke. The lady who served us was buxom and smiling, and wheezy as an old pair of bellows. Even my hot chocolate tasted vaguely of nicotine.

We cycled beside the river Marne on a path even more lumpy and bumpy than the previous one. It was peaceful and

169

pretty, and we weren't in any particular hurry. Terry led the way, seeking the smoothest part of the track. I could see that he was going to fall as his front wheel hit a rock hidden in the long grass, unbalancing him and sending the bike wobbling wildly. The weight of the panniers took over, and the whole rig tilted and sank gracefully towards the river bank, with nothing between it and the water except a few mounds of grass. Terry was going into the river, with his bike, camera, all our clothes and money. Unable to do anything useful, I shrieked to show moral support. He somehow managed to find a space for his left foot on a sliver of firm ground and gingerly pushed himself to the right, away from the edge, while I held my breath as if doing so would somehow be helpful. In slow motion he inched to safety, leaving only his torch poised over a clump of weed bending beneath its weight.

"Leave it!" I yelled as he dangled over the bank trying to get it. "Just leave it – you'll fall in!" But he didn't. His arms seemed to stretch elastically until he was able to get a grip on the torch and land it safely.

We cycled on through patches of woodland, beside the ever-green, barely moving river. Flotillas of ducks broke formation to make way for teams of skinny boats rowed by vested men. Houseboats and fisherman sat motionless on the water. At Noisiel we stopped to admire the glorious old building that was once the seat of a great chocolate dynasty. The Menier chocolate empire started life as a pharmaceutical company who used cocoa powder as a medicine and a coating for pills. In the mid-nineteenth century they discovered a technique for making bars of solid chocolate. These became so popular that the pharmaceutical side was closed down to concentrate entirely on producing chocolate bars, and Menier became a French household name. Two World Wars and growing foreign competition killed it in the end, and the company was sold off, finally finding its way into the clutches of Nestlé at the end of the 20th century. Much as we may not agree with many of Nestlé's practices, we did applaud them

170

for preserving as their French headquarters this delicious confection of industrial architecture, a great chocolate box of ornate, polychrome ceramic bricks.

A short way down the track we arrived in a strange and rather sinister area. Large mobile homes skulked in gloomy woods, and growling dogs ran backwards and forwards on chains. Each neglected garden housed several expensive cars that looked incongruous in this setting. None of the people standing around responded to our "*Bonjours*," but stared silently, with suspicious, unfriendly eyes. A hard-faced woman in a shiny new Mercedes drove on the wrong side of the road just for the fun of almost knocking us off. There was an atmosphere of menace and aggression there that reminded me of the film "Deliverance."

Just a few hundred metres further on we crossed a small bridge into the sunny, peaceful suburb of Gournay-sur-Marne. From there we continued beside the river on the last leg of our day's journey that would take us to Joinville-le-Pont, where I had booked a hotel for two nights.

CHAPTER FOURTEEN
A Tall Dark Stranger

"There is no such thing as accident; it is fate misnamed."
Napoléon Bonaparte

SIX weeks earlier, when I had booked the hotel it was under French ownership and management, with an Italian name – Hotel del Ponte. When we arrived, however, the sign outside said "Auberge Slave" and a notice announced that the languages spoken were English, Bulgarian, Polish, Russian and Serbo-Croat. In the pretty, vine-covered courtyard terrace two swarthy men who looked like bandits sat in a blue fog of smoke, staring at us with steel-blue eyes and unsmiling mouths. They sipped from small glasses of clear liquid, looking as if they would as cheerfully and casually cut your throat as they would stomp out a cigarette butt. I was excited at the thought that behind its pleasant rustic façade, this hotel might be a front for a den of evil. Caches of weapons, drugs, white slave traders, who knew what we might find inside?

Putting down the cloth with which she had been wiping the tables, a sweet-faced girl with a wide smile listened while I explained who we were. While I did so the bandits yelled and bellowed at her constantly. She ignored them with exquisite disdain, and showed us up to our room. The décor was Skegness meets Tyrol, circa 1950. To be truthful, I've never been to either Skegness, nor the Tyrol in the 1950s or at any other time, so I'm just making that bit up. I think it gives a fair idea of what it looked like, though. But the room and en-suite bathroom were clean and airy, and overlooking the river. The new owners had taken over the hotel just ten days before our arrival, said the Slave girl.

After luxuriating in the bath, we went to explore the town. The bandits in the courtyard were still drinking, smoking, staring ferociously, and bellowing at the girl as she calmly tackled a heap of ironing which seemed to have no frontiers. Over the racket, she continued ironing placidly.

Beneath the bridge the lazy waters of the Marne make their way towards Charenton a few miles away. From there they vanish into the Seine. The river almost encircles Joinville le Pont in a great loop, and the town claims to be the only one in France through which the same river passes in opposite directions, flowing upstream to the east, and downstream in the west. In 1910 these waters, up to two metres over their normal height, had swirled, brown and sullen through the windows of the town's buildings. That was during the great centennial flood – a flood that occurs every hundred years - that had swamped Paris, causing the Seine to "jump out of her bed" as they say in France. Now the vast man-made Lac de Der-Chantecoq at St Dizier, two hundred kilometres away, collects the flood waters from the Marne, and forms a haven for waterbirds and twitchers.

In its halcyon days at the beginning of the 20th century, Joinville was an important centre for the newborn film industry. Great cinematographic pioneers like Pathé had their studios there. Although they are long since closed, a thriving post-production and digital imaging industry remains. We found the town to have an enchanting olde-worlde feeling about it - a slow, untroubled world inhabited by slow, untroubled people.

We cycled along the river bank beside large, quiet houses in Norman and Basque styles, slate-roofed, timbered, with boat garages and mysterious windows. Families strolled beside the river, and we stopped to watch a young couple standing by the edge of the water rustling a brown paper bag. Half a dozen ducks paddled rapidly towards them, croaking excitedly. At the same time the surface of the water was broken by three large, smooth heads of coypus that swam quickly to the bank. All the creatures shared the bread sociably. Where we live, the poor coypus are regarded as vermin, and are poisoned, trapped or shot and often eaten as a pâté by locals. They are seen as both a gastronomic treat, and a pest because of the damage they do to river banks and ponds. Here on this section of the Marne they seemed to be safe and popular. As we stood watching them swimming around, an elegant lady wearing high heels and a smart two-piece suit arrived with two little coiffed dogs on leads. Stopping a few metres further along the bank, she opened her handbag, and called out "*Venez, mes beaux!*" Up popped the heads again, and sped to where she stood. They and the dogs sniffed each other politely, as if they were old friends. The lady dug into her handbag and bent down, letting the creatures take the food from her hands. All around her the ducks quacked, and pigeons strutted, and sparrows snatched fallen crumbs. This was one of the rare occasions when neither of us was carrying a camera, and I would have loved to have had a photo of that scene.

As well as being within easy cycling distance of Paris, Joinville-le-Pont is home to the few remaining *guinguettes* on the river Marne. We hoped to spend an evening watching elderly gents with moustaches dining their young mistresses, and lovers twirling to the waltz, or writhing to the java or tango. During *La Belle Époque*, on Sundays Parisians escaped the stresses of the capital and took the train to Joinville on the new Bastille line, to stroll along the embankments, or indulge in the new pastime of rowing on the river. The working classes came to let their hair down and kick up their heels, fuelled by plates of fried fish and glasses of cheap wine. The middle classes came to share the racy atmosphere. *Guinguettes* symbolised *la fin de siècle*. Gentlemen wore striped blazers and boaters. For the ladies bountiful bosoms and tiny waists were *de rigueur*, as were saucy little hats, taffeta bustles, and parasols. The horror of world wars was still unknown, and nobody had heard of global warming.

The oldest surviving *guinguette* in Joinville, Le Petit Robinson had celebrated its centenary in 2004. Ancient accordions hung from the ceiling. The walls were covered with sepia photographs of maestros of the accordion of yesteryear, and faded posters advertising forthcoming events. In the centre of the main restaurant was a spacious dance floor. Each dining chair bore a small plaque engraved with the name of a celebrated musician. Including a terraced dining area and tables right beside the edge of the river, there was a total seating capacity for 600. We were the only two people in the whole place, outnumbered three-to-one by the waiters. Surrounded by 598 empty chairs, you can feel very conspicuous and rather lonely. The waiters stood like a conclave of cardinals on the path watching hopefully as people strolled towards them, then turning sadly to watch their backs disappearing into the distance. It was surprising for a Friday night in mid-June and we began to wonder whether there was something about Le Petit Robinson that we didn't know. However our food was delicious and beautifully cooked, and our friendly waiter was as attentive as he could well afford to be.

When we arrived back at the hotel at 10.30 pm the Slave girl was still ironing. I asked her the best way to get to Paris by public transport the next day. We weren't taking our bikes as they'd be an encumbrance if we wanted to visit buildings. She recommended the RER - *Réseau Express Régional*. I was sure I'd heard that this train network goes underground in places. No, she said, only through a few very short tunnels – no more than a couple of seconds. Otherwise it is overground all the way. Nothing at all to worry about. She herself didn't like being underground, but I'd find it comfortable, quick and completely safe. She smiled encouragingly.

What should I wear for a day in the world's most chic capital? The choice was between the unflattering cycling gear, or the equally unflattering chiffon skirt and black top. It wasn't much of a choice. I decided on the skirt and top. My trainers were dirty. The moccasins were too thin-soled for hours of walking. That left the grotesque sandals. I looked like nothing on earth. I considered wearing a paper bag on my head.

We hiked up the hill to the station, and saw that the trains were indeed travelling above ground. After a kindly gentleman had explained the mysteries of the ticket machine, we hopped aboard, and watched from the windows as the pleasant suburbs of Nogent-sur-Marne and Fontenay-sous-Bois shot past. As the girl had promised, we passed through a few brief tunnels. Just as I was relaxing and breathing a deep sigh of relief, the train plunged into darkness, and halted at a station. Then I knew my worst nightmare had come true.

Probably it was no more than five minutes that we moved through the sub-terrain, but it might as well have been an hour. My whole body was awash with perspiration, and I began to pant like a hot dog. By the time the train rolled into the Gare du Lyon, I was a nervous wreck, frantic to get up the several escalators and through a maze of tunnels out into fresh air. So it wasn't the best time for Terry to choose, very uncharacteristically, to throw a fit of temper. We were standing on a concourse, looking for an exit, when he asked: "Where do we go from here?"

"I don't know yet," I replied, still searching for an exit to somewhere, anywhere at all, that wasn't enclosed.

"What do you mean, you don't know? I thought you were organised." His tone was sharp and irritable.

"Well, I've never been here before in my life. How on earth do you think I can instantly find my way out? You are nowhere near wanting to get out of here as badly as I am. Shut up and let me think." I estimated that at most I could last another 30 seconds without being able to breathe fresh air. Any longer and I really would lose the plot and run amok.

Like a tiny star, at the end of a short tunnel shone a glimmer of daylight, and I sprinted for it. Wherever it led, it didn't matter, as long as it was out. As we emerged into a busy street, Terry asked me again which direction we should take.

"What on earth is wrong with you?" I snapped, trying to relate street signs to the sweaty map that I was carrying.

"I don't like feeling out of control, and if I don't know where I am, I feel out of control."

"Fine. You're out of control, but I'm not, so stick with me

176

and shut up."

We marched along in frosty silence.

"Would you like a coffee?" Terry asked.

I shrugged, then realised he was hungry! The only thing that really ruffles him – apart from generals - is an empty belly.

"Only if we can have some lovely buttery croissants with it, or *pain au chocolat*. Come on, I've worked out where we are."

We sat at a table outside a café on Avenue Daumesnil. After almost three weeks of cycling past the world, it was relaxing to sit and watch it go by from a stationary viewpoint, and to have an opportunity to observe the intriguing behaviour of some of the people around us. For instance, there was the woman in her twenties who looked normal enough, dressed in a neat skirt and T-shirt, who crossed the road at the traffic lights. When she reached the other side, she waited for the lights to be in her favour again, then crossed back. She kept on doing this, and must have made the journey six or seven times in the 15 minutes we sat there. Just walking backwards and forwards across the road, in the same place. Now, why do you think she was doing that?

A few metres from us a shifty man in a track suit stood at the corner, watching something across the road and talking furtively into a mobile phone. Was he a criminal plotting a dastardly deed, or an undercover cop watching a villain? Or just a shifty man talking on a mobile phone? A beggar woman in layers of ragged clothes, with a red woolly scarf wrapped around her head dragged behind her a tartan shopping bag on wheels, with bundles dangling from it. She stopped next to our table, spat what sounded like a curse in our direction, and went into the tobacconist next door. She emerged with six large cartons of cigarettes under her arm. These she attached to her trolley with a bungee cord, talking to herself as she did so. We both offered her a neighbourly *"Bonjour, Madame,"* and received in reply another curse as she wandered away to who knew where.

Our earlier *petit contretemps* was forgotten, and Terry's good humour restored. It was tempting, and would have been pleasant and interesting to sit there all day, nibbling, sipping and speculating, watching the pedestrians and traffic. Who needs to pay for entertainment when you can sit and observe real life dramas, comedies and mysteries for nothing? Still, we hadn't come here to sit about all day enjoying ourselves. We had places to go and things to see. Mostly we, or more correctly I, wanted to visit the buildings where Marie-Antoinette had spent the last miserable months of her short life.

We strolled down the road towards the Bastille. I'd heard that the opera house there was horrible – "a hippopotamus in a bathtub" was one description. Now, I can conjure up a very charming image of a hippo in a bathtub, surrounded by bubbles and scrubbing its back with a long-handled brush. But one of the many attributes lacking in the Opera building is charm. I thought it simply hideous, a mongrel cross between an atomic power station and 1960s municipal swimming baths. And plonked in the centre of such an historic area. Come on, *citoyens* of Paris, pull it down! Burn it! You've done it before! *Allez-y*!

I turned to look at where the Bastille prison would have been were it still there. Closing my eyes for a few moments, and concentrating very hard, I was certain that I could hear, beneath the roar of Parisian traffic, the shrieks and screams of the mob attacking the prison in 1789.

Doubtless I looked rather strange, apart from my general appearance, standing on the pavement, with my eyes closed and sniffing the air. A beautifully-modulated voice asked if Madame was feeling unwell. When I opened my eyes Terry was fifty metres away, fiddling with his camera, and a very thin, tall man with lots of wild black hair and designer stubble was looking at me with some concern. If my face wasn't already scarlet, I would have blushed with embarrassment, but I was past caring. I explained that I was merely trying to soak up some ancient atmosphere of the infamous old prison building.

"But it was not so sinister, really," said the tall man, switching instantly into perfect English. (So humiliating after living here for so long that a Frenchman instantly recognises from my accent that I'm English.)

"The Bastille has a bad reputation, but it was built to protect the people of Paris – from the English," he smiled, "during the war of one hundred years."

"But surely it was the worst prison in France?" I said.

"No, not at all. In fact it was not really so bad. The people who were sent there were usually *aristos*, political prisoners, and their conditions were good. They could bring their own furniture and they had fine food – and wine! They lived well."

Well, maybe that was true. However, it was a place where people could be imprisoned without knowing why or what for, just because the King so wished. If and when they were lucky enough to be released, it was only on the condition that they never talked of their arrest and imprisonment. If they did, they'd be whisked back in again faster than they could say Jacques Robinson. The mysterious man in the iron mask spent thirty-four years of uncomfortable captivity there until he was released by the Grim Reaper. I call that a pretty sinister kind of place. But I didn't want to argue with this new-found friend.

Where the grim walls and turrets once stood there is now a towering column – *la Colonne de Juillet*. It's topped by a bronze sculpture of a naked, winged, and as my new friend pointed out, manifestly masculine figure known as The Spirit of Freedom. I glanced around and waved to Terry.

"That's my husband," I said.

He nodded, and continued: "Do you know what this monument means?"

"Well, yes, it's to commemorate the French revolution, isn't it?"

"Yes, it is! But which one?"

"Was there more than one?"

"Oh, we are quite good at having revolutions! This column remembers the people who died in the revolution in 1830. But

179

that was quite a small one, it only lasted three days and not too many people died." (After Napoleon's defeat and exile, the Bourbon dynasty was restored to the French throne under Louis XVI's brother, Louis XVIII, who died in 1824. His younger brother, Charles X took over and was an unpopular monarch who abdicated and fled the country following the July 1830 revolution, called The July Revolution. His son was king Louis XIX for an ignominious 20 minutes, before he too abdicated and fled abroad. It was all rather a mess. In 1848 the then king, Louis-Phillipe 1 succeeded in sparking yet another revolution, the February Revolution, and scuttled out of France, having named his 10-year-old grandson as his successor. But by then the French had had quite enough of the monarchy.)

I asked him if he was a historian, and he replied that he was a lover of history, but that his job was something to do with the SNCF, the French national railway network.

"It is a pity that I have to go to work today, because otherwise I would be so happy to show you and your husband," – he nodded towards Terry, who had arrived and was wondering why I was talking to a strange man – "anywhere in Paris that interests you."

Terry was glaring rather belligerently. I introduced him to my friend, whose name was Arthur. When I explained that today we were interested primarily in Marie-Antoinette's last months in Paris, he nodded.

"It was a terrible thing, a great miscarriage of justice, I believe. But they were very bad times. So, you will visit la Conciergerie, of course?"

"Yes, and La Chapelle Expiatoire. But first of all we're going to les Tuileries."

"Did you already visit Versailles?"

I nodded.

"Ah, it's very wonderful, isn't it?"

"Yes," I agreed politely. "It is quite spectacular."

He looked at his watch, and said ruefully: "I must excuse myself, because I have to be in my office. It has been a great pleasure to talk with you, and to find English people who are so interested in our history. I wish you a very enjoyable stay, and many good visits today." He loped away with a wave. What a delightful man.

We wandered along to the Rue St Antoine, where, although it had nothing to do with Marie-Antoinette, a most dramatic episode in French history had taken place. It warranted at least a few minutes of our time.

Whether you believe Nostradamus' predictions were genuine, or merely clever, airy-fairy mumbo-jumbo that could be interpreted to fit a particular situation, I thought that he came fairly close to the mark when he foretold in 1558:

"The young lion will overcome the older one,

On the field of combat in a single battle;

He will pierce his eyes through a golden cage,

Two wounds made one, then he dies a cruel death."

Just one year later, celebrations were in full swing to mark a newly signed peace treaty between France, Spain and England. Ignoring the warnings of Nostradamus and others who foresaw his death, and the entreaties of his wife, King Henri II took part in a joust. The lance of his opponent, Gabriel Montgomery, of the King's Scottish Guards, accidentally entered the King's golden visor. The lance splintered, piercing the King's eye and exiting through his ear.

Notwithstanding the attentions of the most skilful surgeons in Europe, Henri died a lengthy and agonising death. While his great love, Diane de Poitiers was sidelined, his wife Catherine de Medici, breaking free from her back-room role, went to ingenious lengths to try to save him. She had surgeons experiment on the newly decapitated heads of criminals, poking into them splintered pieces of wood to try and reproduce Henri's wounds and find a way to cure them. But his injuries were far beyond the help of man, and on the eleventh day after the event, the King died. In her excellent book "Catherine de Medici," Leonie Frieda gives a riveting account of the incident, and the effect it would have on the future of France.

181

Whilst I quickly get bored looking at historic buildings and sights per se, when I close my eyes and visualise the events that have taken place there, and the characters involved, they become magical. I imagined the initial disbelief of the spectators when the King swayed in his saddle. The dawning horror as the extent of Henri's injuries was discovered; the shock and grief of his family and mistress; the terror of his opponent when he realised the enormity of what he had done. I could picture people running in all directions, spreading the news in shouts, in whispers and in written messages. Messengers galloping to find the surgeons, and diplomats hastening to send word to their countries, already scheming and plotting how this tragedy could be turned to their advantage. And all this had happened where we were standing.

At school history and geography were my most hated classes. Both teachers were patently bored by their own subjects and their pupils. It was only the spotty swots who applied themselves to learning the long lists of dry facts and dates that held no interest or inspiration for those of us who were not by nature academics. But to stand on the spot where an event of such dramatic and historic enormity had taken place, and to let my mind travel back to that time makes my hair tingle and stand on end. Absolutely thrilling.

We had agreed that we would, as far as possible, follow Louis and Marie-Antoinette's trail in chronological order. We had more or less done that so far, and I wanted to continue doing so in Paris. It was from the Tuileries that she and Louis and their family had made their escape attempt, and it was to the Tuileries that they had been brought back, so that was our first call.

Strolling along, we passed a tiny park, really no more than a handkerchief-sized patch of grass with a couple of benches shaded by trees. There a handsome man in a crumpled cream linen suit and Panama hat sat mournfully playing a flute, as if he was the saddest man in the world. His plaintive notes trailed behind us, like small lost children.

Across the river from the resplendent Town Hall we could see the Conciergerie, and Terry said it would make sense go straight there, as it was so close. I insisted that we had to see places in the correct order. Terry sighed and said that he thought that was a daft idea, but he couldn't persuade me to change my mind. Nobody can once it's made up. It was rather illogical, I knew, but something inside me said that it was important for this personal pilgrimage to be done in the correct sequence.

We took the Batobus down the Seine. It was a heavenly day of cloudless blue skies and brilliant sunshine. As we motored along I noticed that my knees were turning an interesting shade of pink that harmonised with the various red shades on my upper half, and contrasted dramatically with the startling pallor of my lower legs.

At the Louvre we disembarked and walked to the Tuileries gardens. After her husband's shocking death, Catherine de Medici commissioned the building of the Tuileries Palace on the site of an old tile factory from which it took its name. The gloomy great building had been highly significant in the story of Louis and Marie-Antoinette, so I was irritated that like the Bastille, angry Parisians had wrecked and burned it during one of their sporadic insurrections. The remains were demolished in 1883. There must have been restless spirits in the building. Some of the ill-fated material found its way to the island of Corsica, where it was used to build the Château de la Punta, which seems to have inherited the curse of the palace. Ravaged by fire several times, in 1978 it suffered such severe damage that it has been uninhabited ever since.

Since 2003 there have been discussions about rebuilding the Tuileries; the cost would be enormous, but who cares? Let's have it back again. It's an integral part of the turbulent history of Paris.

After their brief overnight stop and early morning departure from Meaux, the Royal captives continued their journey to Paris. Notices throughout the city warned: "He who applauds the King will be beaten. He who insults him will be hanged."

During the return journey one of the three deputies, Antoine Barnave, an influential member of the Assembly, became increasingly well-disposed towards his charges.

"At the moment of entering Paris, Barnave claimed the principal seat. It was no longer the place of honour; it was the place of danger. If a fanatic fired on the King, which was not likely, or at the Queen, which was possible, he would be there to receive the bullet." [10]

Prepared to risk his life for the King and Queen, Barnave's royalist sympathies would cost him his head in 1793, when he'd climb the steps to the scaffold.

Louis noted in his diary in his habitually concise fashion: "Left Meaux at half-past six. Reached Paris at eight, without halting on the way."

His daughter, Marie-Thérèse described their day rather more eloquently:

"We started at six, and though it is only ten leagues from Meaux to Paris, we did not reach Bondy, the last post, till midday nor the Tuileries till half-past seven at night. At Bondy the populace showed its desire to massacre our three *Gardes du Corps*, and my father did all he could to save them, in which, it must be owned, the deputies eagerly seconded him. The crowd we met along the road was innumerable, so that we could scarcely advance. The insults with which the people loaded us were our only food throughout the day. In the *faubourgs* of Paris the crowd was even greater, and among all those persons we saw but one woman fairly well-dressed who showed by her tears the interest she took in us.

On the Place Louis XV was M. de la Fayette, apparently at the summit of joy at the success of the blow he had just struck; he was there, surrounded by a people submissive to his orders; he could have destroyed my father at once, but he preferred to save him longer in order that he might serve his own designs. We were made to drive through the garden of the Tuileries, surrounded by weapons of all sorts, and muskets

---

10 The Flight to Varennes by Alexandre Dumas père

which almost touched us. When the deputies said anything to the people they were instantly obeyed, and it is no doubt to their intentions (good or bad) that my father owed his preservation at that moment; for had those deputies not been with us it is more than likely we should then have been murdered. It was they also who saved the Gardes du Corps. On arriving at the Tuileries and getting out of the carriage, we were almost carried off our feet by the enormous crowd that filled the staircase. My father went up first, with my mother and my brother. As for me, I was to go with my aunt, and one of the deputies took me in his arms to carry me up. In vain did I cry for my aunt; the noise was so dreadful she could not hear me. At last we were all reunited in the King's room, where were nearly all the deputies of the National Assembly, who, however, seemed very civil and did not stay long.

My father entered the inner rooms with his family, and seeing them all in safety, I left him and went to my own apartments, being quite worn out with fatigue and inanition. I did not know until the next morning what took place that evening. Guards were placed over the whole family, with orders not to let them out of sight, and to stay night and day in their chambers. My father had them in his room at night, but in the daytime they were stationed in the next room. My mother would not allow them to be in the room where she slept with a waiting-woman, but they stayed in the adjoining room with the doors open. My brother had them also, night and day; but my aunt and I had none. M. de la Fayette even proposed to my aunt to leave the Tuileries, if she wished to do so, but she replied that she would never separate from the King."

Observers reported that the King showed no sign of distress, but imperturbable as ever enjoyed chicken for dinner. His wife took a bath to wash away the grime of the journey. Under the new regime, she was required to leave the bathroom door open. There was a visible indication of how the trauma of their capture had affected her. Her once-blonde hair had, during the previous five days turned white.

In her new circumstances, the Queen had to become something that by nature she was not. She had to develop courage in order to cope with the family's new situation. Her husband was regarded as a benevolent simpleton. It was she who must use her wits and charm, and try to learn the art of statesmanship, to protect her family. She had to become the man her husband wasn't. From a frivolous and carefree bubblehead, she transformed herself into a woman of dignity and pride.

In a sketch made in 1791 Marie-Antoinette is unrecognisable from the previous portraits of an overdressed and rather vacant-faced doll. It shows a serious and very regal looking woman whose expression seems to indicate that she already knows how her story is going to end.

Safely in Belgium, the King's two horrid brothers rejoiced in his capture, each with their eyes fixed on the crown of France. Fersen wrote: "There has been the most unseemly joy manifested because the King was taken prisoner; the Count of Artois is positively radiant."

Marie-Antoinette had written to Fersen to reassure him that she was safe. She warned him not to return to Paris, as his part in the escape attempt was known and he would be arrested immediately if he was seen. But in February 1792 he did return in disguise, and managed to get into the Tuileries. He recorded in his diary that he spent the night and the following day with the Queen in her apartments. It was the last time they would see each other, and the date was February 14th – Valentine's day.

Assassination attempts on Marie-Antoinette were thwarted. A man carrying a knife was discovered in the corridor outside her room one night. It was suspected that her food may be poisoned. "The Austrian," "the bitch," "Madame Deficit," "the lesbian," "the whore," as she was variously named, knew that it was she who was the target of the people's hatred far more than the King. She was perfect fodder for the gutter press, the 18th century red-tops, and no accusation was regarded as too vile to level at her.

Political events, both domestic and foreign, which were beyond their control, kept nudging the royals closer and closer towards their fate. In response to warnings by Marie-Antoinette's brother, the Holy Roman Emperor, that any harm done to the King would have severe consequences, France declared war on Austria. Émigrés who had escaped the Terror plotted and planned to restore Louis to the throne. These actions succeeded only in further angering and alarming the Revolutionary citizens.

On 20th June of 1792, the first anniversary of their escape attempt, a crowd stormed the Tuileries. Marie-Thérèse remembered:

"Suddenly we saw the populace forcing the gates of the courtyard and rushing to the staircase of the château. It was a horrible sight to see, and impossible to describe – that of these people, with fury in their faces, armed with pikes and sabres, and pell-mell with them women half unclothed, resembling Furies."

Madame Campan describes the incident similarly, adding:

"The horde passed in files before the table; the sort of standards which they carried were symbols of the most atrocious barbarity. There was one representing a gibbet, to which a dirty doll was suspended; the words '*Marie Antoinette à la lanterne*' were written beneath it. Another was a board, to which a bullock's heart was fastened, with 'Heart of Louis XVI' written round it."

With splendid courage and sang froid, almost alone Louis faced these ghouls who had been fuelled with alcohol and primed to assassinate him. Whilst they rampaged through the palace screaming the vilest insults at the royal family he humoured them – putting on the silly red cap that was their symbol. He remained unruffled and courteous in the face of the contempt and jeers of his subjects until the mob eventually disbanded.

The family lived in continual anxiety and fear, knowing that their situation would continue to worsen. Marie-Antoinette, like her husband, had been planning to write her

187

memoirs. Following the attack of 20th June, she burned many of the letters and reports that she had collected together. What a loss! What would historians give now to read their stories in their own words, and what an insight it would have given us into their thoughts and feelings.

On the first anniversary of the fall of the Bastille – 14th July – their captors forced the royal pair to appear at the celebrations. Anticipating that attempts would be made on their lives, they both wore protective breastplates to resist blade or bullet. Louis wore his only to put his wife's mind at rest. By now the portrait of Charles I of England had obviously made a deep impression on him. He recognised that what had happened to England and its monarch was happening in France and would happen to him. He knew that his death was already planned, but that it would not be by assassination.

August 10th 1792 turned up on the calendar, and with it a vast crowd of heavily armed Parisians screaming for blood, bearing down once again upon the miserable Tuileries palace. Louis dithered, dillied and dallied, waiting until the last moment before he and his family fled the Tuileries for the final time. They ran next door to the protection of the National Assembly, where there they spent 18 hours crammed into a tiny cubicle normally used by journalists.

Behind them fierce fighting was taking place at the Tuileries between the mob and the loyal Swiss Guard. Hoping to avoid further bloodshed, Louis signed an order for the Swiss Guard to lay down their arms. It was the death warrant for his royal bodyguard. Once they surrendered they were brutally massacred and their bodies mutilated.

Meanwhile, throughout their long and intensely uncomfortable ordeal, Louis managed to chomp his way contentedly through several meals. To her friends, his wife confessed that she was much disturbed by the fact that no situation, no matter how grave, could blunt the King's appetite. This gave an entirely false and very unfavourable impression to those who did not know him.

As their situation became increasingly precarious, she must have been wondering just how long the nightmare was going to continue, and how much worse it could get. The answer was not much longer, but very much worse.

All these extraordinary events had happened on and around the ground on which we were standing. During her imprisonment the Queen would have walked on the same ground where we now walked. I wondered what thoughts had gone through her mind when she did so. I tried to imagine how she would have felt as the preparations for the escape had advanced. Was she confident they would succeed, or was she was afraid? What was she thinking when she ran through the corridors and streets to find the carriage waiting to take them out of Paris on the first stage of their flight? Did Axel Fersen walk on these same paths when he came to visit her? Did they stand beside each other at a window in the palace, looking down onto the gardens?

The footsteps of the good and the great and the low and wicked had all left their imprints in the garden of the Tuileries, and the bodies of several hundred Swiss Guard had lain here in their blood.

I felt as if we were standing on a vast stage, empty now, the cast having taken their final bow and disappeared behind the curtains. If we looked around we would see them dispersing, dressed in finery, uniforms or rags, climbing into their carriages, marching away with their pikes over their shoulders, shouting or singing, or climbing onto waiting horses and clattering away on the cobbles.

It would be easy, but a shame to only see in the garden sculptures and trees, ponds and fountains, velvety lawns, neat paths, and views to the Arc de Triomphe. Because it is far more than that: it is the arena where one of France's greatest dramas was enacted.

CHAPTER FIFTEEN
With Their Heads Held High

"All our life is but a going out to the place of execution, to death."
John Donne

"When fate summons, monarchs must obey."
John Dryden

NO longer safe at the Tuileries, the prisoners were moved to the sinister Temple prison. There they would suffer their cruellest and most brutal treatment. For father and son, it would be their final address.

With the family went a handful of loyal companions, including the Queen's closest friend, the Princess de Lamballe. Three servants accompanied them, but very quickly all except one were removed until only a single valet remained. Heavily guarded, as much for their own protection as to prevent a further escape attempt, the King and Queen were free to walk in the gardens, play cards, and educate and entertain their children. Although their gaolers delighted in insulting and humiliating them as often and offensively as possible, Marie-Thérèse noted that her father "suffered it all with gentleness," and her mother bore it with dignity. Not only did he have access to a fine library, but Louis' appetite was well-catered for. A staff of thirteen ensured that his mid-day meal comprised an excellent and huge selection of dishes and wines.

Briefly the family were able to lead a fairly undemanding life, apart from living in perpetual fear of what would happen to them next.

They were right to be fearful, because things would soon become very nasty indeed. The Princess de Lamballe went to England in an attempt to raise support for the French royals.

Against the advice of her friends, she returned to France where she was arrested and taken to the La Force prison. There, refusing to denounce the monarchy, she met a most gruesome and violent death. While the King and Queen were playing cards in the afternoon they were disturbed by shouting outside the prison. Through the high window they saw the severed head of the princess being waved on a spike by a mob who wanted to show their Queen what they had done to her dearest friend.

In their adversity, the family were strong and united. The Queen and her daughter mended and patched their clothing and cleaned their rooms. Louis lamented the fact that Marie-Antoinette had been brought so low because she had married him. She responded that hers was the glory and noble honour of being the wife of one of the best and most persecuted of men. I found the mutual loyalty and support of this odd couple very touching. Each of them could have justifiably blamed the other for their dire situation.

His wife was not blind to Louis' weaknesses, but explained:

"The King is not a coward; he possesses abundance of passive courage, but he is overwhelmed by an awkward shyness, a mistrust of himself, which proceeds from his education as much as from his disposition. He is afraid to command, and, above all things, dreads speaking to assembled numbers. He lived like a child, and always ill at ease under the eyes of Louis XV, until the age of twenty-one. This constraint confirmed his timidity. Circumstanced as we are, a few well-delivered words addressed to the Parisians, who are devoted to him, would multiply the strength of our party a hundredfold: he will not utter them."

France proclaimed herself a Republic on 21st September 1792. Louis was no longer a king, and with his crown gone, he no longer had need of a head. He was accused of treason and sent to trial, doubtless well aware of the inevitable outcome. While he waited to learn his fate, he is said to have asked his defence counsel, M. de Malesherbes:

"Have you not met near the Temple the White Lady?"

191

"What do you mean?" replied he.

"Do you not know," resumed the King with a smile, "that when a prince of our house is about to die, a female dressed in white is seen wandering about the palace?"

Isolated from his family, Louis spent a solitary Christmas day writing his will. On the 20th January, 1793 he was allowed to see his wife, his children and sister. The following day, at just after 8.00 am, apart from shedding a tear at being unable to say a final farewell to his family, he set off from the Temple to his execution. He bore himself with his habitual composure, as if he was going to play a game of cards. In the carriage with him went Henry Essex Edgeworth de Firmont, a cleric of English birth, long time friend of the royal family, and Louis' confessor. Edgeworth was the rather reluctant vicar of Paris, a position bequeathed to him by the city's Archbishop who had fled the country to save his own life. Like Malesherbes, Edgeworth expected to pay with his life for his loyalty to the King. He recounted Louis' journey to the scaffold, and his execution:

"The King, finding himself seated in the carriage, where he could neither speak to me nor be spoken to without witness, kept a profound silence. I presented him with my breviary, the only book I had with me, and he seemed to accept it with pleasure: he appeared anxious that I should point out to him the psalms that were most suited to his situation, and he recited them attentively with me. The gendarmes, without speaking, seemed astonished and confounded at the tranquil piety of their monarch, to whom they doubtless never had before approached so near.

The procession lasted almost two hours; the streets were lined with citizens, all armed, some with pikes and some with guns, and the carriage was surrounded by a body of troops, formed of the most desperate people of Paris. As another precaution, they had placed before the horses a number of drums, intended to drown any noise or murmur in favour of the King; but how could they be heard? Nobody appeared either at the doors or windows, and in the street nothing was to be seen, but armed citizens - citizens, all rushing towards the commission of a crime, which perhaps they detested in their hearts.

The carriage proceeded thus in silence to the Place de Louis XV, and stopped in the middle of a large space that had been left round the scaffold: this space was surrounded with cannon, and beyond, an armed multitude extended as far as the eye could reach. As soon as the King perceived that the carriage stopped, he turned and whispered to me, 'We are arrived, if I mistake not.' My silence answered that we were. One of the guards came to open the carriage door, and the gendarmes would have jumped out, but the King stopped them, and leaning his arm on my knee, 'Gentlemen,' said he, with the tone of majesty. 'I recommend to you this good man; take care that after my death no insult be offered to him - I charge you to prevent it.' As soon as the King had left the carriage, three guards surrounded him, and would have taken off his clothes, but he repulsed them with haughtiness - he undressed himself, untied his neckcloth, opened his shirt, and arranged it himself. The guards, whom the determined countenance of the King had for a moment disconcerted, seemed to recover their audacity. They surrounded him again, and would have seized his hands. 'What are you attempting?' said the King, drawing back his hands. 'To bind you,' answered the wretches. 'To bind me,' said the King, with an indignant air. 'No! I shall never consent to that: do what you have been ordered, but you shall never bind me.'

The path leading to the scaffold was extremely rough and difficult to pass; the King was obliged to lean on my arm, and from the slowness with which he proceeded, I feared for a moment that his courage might fail; but what was my astonishment, when arrived at the last step, I felt that he suddenly let go my arm, and I saw him cross with a firm foot the breadth of the whole scaffold; silence, by his look alone, fifteen or twenty drums that were placed opposite to me; and in a voice so loud, that it must have been heard it the Pont Tournant, I heard him pronounce distinctly these memorable

193

words: 'I die innocent of all the crimes laid to my charge; I Pardon those who have occasioned my death; and I pray to God that the blood you are going to shed may never be visited on France.'

He was proceeding, when a man on horseback, in the national uniform, and with a ferocious cry, ordered the drums to beat. Many voices were at the same time heard encouraging the executioners. They seemed reanimated themselves, in seizing with violence the most virtuous of Kings, they dragged him under the axe of the guillotine, which with one stroke severed his head from his body. All this passed in a moment. The youngest of the guards, who seemed about eighteen, immediately seized the head, and showed it to the people as he walked round the scaffold; he accompanied this monstrous ceremony with the most atrocious and indecent gestures. At first an awful silence prevailed; at length some cries of *'Vive la Republique!'* were heard. By degrees the voices multiplied and in less than ten minutes this cry, a thousand times repeated became the universal shout of the multitude, and every hat was in the air."

Louis' body was thrown into a large pit at the cemetery of the Church of the Madeleine, close to the wall of the Rue d'Anjou, then smothered in quicklime. He was 39 years old.

Edgeworth managed to escape from Paris and, eventually, from France. M. de Malesherbes was not so lucky. He had known that by acting as the King's defence counsel he was signing his own death warrant. But could he have foreseen that before he laid his 73-year-old head on the block he would be forced to sit beside the guillotine and witness the deaths of his daughter, grand-daughters and their spouses?

When Louis went to his execution, his son, the Dauphin became the de facto King of France, Louis XVII. Six months after his father's death, he was taken from his mother to another part of the prison, and put into the care of rough guardians. He would never see any of his family again, although his mother stood for long hours at the window trying to catch sight of her son. Two years later, in his tenth year, Louis died in the Temple from illness, cruelty and neglect. Frightened, lonely, tormented, corrupted, dressed in rags and most of the time in solitary confinement in the dark. How could that have been allowed to happen to a small boy?

Despite her dismal circumstances, and prematurely white hair, Marie Antoinette had many admirers, even amongst those who had once been her fiercest enemies.

"As soon as the most violent Jacobins had an opportunity of seeing the Queen near at hand, of speaking to her, and of hearing her voice, they became her most zealous partisans; and even when she was in the prison of the Temple several of those who had contributed to place her there perished for having attempted to get her out again." [11]

She had always inspired love and admiration among many men and women who knew her. One particular gentleman had stalked her devotedly for over ten years. Slightly barmy M. Castelnaux declared himself to be her lover, and popped up wherever she went, whether it was at one of the palaces, the theatre or walking in her garden. Told that his constant attentions were unwelcome to the Queen, he promised to desist. However, half an hour later he retracted, saying that his love for her was too strong to deny him her presence. She was generous enough to tolerate his tiresome attentions, and when he learned of her arrest he tried to starve himself to death.

More than once when facing hostile crowds, Marie Antoinette's dignity and humour won them over. Men were still prepared to risk their lives attempting to rescue her. But their plans were always discovered, leading to further punishment and deprivation for the Queen and making her situation more wretched.

They came to the Temple at 2.00 in the morning on 2nd August 1793, to waken her and tell her she was to be taken and tried before the Revolutionary Tribunal. Saying farewell to her daughter and her sister-in-law, she collected a small bundle of clothes and went without protest to her next address – the notorious Conciergerie.

---

11 Memoirs of the Private Life of Marie Antoinette by Madame Campan

We did not go to the Temple. It was demolished on Napoléon's orders to prevent it becoming a place of pilgrimage for royalists. I wish the French hadn't demolished so many historical buildings. Now it is merely the name of a station on the Metro. Surely the ghosts of the White Lady and a little boy must lurk there. Instead we set sail for the Conciergerie.

From the Batobus our first view of the building quite startled me. I had visualised a sinister place of grimy stones and mean proportions. But reclining beside the river the long building with its witchetty-hatted turrets looks nowhere as grim as I expected. It is rather handsome.

Terry opted to sit in the sun at a nearby café while I visited Marie-Antoinette's last home. Although he had fairly patiently indulged my whim to follow the path of the unfortunate woman, he didn't want to stand in the long and good-natured queue shuffling towards the ticket office. When I pushed through the heavy door, the interior was as much of a surprise as the outside. Far from being dank and slimy-walled, the Guard Room and the Hall of the Men at Arms are beautiful examples of Gothic architecture. Beneath a vaulted ceiling supported on elegant pillars, sunlight fell in warm rays on creamy flagstones.

Most of my fellow queue shufflers stampeded straight through to other parts of the building. Almost alone in the two great empty halls, I tried to visualise the scenes here during The Terror. I wondered who had stood on the spot where I was now standing. There must have been sobs, entreaties, threats, bribes, hopes raised, hopes dashed. But I could pick up not a single frisson. This silent place felt as peaceful and safe as a cloister. But then, of course, I was free to walk out of here at any time I wished. The building looked and felt as if it had been vigorously scrubbed and polished to remove any trace of the ignoble events that had taken place there, to erase them forever.

The most powerful and feared figures of the Revolutionary tribunals, whose names turned people's blood to ice, had zealously despatched nearly 3,000 victims from here to the guillotine. What terror, hate, fear, treachery and despair these stones had witnessed. And what great reverses in fortune, and for some, almost-divine retribution. Hateful Fouquier-Tinville, blood-thirsty Robespierre, vile Hébert and vacillating Danton must all have strutted and swaggered over these stones, confident of their supreme power over the lives of their prisoners. How much less cocksure they must have been when the scales began to tilt against them, when power slipped through their fingers and they found themselves setting off in the tumbrel for their own personal appointment with the "National Razor." Robespierre, sentenced without trial, was already half-dead of a gunshot wound when the guillotine finished him off. He faced the executioner with a blood-curdling yell. Marat, if he had been given the choice, might have preferred to lose his head ceremoniously on the scaffold rather than to die so embarrassingly, sitting in his bath with his itchy bottom. I found it most satisfying to know that these loathsome people had met such harrowing ends. Still, it needed an extreme effort to envisage such events in this elegant but sterile place.

Upstairs a few reconstructed cells show how prisoners lived while awaiting trial. Members of the riff-raff element slept upon piles of straw on the floor. The middle classes who were able to afford a little comfort could have a bed, and wealthy *aristos* had the luxury of chairs and writing desks too. What happened to the "liberty, equality and fraternity" which was the slogan of the Revolution?

Once prisoners had been condemned, they had little time to fret. They went to their death the following day, after emptying their pockets and having a final haircut in that last chance saloon, the tiny and sparse *Salle de la Dernière Toilette*. From there they passed through a small doorway leading out to the street where the tumbrels waited. The doorway is still there. I thought I might have caught, from the corner of my eye, a transparent figure passing through it.

The twenty-one Girondist deputies became victims of the

same Revolution that they had been instrumental in unleashing. They are pictured having a jolly party in their chapel on the eve of their execution. Elegant and relaxed, they sit at, or stand around a long table whose white cloth is covered with dishes, plates and glasses. Numerous empty bottles are in evidence; perhaps these contributed to the high spirits with which the men went singing to the scaffold next morning. Only one of them wasn't enjoying the party. He had already stabbed himself to death, and his body lies in a barrow. He didn't succeed in cheating the guillotine simply by killing himself, though. Next day his dead head was chopped off.

When Marie-Antoinette arrived at the Conciergerie she was lodged in the semi-subterranean former Council Chamber. It is no longer visible today. In its place stands a plain and rather chilly-looking commemorative chapel, built on the orders of her brother-in-law, Louis XVIII. There is a reconstruction, though, of the tiny room in which she spent the last 76 wretched days of her life. The figure of a woman dressed in black is seated at a desk, her back to viewers. To one side is a narrow, uncomfortable-looking bed. Behind the Queen, Prisoner No. 280, Widow Capet, or whatever other name her gaolers chose to use, is a folding screen. This could not have offered her any privacy whatsoever, as it only reaches to the chin of the guard permanently stationed behind it to watch over her. The contrast between this room and the opulence of Versailles couldn't have been stronger. Yet there was one similarity - in both places she was under constant observation, like an animal in a zoo.

According to Madame Campan's Memoirs of Marie-Antoinette:

"The Queen was lodged in a room called the council chamber, which was considered as the most unwholesome apartment in the Conciergerie on account of its dampness and the bad smells by which it was continually affected. Under pretence of giving her a person to wait upon her they placed near her a spy, – a man of a horrible countenance and hollow, sepulchral voice. This wretch, whose name was Barassin, was a robber and murderer by profession. Such was the chosen attendant on the Queen of France! A few days before her trial this wretch was removed and a gendarme placed in her chamber, who watched over her night and day, and from whom she was not separated, even when in bed, but by a ragged curtain. In this melancholy abode Marie Antoinette had no other dress than an old black gown, stockings with holes, which she was forced to mend every day; and she was entirely destitute of shoes."

Madame Campan does not mention the young serving girl, Rosalie Lamorlière, who was the nearest thing that Marie Antoinette had to a maid. The girl later related the events she witnessed during the Queen's stay in the Conciergerie. She described her gentleness, her attempts to keep herself decent as her clothes fell to pieces, her occasional despair and the admiration and pity her plight awoke in her gaolers. However, anybody openly sympathetic to her risked the most severe punishment, thus any small kindnesses had to be most discreet. The few small treasures she still owned were confiscated after a bungled rescue attempt. Stefan Zweig relates how she found temporary escape from the loneliness and hopelessness of her situation by avidly reading true adventure stories.

There was no question that Marie Antoinette would be condemned to death at her trial, but she decided to defend herself anyway. Her ordeal had transformed a vivacious young queen into a prematurely-aged, exhausted and ailing woman. The only assets she retained were dignity and courage. She responded to the indictments cautiously but with spirit. When outrageous charges of incest with her young son were read out, she treated them with contempt. Even those women who had come to see her humbled were so shocked by this disgusting charge that they became sympathetic to her.

It was 4.00 in the morning when, after a trial lasting two days, she was summoned before the tribunal, pronounced guilty and sentenced to die. She spent some time writing a farewell letter to her sister-in-law who was still in the grim Temple prison. She wrote that she hoped to die with the same courage as her husband, and she would do so with a clear conscience, devout in her Catholic faith. She refused the ministrations of a priest who had taken the oath of allegiance to the Constitution. Her greatest sadness was in leaving her children.

The letter was never delivered to Madame Elizabeth, who would lose her head the following year. (At her execution, the King's sister was seated beside the guillotine, to benefit from a close-up view of the machine in action as it decapitated all her companions first.) Marie-Antoinette's letter was handed to the public prosecutor, and only reappeared twenty-one years later when it arrived in the hands of Louis XVIII.

The new Republic had almost finished with Marie Antoinette. Just a few more hours of her life remained, and her enemies would make them as humiliating and painful as they possibly could.

Apart from the prison guards, Rosalie was the only person who witnessed the Queen's preparation for her execution. On the morning of October 16th 1793, the girl encouraged Marie Antoinette to eat a few spoonfuls of soup. A guard stood in the cell watching as she changed her undergarments, stained from haemorrhages she had suffered. She dressed herself carefully, in white, with her best shoes and stockings. How poignant is that – a woman taking pains to look her best on her way to the guillotine? A grey-haired old lady two weeks before her 38th birthday. It had been four years, almost to the day, since the family were driven out of Versailles.

Looking at the mocked-up cell did nothing for me. I could not relate it in any way to the above events. It felt as if Marie Antoinette had deliberately refused to let any part of her spirit exist in this bleak place.

After a brief visit to the rest of the building, I went off to find Terry. He was happily standing by the bridge in the sunshine, chatting to a blonde French lady.

"Shall we go for lunch now?" he asked, hopefully. Like a

baby bird, he needs feeding at short and regular intervals.

"Not just yet. In a while. We'll walk a little first."

"Where to?"

"You'll see," I said, setting off at a brisk pace because I was quite hungry too.

"So, what did you think of the Conciergerie?"

"Hm. The architecture of the two great halls is magnificent, but I couldn't feel any atmosphere in there. It seemed too sanitised."

"What, no rusting chains or messages scratched on the walls?"

"No, nothing at all like that. It's as if every trace of anything unpleasant has been whitewashed out, and all the history sucked away. I'd like to have seen it as it was during the Revolution."

We followed the route the tumbrels had taken when they left the Conciergerie, crossing the Pont au Change to the north bank of the river and picking up the Rue Saint Honoré.

"Why are we walking here? I'm hungry."

"So am I, but we are walking here," I explained, "because this is the route on which Marie-Antoinette was taken to her execution."

"I hope she went in style."

"She certainly did, but not in the style that you are thinking, nor to which she was once accustomed."

Unlike Louis who had travelled in a carriage accompanied by a priest, the hated Austrian woman was led from the prison by the executioner, holding her by a cord binding her hands behind her back. She was helped onto the back of a crude cart pulled by a draught horse.

Like that of her late husband, her journey was designed to give as many spectators as possible a chance to enjoy the spectacle, which lasted for two hours. All along the roads people lined up, laughing and shouting at her. They revelled in her humiliation – albeit she had never personally done them any harm. Throughout this degrading ordeal she maintained an air of complete indifference. With her back

201

straight and her chin up, the only sign of her inner torment was the way her cheeks alternately flushed and paled.

I looked up at the elegant buildings, visualising coarse, jeering ghouls leaning from the windows to watch the miserable procession on its way to the guillotine in the Place de la Révolution. Amongst the spectators, I wondered, were there were any who had felt sympathy for the woman on the cart?

Marie Antoinette on the Way to the Guillotine,
sketch by Jacques-Louis David, Louvre.
Image in public domain taken from Wikipedia

Eye-witnesses told that the Queen went to her death with royal dignity and great courage. Even that most spiteful man, Hébert, wrote: "The whore, for the rest, was bold and impudent to the very end."

In contrast, her old bête noire Madame du Barry, who followed her to the guillotine a couple of months later, made a hysterical exhibition of herself on the scaffold, running around screaming and begging for mercy.

After Marie-Antoinette's death her body was tossed onto a cart with her severed head placed between her legs. Her remains were put into the meanest coffin and buried in a common trench beside her dead husband and other victims of The Terror.

We arrived at the Place de la Concorde where the guillotine had once practised its grisly trade. It felt as if we were standing beside the Tower of Babel. Foreign tongues filled the air, tourists clicked their cameras, backing and bumping into each other as they manoeuvred for the best angle. Amongst the polyglottal chatter there were French voices too. As we listened to and watched smiling, sophisticated Parisians talking on their mobile phones, laughing and strolling in the sunshine, I couldn't help wondering what their ancestors had been doing at the time of the Revolution.

Despite the heat of the sun, chilly little fingers ran over my flesh as I reflected on the horrors that had taken place in this elegant square. There had been a time when the smell of blood was so powerful that cattle refused to walk there. In particular I thought how terribly lonely Marie-Antoinette must have felt as she climbed the scaffold's steps amongst a sea of hostile faces waiting excitedly to watch her have her head cut off. And it seemed extraordinary that this barbaric event took place not in the Middle Ages, but only eight years before the birth of the 19th century. And in a country that has produced some of the world's greatest writers, artists and philosophers.

"I'm hungry," repeated Terry, unmoved by events of the past. "Let's go and eat."

Because it was such a glorious a day, we forwent our planned lunchtime treat of a meal in a restaurant. Instead we picnicked in the garden of the Tuileries, tossing crumbs to fat and expectant pigeons. I noticed that the spaces between the straps of my ugly-sandaled feet were sunburned to Dayglo-pink, and so were my shoulders.

I had forgotten the precise address of the next stage of our safari, so we wandered along to a small tourist office in the Elysian Fields. The man there was polite but baffled, and said he'd never heard of the place I mentioned. However after burrowing into a drawer he consulted some papers, then sketched a map. Following his directions, we unexpectedly found ourselves at the gates of the Elysée Palace, eyeball to eyeball with a policeman who stared back unblinkingly. There was no sign of any activity within the building. Presumably M. Chirac was either inside busily running the country in his oleaginous way, or on one of his frequent overseas jaunts.

The map drawn by the man at the tourist office led us around in circles. We asked several pedestrians and a policeman for directions, and were surprised by two things: firstly their courtesy. Where were the rude Parisians we hear so much about? Without exception, from the railway staff to the Batobus staff, the people in the Tourist Office, the shopkeepers, the *flics* and the pedestrians we spoke to, they were all charming, polite and as helpful as they could possibly be. The second surprising factor was that none of them could easily remember, or even appeared to know where to find the place we were looking for. A vague idea was the best that most of them could summon up. By putting all the little clues together, we eventually arrived at the dark and leafy little Square Louis XVI, at the junction of Boulevard Haussmann and Rue d'Anjou.

At the beginning of the 18th century the cemetery here welcomed about 160 new residents each year. In May 1770 there was a rush for places by the 133 people who had died at the giant firework display for the nuptial celebrations of Louis and Marie-Antoinette. But this was as nothing in comparison with the demand for space during The Terror. It was to this cemetery, only 45 by 19 metres, that the tumbrels delivered the heads and bodies, in separate baskets, of the recently-executed for burial in a large communal pit.

During the final seven weeks of the madness, the guillotine despatched an average of 46 people each day. [12] Quite a

---

12 A Popular History of France by François Guizot

logistical challenge to find somewhere to put them. The 900 massacred Swiss Guard, who had needlessly died at the Tuileries were buried here. Men and women, rich and poor, young and old, educated and illiterate, famous and infamous. There had been no discrimination. Many of even the most conscientious and vociferous Revolutionaries would end up mingled with their victims in a companionable and democratic tangle in the melancholy square where we were standing.

Beneath our feet had lain the unidentifiable remains of more than 2,000 victims, including Louis and Marie-Antoinette. However, a vigilant Royalist resident in a nearby street had kept his head and noted the place where the King and Queen were buried. Once the Terror was over he marked the spot by planting some willow and cypress trees. What little remained of the royal bodies was exhumed in 1815 and buried in the Royal necropolis at St Denis.

Still, it's hard to believe that with so many corpses crammed into such a relatively small area, and the heads arriving independently of the bodies, there could not have been some room for error. Also, if Louis' body was smothered in lime, very little of him would have been left. Marie Antoinette's remains were supposedly identified by a piece of garter. It's unlikely that she alone of all the female victims was wearing a garter. With no DNA testing at that time, who knows whether the disinterred remains were indeed royal, or just some unfortunate commoner who had shared their fate? If you visit the chapel in the square, and read the information sheets there, it says very clearly "The King and Queen's bodies (or at least the presumed bodies, at least for the King's) were excavated."

The chapel, built in the style of a Roman temple with a pinch of Greek influence, lies at the far end of a lawned area divided by a path. A series of mini-temples containing the tombs of the Swiss Guard flank the outer edges of the grass. I tried not to think of what and who lay beneath us as we walked through the profusion of white roses bordering the path leading to the steps of the chapel.

Inside, statues of Louis and Marie-Antoinette on their way to their heavenly repose live in niches in the walls. The interior is brightly illuminated by rays of light from a series of small circular windows in the domed ceilings above. It solemn without being mournful. I thought that if she were alive, Marie Antoinette may have been quite content sitting here reading or writing, while her children and pet dogs played on the lawn.

A reproduction of Louis' Will is on display. In this poignant document he commends his soul to his God, pardons those who have done him harm and begs forgiveness of anyone whom he has unwittingly harmed. He commends his children to the loving care of their mother and aunt, advises his son not to seek revenge for his death, and bequeaths what few tiny possessions remain to him to his valet Cléry. The following paragraph intrigued me:

"I beg my wife to forgive all the pain which she suffered for me, and the sorrows which I may have caused her in the course of our union; and she may feel sure that I hold nothing against her, if she has anything with which to reproach herself."

Now, with what could he have felt she might reproach herself?

Chopping off heads, confiscating, denouncing, looting, terrorising were not the only sports practised during the French Revolution. The guillotine was by no means the worst form of execution. Slower and more painful methods included burning, beating, shooting, stabbing, trampling with horses. In Nantes, enemies of the Republic, or people who were in the wrong place at the wrong time, were condemned to death by the horrifying "*noyade*" - sealed into the holds of old barges that were then sunk. In the "Republican marriage" version of this, naked men and women, often clergy and nuns, were chained together and thrown into the water to drown. The guillotine had been conceived as a quicker and more humane death – but of course, it was a matter of taste.

Under the new regime, it wasn't only the aristocracy who had to be eliminated. There was no place for clergy unless they renounced their religion and embraced the new Revolutionary creed. Christianity had to go. First it was replaced by the Cult of Reason, which was followed by the Cult of the Supreme Being. The French Revolution was no longer about a shortage of bread or the depravity of the *aristos*. It had become a war of ideologies between the most powerful men of the time.

With the outlawing of Christianity, out too went the Gregorian calendar based on the birth of Christ. The Revolutionary calendar came into existence in 1792, on the 22nd September to be precise, the autumnal equinox, and the birthdate of the Republic following the abolition of the monarchy.

This new calendar retained the twelve-month format, but each month was divided into units of 10 days known as *décades*. The months were given rather beautiful and appropriate new names, by a French poet called Fabre d'Eglantine:

Vendémiaire - vintage month
Brumaire - foggy month
Frimaire - sleety month
Nivôse - snowy month
Pluviôse - rainy month
Ventôse - windy month
Germinal - seed month
Floréal - blossoming month
Prairial - pasture month
Messidor - harvesting month
Thermidor - hot month
Fructidor - fruity month

Across the Channel the irreverent English called them Wheezy, Sneezy and Freezy; Slippy, Drippy and Nippy; Showery, Flowery and Bowery; Wheaty, Heaty and Sweety.

Having twelve months each of thirty days meant that at the end of every year there were five, or in a leap year, six "spare" days. These were known as *Sans-Culottides*, and were national holidays. Each day of the year was given the name of an animal, an agricultural implement or a plant. Even time found itself subject to change. Henceforth there would be ten hours to the day, one hundred minutes to the hour, and one hundred seconds to the minute.

The new calendar was unpopular with workers. With the *décade* replacing the week, it meant they had to work for nine days instead of six before earning a rest day, and the management of leap years was extremely complicated. So it was perhaps fortunate that these new arrangements only lasted for 14 years until Napoléon reinstated the Gregorian calendar and Christianity. However, d'Eglantine would never know that his beautifully-named months had reverted to their previous names, as he trundled off to the guillotine in 1794 on falsified charges of forgery and misuse of public funds.

Although France reverted to the Gregorian calendar and the twenty-four hour clock, one major invention of the Revolution survived – the metric system, which implemented uniform weights and measures to replace previous archaic and haphazard forms of measurement. Those of us who grew up using Imperial measurements – pounds, shillings and pennies, pounds and ounces, miles, yards and inches, were perfectly at ease with their intricacies. However, there is, I feel, far more logic in a measurement system that works on the simple basis of adding or subtracting noughts, and where freezing point is 0° and boiling point 100°, instead of the equivalent Fahrenheit measurements of 32° and 212°.

Nevertheless, even after 15 years of living in France, unlike Terry I still think in feet and inches and can more readily understand the temperature in Fahrenheit.

The royal necropolis at St Denis was too far for us to travel today. Even if we had our bikes, it was over 10 kilometres north from where we were, through some of the busiest suburbs of Paris. We had no idea how we could reach it via overground public transport. Neither would we have time to visit tomorrow, the final day of our trip, so we agreed that we'd return later, by car, to see where the unfortunate royals had eventually come to rest for once and for all.

CHAPTER SIXTEEN
Tourists

"Travelling is like flirting with life. It's like saying, "I would stay and love you, but I have to go; this is my station."
Lisa St Aubin de Terán

OUR onward wanderings took us to the spot where Diana, Princess of Wales, was killed. Terry pointed to a giant golden pumpkin, sitting on a pedestal surrounded by bunches of withered flowers and some plastic skittles with ribbons, balloons and messages tied to them. "What on earth is that strange thing?" he asked.

The gilded lump is a replica of the top of the flame on the Statue of Liberty, a gift from the International Herald Tribune newspaper as a mark of the enduring friendship between France and the United States. Although the ungainly blob had absolutely nothing at all to do with the late princess, it has become an unofficial memorial to her purely because of its location. I wondered whether the princess would be aghast if she saw it, or whether she'd giggle behind her hand. Idly, the thought crossed my mind that she and Marie-Antoinette had much in common. Both controversial, beautiful and arousing strong partisan feelings, both married off as royal breeding stock, both trying to make the best of difficult marriages, and both meeting premature and gruesome deaths.

For the conspiracy theorists, Diana's fatal accident couldn't have happened in a better place. In pagan times the Pont d'Alma was a place of human sacrifice for worshippers of the mythical Greek goddess Artemis, whom the Romans called Diana.

The original Alma bridge was built during the 19th century to celebrate an Anglo-French victory over the Russians in the Crimean war. During the 1970s it was demolished and rebuilt. As well as its function of facilitating traffic from one side of the river to the other, it serves as an indicator of the level of the Seine, according to how high the waters reach up the statue of the Algerian soldier standing on one of the piers of the bridge. When it reaches his knees, it's time to take to the lifeboats. During the great flood of 1910 that had ravaged Joinville-le-Pont, the waters had swirled around his neck.

As we crossed the bridge, a young Japanese man just ahead of us was looking perplexedly at something in his hand. He held out a gold wedding ring and tried to force it onto Terry. He spoke urgently in French with a Japanese accent; or it could have been Japanese with French accent. We couldn't understand him. Terry pushed the ring back and tugged me quickly after him, saying that it was some kind of trick. The poor man looked absolutely distraught, and called after us plaintively. Terry ignored my insistence that we should go back. We had a lively argument on the bridge, during which I accused him of being far too cynical, suspicious and callous, and he said I was far too naïve. While we were in full spate, the subject of our disagreement approached another person, who shouted at him. Off ran the ring-bearer as fast as his Japanese legs would carry him. Later I learned that Terry was quite right. The "gold ring" is a well-known scam.

Terry wanted to go to the top of that most Parisian of Parisian landmarks, the Eiffel tower. While he queued I wandered around the Champs de Mars amongst ice-cream lickers and tourists flicking through guide books, clicking cameras and examining maps. Parents tried to placate tired little wailing children, or bribe them with promises of treats if they'd just for heaven's sake be quiet. An excited family festooned with cameras and guide books ticked off on a list all the sights they'd seen so far that day, and those still to be crammed in before they went to "do" the châteaux next day. Coaches spilled out streams of school children and old people. Japanese, Chinese, Russian and German people all chirruped excitedly as tour guides chivvied them into order. Coach drivers lounged against their vehicles, smoking, chatting with each other, or simply looking bored.

After roaming around the park for twenty minutes, I went and stood beneath the tower. Looking up at it I thought firstly that it is a spectacular piece of engineering ingenuity. Secondly I thought, what a shame it isn't somewhere else. A huge iron pylon stuck in the middle of the beautiful buildings and parks of Paris and in my eyes, utterly incongruous.

It is a view that was shared by a number of French luminaries. When the plans for the tower were first published Parisians by no means took it to their collective heart. Once it was built people living in the vicinity watched it swaying before the wind, wondering whether it might topple onto their houses.

Aghast at its ugliness, Guy de Maupassant's first inclination was to leave Paris. However, instead he compromised by eating in the second-floor restaurant of the tower, the only place from where the structure itself could not be seen.

Many illustrious people protested in the strongest possible terms, calling it "a truly tragic street lamp," "a mast of iron gymnasium apparatus, incomplete, confused and deformed," "a high and skinny pyramid of iron ladders, a giant ungainly skeleton upon a base that looks built to carry a colossal monument of Cyclops, but which just peters out into a ridiculous thin shape like a factory chimney," "a hole-riddled suppository," "a bald umbrella."

They formed a committee to oppose the building, and expressed their quivering outrage with delicious eloquence:

"We come, we writers, painters, sculptors, architects, lovers of the beauty of Paris which was until now intact, to protest with all our strength and all our indignation, in the name of the underestimated taste of the French, in the name of French art and history under threat, against the erection in the very heart of our capital, of the useless and monstrous Eiffel Tower. Is the City of Paris any longer to associate itself with the baroque and mercantile fancies of a builder of machines, thereby making itself irreparably ugly and bringing dishonour? To comprehend what we are arguing one only needs to imagine for a moment a tower of ridiculous vertiginous height dominating Paris, just like a gigantic black factory chimney, its barbarous mass overwhelming and humiliating all our monuments and belittling our works of architecture, which will just disappear before this stupefying folly. And for twenty years we shall see spreading across the whole city, a city shimmering with the genius of so many centuries, we shall see spreading like an ink stain, the odious shadow of this odious column of bolted metal."

M.Eiffel riposted stoutly:

"For my part I believe that the Tower will possess its own beauty. Are we to believe that because one is an engineer, one is not preoccupied by beauty in one's constructions, or that one does not seek to create elegance as well as solidity and durability? Is it not true that the very conditions which give strength also conform to the hidden rules of harmony? Now to what phenomenon did I have to give primary concern in designing the Tower? It was wind resistance. Well then! I hold that the curvature of the monument's four outer edges, which is as mathematical calculation dictated it should be will give a great impression of strength and beauty, for it will reveal to the eyes of the observer the boldness of the design as a whole. Likewise the many empty spaces built into the very elements of construction will clearly display the constant concern not to submit any unnecessary surfaces to the violent action of hurricanes, which could threaten the stability of the edifice. Moreover there is an attraction in the colossal, and a singular delight to which ordinary theories of art are scarcely applicable."

I am often shocked by the fact that I have a certain amount in common with Adolf Hitler, being an Arian, opposed to blood sports, and an animal lover. When he saw the Eiffel Tower, he remarked succinctly: "Is that all it is? It's ugly!" I agree. If I could, I'd move it elsewhere, maybe to one of the Channel ports, or in a very large field where people could go and look at it if they wanted to – like Stonehenge.

Terry had given up after a 30-minute wait to catch a lift to the top of the tower with no noticeable movement in the queue ahead of him. He found me trying to give directions to the Louvre to a couple who didn't speak any language that I recognised. I think they must have been from one of the Balkan states. The only word I could understand was "Louvre," which they repeated insistently. I pointed to it on my ragged little map, then pointed to the river and repeated "Batobus" loudly and slowly, making wave-like movements with my hands and a gentle engine noise to help them. But they obviously didn't understand, and responded with streams of angry-sounding guttural noises. I wondered why they'd chosen me - perhaps it was my outlandish footwear. Then again, maybe I'd misunderstood and they didn't want the Louvre at all. With an apologetic shrug, rueful facial contortion and a final long, slow "B-A-T-O-B-U-S," I abandoned them and walked around with Terry while he photographed the "odious column" from a variety of unusual angles.

I admit to not being easy to impress. Many places described in glowing terms have not lived up to my expectations, which were obviously unrealistic. Venice I'd found grubby, malodorous, outrageously expensive and infested with very rude people. I'd ended up buying two sets of coloured decanters and matching glasses that I didn't like, as the only means of escape from a limpet-like and increasingly menacing salesman. Mind you, that was in 1968 and under unfortunate circumstances. I expect it's much nicer there now. I've seen Mount Kenya and Mount Kilimanjaro topped with snow, and they weren't quite as big or quite as majestic as I expected - and they were very big and very majestic. Until now, the most beautiful place I had ever seen was the Suez Canal. At dusk, with silhouetted camel trains swaying along the banks and the setting sun reflected in the turquoise waters, it was magical.

But already, even from the relatively small part of Paris that we'd seen, I was absolutely knocked sideways. It was beautiful and elegant beyond anything I could have imagined, and lived up to every glowing description I'd ever heard. Each corner revealed another perfect vista, one glorious building standing beside another; space and light and perfect proportions. Every stone throbbed with history. Like a magician pulling endless rabbits from his top hat, Paris delivered one visual thrill after another. The few buildings that failed to enchant us could not detract from the wonder of this luscious city. And that wasn't all. There was a feeling of pure pleasure all around, a relaxed atmosphere as if on that day the whole world overflowed with *joie de vivre*.

Towards late afternoon we began making our way homewards. As we climbed down into the Batobus, kindly passengers swung their feet out of the way and smiled sympathetically, looking at my peculiar shoes, sunburned limbs and scarlet face.

Although we hadn't planned to visit Notre Dame today, it was right in front of us and just a question of hopping off the boat. We clambered up the steps to the quay and stood for a few moments staring up at the great cathedral. I knew that somewhere embedded in the cobblestones, amongst the milling feet of the crowds, is the absolute geographical centre of the city. On French road signs giving the distance to Paris, the measurement is taken from this point. It was rather a nuisance that it was hidden by all these thoughtless people, and it took a few minutes before we spotted it underneath the wheels of a twin baby-buggy. While the parents were photographing each other against the backdrop of the cathedral, I nudged their infants forward a few centimetres to expose a circular stone engraved with the words: "*Point zéro des routes de France.*" At its centre is a bronze sun. As I wheeled the babies back over it, I wondered how many people notice the marker.

Inside the candle-lit cathedral a solo female voice soaring to the ceiling sent shivers up and down our spines. It was impossible to move around through the dense crowd, so we stood at the back for a few minutes, listening and watching the flickering flames.

Then Terry nudged me and whispered: "Come on, I'm getting hungry. Let's get back and go and have dinner."

215

The last Batobus of the day was due to leave in 10 minutes. In the small ticket office, I tried to buy a bar of chocolate from a machine, to fill "*un petit creux*." The machine greedily swallowed our coins, but refused to spit out the Mars bar which became stuck in transit between a collection of M&Ms and some Fruity Fruits. We couldn't dislodge it even when we banged our fists on the glass panel.

At the counter ahead of us was a long queue of Japanese girls with perfect skin and hair, all wearing jeans and hooded tops. I thought it was a pity that Western clothing is displacing traditional costumes, because they would have looked exquisite in kimonos. They weren't there to buy tickets, but only wanted information. The man at the counter very patiently showed them timetables and answered their halting questions. He waited while they conferred in their own language, answered more questions, and finally wished them "*Bonne soirée*" as they chattered noisily out of the office, like a bunch of starlings returning to their roost.

Apologetically I explained about the Mars bar and pointed at the machine. No problem, he smiled, he would retrieve it. It would be no trouble at all. He locked the till, locked the office, closed the barrier, exited through the rear of the booth, come round to the front, tilted the whole machine forward and administered it an almighty thump with his fist. The Mars bar disentangled itself and plopped into the slot, from where he extracted it and presented it to me with a small bow. What a charming gentleman.

It was as much comfort food as to quell any hunger. For the last hour or so I had been contemplating with increasing gloom the journey back to Joinville-le-Pont on the RER semi-underground train. Tragically, as I climbed onto the Batobus trying to unwrap the chocolate, the wretched thing slipped from the wrapper and slithered into the river without a murmur, as if it had a life of its own and no intention of ending it by being eaten.

We disembarked at Le Jardin des Plantes, where I clutched at the opportunity of delaying our journey just a little longer.

Terry wasn't wildly enthusiastic about visiting the gardens. In fact he wasn't at all enthusiastic. I dragged him in anyway and managed to pass twenty minutes admiring a great number of recently dug-up beds of earth surrounded by keep-out tape, and a large and realistic dragon made from recycled waste materials.

Over Charles de Gaulle bridge we dawdled on our way to the station. Even the vile but comfortable sandals had failed to save me from a nice springy blister that had developed under the ball of my right foot from all the hours of walking around in the heat. I walked with a strange gait, taking all the pressure on my right heel. Terry knew how panicky I was feeling about our return journey. I knew he knew, and he knew I knew he knew. But neither of us mentioned it. Instead we discussed the sights we'd seen, and how funny I looked shuffling, hobbling and limping along. All the time, like a drum-roll before an execution, the word "underground" repeated itself over and over in my mind.

The labyrinthine station expected you to know instinctively which line you needed to choose in order to reach your destination. There were a number of coloured circles with different letters in them, none of which, as far as we could find, told you which went where. It was like playing a complicated board game without knowing the rules. We anxiously scoured notices and diagrams to try and find the route that would take us back to Joinville-le-Pont. A pencil-slim lady with a blonde chignon and grey eyes overheard us, and pointed out the right direction with a perfectly manicured hand and a dazzling smile. As we glided down the escalators, I tried to avoid mentally measuring how far beneath the surface we were going; the descent seemed to take forever.

Fortuitously, because it did divert my mind slightly, when we arrived on the platform there was a lunatic, unshaven and dressed in filthy clothing. He was shouting and waving his finger, pointing at people and occasionally spitting quite an impressive distance.

"Do not," warned Terry, "attract his attention. I know what

217

you're like when it comes to collecting peculiar people."

"Terry, I don't attract their attention. You know that perfectly well. It is they who cluster to me like moths around a flame."

"I won't be surprised if he makes a pass at you, with those shoes you're wearing."

He tugged me further down the platform out of range as the spits were getting closer. We chattered about all the places we'd seen since we had first set out from Versailles, and our journey home the next day. I knew he was trying to relax me, but nothing less than a general anaesthetic could have done so and the "underground" drums beat louder than ever. I concentrated surreptitiously on the crazy man, without attracting his attention because I didn't want to get spat upon. It looked as if he was a regular, or else they were ten a centime, because nobody was taking the slightest notice of him. By this time he was angrily ripping a newspaper into shreds, hurling it all over the place, and eating selected pieces.

The train rumbled to a stop. We climbed in and sat down. A lady opposite looked at my burned feet and smiled sympathetically. The doors closed. Nothing happened. Instantly, I felt very, very hot. I looked out of the window straight into the eyes of the newspaper-eating madman, who shook his fist and sent a shower of saliva towards us. The lady opposite rolled her eyes, and began to fan herself with a magazine. Sweat poured down my back.

I reminded myself how courageously Marie Antoinette had borne her final ordeal, the two hour journey to the guillotine in the tumbrel. I told myself that if she could hold her head up all the way, I should be able to manage ten minutes underground. The train was like a sauna. It pulled away slowly, and slowly crept along its subterranean rails. Terry tried to maintain a conversation and I tried in vain to reply. My mouth had dried up, and I was sweating faster than the train was moving.

When we arrived at Joinville-le-Pont we had to slide our tickets into a slot in the barrier to raise it. Terry's went through, but mine crumpled up because it was all bent and mushy from being clenched and twisted in my wet hand. Terry's ticket wouldn't work twice, and it looked for a while as if I might have to clamber over the barrier, short too-tight skirt and funny sandals notwithstanding. A very large gentleman with a twirly moustache noticed our predicament. He tapped me on the hand and pushed his season ticket into the slot to release the barrier.

CHAPTER SEVENTEEN
Having a Good Time – Don't Stop Me Now!

*"Quickly, bring me a beaker of wine, so that I may wet my
mind and say something clever."*
Aristophanes

FOR the last night of our journey we wanted to dine again
beside the Marne, so we cycled to Champigny and crossed the
small footbridge leading out to the *guinguette* on the Île du
Martin-Pêcheur – Kingfisher Island. There was a very large
expanse of empty tables, and only two other diners seated. We
hesitated: did we really want to spend another almost solitary
evening? The *maître d'* approached and asked whether we had
reserved, and tut-tutted when I said no. Looking pointedly at
the dining desert around us, I thought he was joking, and
laughed. He glared back, but with much mumbling and
sighing he led us to a table beneath an awning. Then he
disappeared for almost half an hour.

As we sat obediently wondering what would happen next,
if indeed anything at all would happen, more diners began to
arrive. Very soon the place was full to capacity and people
were being turned away. There was a party of affluent, stylish
people who took aperitifs on a small lawn before settling
down in one of the dining rooms. They seemed to be
celebrating a retirement, because every so often somebody
popped up and made a speech directed at a very satisfied-
looking gentleman of a certain age, and bottles of champagne
followed each other in quick succession. At a long trestle table
beside us was a more casually-dressed group of about 50
people, from grandparents down to gurgling babies in
buggies. I'm always surprised by how perfectly behaved
young children are, in France, no matter where, and no matter
the time. They sit, eat what is put in front of them - even

220

andouillettes[13] - and don't make a noise or climb on the table. Even babies seem to know instinctively how to behave.

Just before it expired, our patience was rewarded by the *maître d'* returning. While simultaneously shouting orders to waiters, he waved a menu briefly before us, from which we managed to glimpse what was on offer. It was rather expensive, but never mind, this was our last night. He stabbed at a handheld computer screen with a small pencil and tucked a piece of paper under a clip on our table. Terry asked what I'd like to drink, and I said without any hesitation: "Champagne."

"What – a whole bottle?"

Despite popular belief caused by a malicious rumour spread by one of our previous English neighbours, I am generally abstemious to the point of being almost teetotal. At home I seldom drink unless we have company, and then at most two glasses of wine or a small whisky. When we're alone, I'm happy with a cup of tea or hot chocolate. It is only when we go out, or are travelling, that I occasionally indulge.

"Yes, please," I said. "Let's celebrate the completion of our trip."

Madame Bollinger said of champagne:

"'I drink it when I'm happy and when I'm sad. Sometimes I drink it when I'm alone. When I have company, I consider it obligatory. I trifle with it if I'm not hungry and drink it when I am. Otherwise, I never touch it – unless I'm thirsty."

"I'm happy we've had such a satisfying adventure, and sad that it's almost over. We're in company, and I'm not hungry, but absolutely famished. And I'm very thirsty. I think that satisfies most of the criteria."

Unlike our meal, the champagne came swiftly. By the time our food arrived 40 minutes later, the bottle was empty.

Despite the long wait, I was feeling exceedingly happy, and called out to the grim-faced *maître d'* to bring a second bottle. Terry was looking a little bemused, and I was conscious but

---

13 A rough, lumpy sausage made from pig's colon, from which it gets its characteristic taste/smell of faeces/urine. Probably more appreciated by French than English.

unconcerned that I was behaving rather loudly. I don't recall what we ate, but I do remember thinking what a splendid time we were having.

A pretty girl with a professional camera went from table to table, sweet-talking diners into having their photographs taken, making them eligible to win some undisclosed prize later in the evening. Some people, like ourselves, refused. How could she possibly imagine I'd want a photographic reminder of my appearance? However, many more accepted, including all of the large party next to us. The girl snapped away and beamed, and returned later to show the finished photos. Nobody would buy a copy, and her smiley expression turned to a fixed grimace. As she walked back to the bar, her face set in an angry scowl, I wondered if this was an evening job that enabled her to earn a few badly-needed euros. Did she have a sick child, an old mother, student debts to pay? I felt sorry for her. Should we offer her a glass of champagne? Oh, too late – the second bottle was empty. While I seemed to be getting through it rather quickly, Terry was making his last.

Later during the evening an *accordéoniste* arrived and weaved her way around the tables. With her hair in a loose chignon, and dressed in a floaty, flowery dress with a plunging neckline, she played all the old accordion favourites.

A couple occupied the entire dance floor with their expert tango. Gradually more couples joined in, elders with teenagers, lovers of all ages tangled together, children hopping around holding hands. This was what we had come to a *guinguette* to see. Listening to and watching a couple of hundred people of all ages relaxing and enjoying themselves beside the river on this summer evening was worth the cost of the food, which was unremarkable except for its price and the unbelievably long wait for service.

Madame de Pompadour, who transcended her unfortunate maiden name of Mademoiselle Poisson (Miss Fish) to become the favourite mistress of Louis XV, remarked that champagne is the only wine that leaves a woman beautiful after drinking it. I knew my appearance was beyond redemption, but what a fun evening I was having! I was so amusing, so witty, so confident. My French had never been so smoothly fluent as I chatted with the people around us. I wish you could have been there. I really sparkled. Even my voice, which normally sounds like bagpipes played by a beginner, seemed to be quite wonderful, as I sang along with the music. I couldn't remember the last time I'd found myself quite so entertaining.

I think Terry paid the bill - in fact I'm certain he did. We wheeled the bikes over the small bridge from the island back on to the path. It was quite late, and quite dark, and I couldn't see very well, yet I rode my bike like a circus performer, twisting and turning at speed around and between startled pedestrians, waving and singing to their further astonishment. Terry was calling at me to slow down, but nothing was going to stop me. The groups of people stretching the entire width of the path scattered as I shot through their midst yelling "*Bonne nuit, mes amis!*" and singing "Don't stop me now."

Terry must have put the bikes into the laundry room at the hotel, and I must have somehow got upstairs and into bed. I woke up the following morning with a clear head, a detailed memory of the previous evening, and a feeling of intense mortification.

After we'd loaded our bikes for the last time we chatted with the Slave girl while she served our breakfast, cleared tables, reset them for lunch, and smilingly ignored the bellows of the bandits. I told her how much we had enjoyed staying at the hotel, and her face lit up with pleasure.

"We have only been here 10 days, but we have big plans for modernising it. The last owners did nothing for years."

That was fairly evident. I hoped she'd have some help in the task ahead. I visualised her armed with hammers and saws, ladders and paint pots, buckets and bags, with half a dozen nails clenched in her teeth, cheerfully rebuilding the place in between serving meals and ironing bed linen.

"Please mention our hotel to your friends," she said, as we left. So that's the Auberge Slave, Joinville-le-Point.

CHAPTER EIGHTEEN
The Longest Mile

"Begin at the beginning and go on to the end. Then stop."
Lewis Carroll

IN gentle drizzle we took a last look at the green waters of the Marne and cycled into the Bois de Vincennes where we became entangled inadvertently in the French Psychotic Motorists' Annual Jamboree. Every passing car, klaxoning furiously, forced us off the road, slammed to an unannounced halt in front of us, or changed direction without warning. Only our British bulldog spirit, Anglo-Saxon sang-froid and swift reactions enabled us to maintain our good humour and avoid becoming road traffic accident statistics.

By the time we emerged from the woods and alongside the Seine, the sun had come out. When I'd bought a ticket for the Conciergerie the previous day, it included entrance to the Sainte Chapelle. Because Terry had been waiting for me I hadn't used that part. To my eternal shame, I knew nothing of the Sainte Chapelle, and really didn't mind whether or not I saw it.

"It seems a pity to waste the ticket. Why don't you go and have a look? I'll sit outside with a cup of coffee," Terry said.

We crossed the oldest bridge in Paris, contrarily named Pont Neuf, to the Ile de la Cité. Carefully and gently we leant our bikes against the glass side wall of the café. A waiter came out and pointed at them, and started explaining something that Terry didn't understand, and rather unkindly I left him to sort it out. We had learned by experience that sometimes the best way to deal with an awkward situation is to be unable to understand the language.

I stood obediently for several minutes in a long queue that led round several corners, to go in to the Sainte Chapelle. Then I wondered why I was doing so when I already had a ticket. Smiling simultaneously smugly, triumphantly and apologetically – no easy feat - I made my way to the head of the queue and through security into the chapel. I imagined a dim and musty little place that would warrant five minutes of my time.

The small chapel was commissioned in the 13th century by pious King Louis IX to house what he believed to be Christ's crown of thorns and a relic from the cross, bought for an extortionate price from the Byzantine emperor.

If "Gothic" conjures up a picture of stern austerity, there is nothing of that in this enchanting church. It's Aladdin's cave and Blackbeard's treasure chest all in one. La Sainte Chapelle is the most exquisite building I have ever seen. Breathtakingly, heart-achingly, overwhelmingly, tear-jerkingly magnificent. My jaw had never spontaneously fallen open before. Until then I had thought that "open-mouthed wonderment" was an exaggeration.

The vaulted blue ceilings are decorated with golden heavenly bodies to resemble the night sky. They are supported by pillars painted in voluptuous colours - rich red adorned with golden Castilian castles and midnight blue with golden fleurs de lys. Standing in this glorious church is a truly sensuous experience. It's so beautiful that you feel you want to break off little pieces and eat them.

When it still served as a royal church, the lesser social classes worshipped in this lower chapel. The floor above was reserved for royalty. I climbed the narrow stone spiral staircase. It was worth the momentary panic of claustrophobia because it leads into a radiant jewel-box of brilliant hues. The high walls of the chapel are formed by intricate stained glass windows separated from each other by the most slender of columns, giving the impression that the entire wall is built of one vast pane of bejewelled glass. Sunlight poured through these windows and projected lakes of coloured lozenges that danced on the floor, creating a living kaleidoscope.

I could have most happily spent the rest of the day sitting in and admiring the beauty of this little church in its absolute perfection and almost oriental splendour. My only regret was that I had left my camera behind, so I wasn't able to share the beauty of La Sainte Chapelle with Terry. I went back to find him and tried to persuade him to come back in, but the queues were long, and there was the problem of our bikes. We'd come back again one day.

Of all the sights we saw on our journey, and all the other beautiful buildings I've ever seen, nothing compares to La Sainte Chapelle. As we cycled away, I was trying to rationalise why I had so loved the flamboyant chapel when the opulence of Versailles had slightly repelled me.

We dawdled amongst the old books, magazines and paintings at the *bouquinistes* along the quay, clinging to the last few hours of our journey by our fingernails. With no particular plan, we meandered in a roughly westerly direction to see what happened.

Just past the Eiffel Tower, close to the Bir Hakeim bridge, is a small green square known as the Place des Martyrs Juifs du Vélodrome d'Hiver. The monument marks one of the most shameful events that took place in wartime Paris. In 1942 the French police rounded up almost 13,000 Jewish men, women and children and imprisoned them in the indoor cycling stadium, the Vélodrome d'Hiver, or *"Vél d'Hiv"* as it was known. From there the prisoners were shipped to concentration camps. Very few would survive. The immensely moving life-size sculpture shows a mother cradling a child on her lap, her husband's hand resting on her shoulder. Another child plays forlornly with a doll. A young man comforts an older man, and a young woman lies on the ground, her elbow resting on a suitcase, her arm supporting her head.

The monument bears an explanatory plaque, but anybody seeing it would not need to be told its meaning. Polish sculptor, Walter Spitzer, whose family survived Auschwitz, has perfectly depicted people who are bewildered, exhausted, and in despair.

This little square is a very sad place, but it's well worth a visit to admire the artist's haunting and beautiful sculpture.

We continued cycling beside the river until we arrived at

226

the suburb of Javel, a bustling area of modern buildings and competitive traffic. Before it was swallowed up into the general agglomeration of Paris, the small village of Javel had witnessed the birth of two household names in France.

Towards the end of the 18th century it was a centre for the production of chemicals. A French chemist named Claude Louis Berthollet discovered the properties of sodium hypochlorite, from which he developed the product that has a place in every French home today. He called it *"Eau de Javel."* It is still called that in French; in English it's known as bleach.

By the time World War I broke out in 1914, Javel was an area of mostly wasteland and allotments. An engineer of Dutch/Polish origin purchased a large plot of land there. He built a vast factory to manufacture munitions for the war effort, employing some 12,000 female workers who turned out up to 30,000 shells daily. Their considerate employer provided health care, maternity pay, canteens, crèches and clinics for these ladies. They must have wished that the war would never end.

When it did, their employer needed to find a different product for his workers. What he decided to manufacture was the new-fangled horseless carriage. The logo of André Citroën's new venture was two chevrons, which are still seen today on the front of every Citroën motor vehicle. In May of 1919 the first Citroën Type A went into production, and in 1948 the quirky, iconic 2 CV took France by storm.

Sadly, innovator, caring employer and creator of one of the great names in French industry, André Citroën was a broken and bankrupt man by 1935, victim of market forces and his Achilles heel – gambling. Michelin took over his company, and within a year he was dead at the age of 57. But he left behind an enduring legacy, and a name known and respected throughout the world.

Javel is no longer a small village, but part of the 15th *arrondissement* of Paris. There is no trace there of the chemical factories, nor the Citroën car production plant, which closed down in the late 1970's and relocated out of Paris. The memory of its great founder remains in the local Metro station named after him, and in the futuristic André Citroën park. This innovative design covers about 30 acres, with wide lawns, two vast glass pavilions, and a number of water features. I loved its neatness and clean geometric shapes, and imagined that once man inhabits the moon, this is the kind of park he'll build there.

We sat beside a rectangular lake from which rows of trees grew out of square boxes, watching the residents of the area as they went about their Saturday morning affairs. I was still mulling over the conundrum of the appeal of the Sainte Chapelle as against Versailles, and I thought I'd found the answer. While one had been built to the glory of God, the other was the glorification of self and power.

After this peaceful and pleasant interlude, we started off again, vaguely in the direction of Versailles. Soon we found ourselves on a magical mystery tour where every corner yielded a new surprise. One minute we were cycling along an elegant suburban street, the next at a busy junction teeming with impatient traffic. Then, after a stretch of woodland, without warning we were on a multi-lane highway. High-speed traffic roared past, hooting, drivers glaring at us in their mirrors. In moments of extreme terror my reaction was to scream and scramble off the bike. That is what I did, but Terry, several hundred metres ahead of me, just kept blithely pedalling along. I dragged my bike to the very edge of the road, against a metal barrier, and waited. Passing motorists slowed and stared. I tried to look *insouciante*, as if I habitually hung around on busy motorways dressed like a clown, with a bicycle almost buried beneath bundles of paraphernalia. I wondered how long it would be before Terry recognised my absence, and came looking for me.

It was about five minutes before he hove into sight, backtracking nonchalantly down the narrow strip between the barrier and the cars.

"What's wrong? Why have you stopped?"

Momentarily dumbstruck, I waved my arms at the road,

the vehicles, at our bikes.

"What is the matter with you?" he asked.

"Are you off your head? Can you not see where we are? Do you see anybody else mad enough to be riding a bicycle here?"

"I don't see what you're making such a fuss about. Just follow me, and you'll be fine." He began to swing his leg over his bike.

"I will not follow you. We will not be fine. If we are not killed, we'll be arrested. I'm pretty sure we're on the *périphérique*."

"Rubbish."

"Terry, I am not going on this road. You can continue, if you like. I will find my own way, and meet you back in Versailles."

I heaved my bike around so that it was facing the way we had come, delivering myself an almighty whack on the ankle and enraging drivers who had to swerve to avoid knocking my wheels off. I began pushing it back until I reached a junction with a slightly less frenetic road. Terry would either follow, or leave me. I didn't look back. I climbed back on and pedalled a couple of hundred yards until I arrived at Porte de Versailles. Terry pulled up beside me.

"Shall we have something to eat? I'm starving." The baby bird syndrome again.

With the perpetual problem of being unable to leave the bicycles unattended, we stood on the pavement while a jolly man cooked us a toasted cheese *panini*. He suggested that we should try a slice of ham as well. It was good, tasty, he said, picking up a slice on a fork and flapping it towards us. No, thank you, we were vegetarians. Pah – that was no good for us. In any case, ham isn't meat. That seems to be a common misconception amongst French carnivores. They do not class *charcuterie* or poultry as meat. Our jovial host today was a good-natured man. He argued that not eating meat would weaken us. I countered by pointing out that the world's most powerful mammals, elephants, rhinoceroses and gorillas are all vegetarian.

"Ah yes!" he roared, banging his fist on the counter, "but

229

you don't see them riding bicycles!"

He asked where we were going, and when I said Versailles his face lit up. He tilted his arm up at a steep angle, like someone swearing an oath.

"Hard work! You're going to wish you'd eaten some meat!"

Busy Issy-les-Moulineaux was like any other densely-populated suburb on a Saturday afternoon: pandemonium. Pedestrians festooned with shopping bags stepped off pavements without looking. Cars stopped and started without any indication that they were going to do so. We seemed to be invisible and inconsequential amongst this teeming mass of humanity.

As suddenly as a film scene changes, the human and vehicular traffic faded into a peaceful, almost deserted residential area.

The pleasant little road on which we were cycling rapidly became steeper, until it was approaching perpendicular. We had benefited from an entirely down-hill run when we left Versailles. Now we faced the haul back there, climbing more than 100 metres over a few kilometres. Terry's legs were still pedalling, but even in my lowest gear I could not move the pedals another inch. I climbed off and began pushing. It took all my remaining strength to move forward. I had to keep squeezing the brakes to prevent the bike making its own way back down the hill. Terry gave up and dismounted. He hooked one of the handlebars around a fence post to stop his bike rolling back, and came back down to help me. Together we slogged onwards, panting. My legs wobbled and felt that their knees might bend backward under the effort being expected of them. Every few metres, we both stopped to catch our breath.

With one final push we reached the summit, and remounted.

We cycled back into into Versailles on *décade* III, Nonidi of Prairial in the year CCXIV of the Revolutionary calendar, 750 kilometres and seventeen days since we started out.

If the Zinedine Zidane look-alike had been on duty at the

car park, I know he would have been impressed by how skilfully we managed to open the barrier with our ticket.

CHAPTER NINETEEN
The Lottery of Life

Lottery: A situation whose success or outcome is governed
by chance.
Oxford Dictionary

ON an earlier journey in 2006 we had been to Varennes, the town where Louis and Marie-Antoinette were captured when they were so close to freedom. I remember how I had dismissed their fate as insignificant when compared to the loss of life at our previous stop, Verdun. [14]At that time I knew nothing about Marie-Antoinette and her royal spouse, other than that they lived a pampered life whilst their subjects starved. So we had visited every place of significance in their lives - apart from places that were no longer there - except their final burial place at St Denis. As well as being the royal necropolis, St Denis is the place where the coronation regalia was kept and French queens were crowned. Great names came there to settle for eternity.

I had a mental image of the church: solemnly magnificent, a bright white temple standing on a small mound, surrounded by well-tended lawns.

It was a long drive, but until we had seen where Louis and Marie-Antoinette's mortal trail had finally ended, I didn't feel we had completed our journey. So a couple of weeks after our return, we set off one Sunday morning at a distressingly early hour.

When we left home, it was a cool grey day, punctuated by heavy showers; in Paris, it was a grey wet day punctuated by occasional dry spells.

Here is a useful tip if you decide to visit St Denis: don't try to find any signs to it. Instead look for "Le Stade de France." The great stadium built to host the 1998 World Cup has the

---

14 A Perfect Circle, published by Bantam Books 2006

232

appearance of a giant flying saucer that has alighted in the northern suburbs of the capital. Signs to *Le Stade* abound. Conversely, to find the church took canine determination and tireless tenacity.

Having arrived in the St Denis neighbourhood, we admired the stadium from every possible angle as we drove around it several times in a fruitless search for our destination. We came upon a large unshaven man in a powder-blue shell suit and asked him for directions. He barked out an unintelligible response, and gobbed on the pavement next to the car. A female taxi-driver with a tiny apricot poodle draped over her shoulder like a stole was more helpful. She led us into an area of narrow, mysterious streets where there were no people at all. There we found a parking place and a small, insignificant sign pointing to the direction of the church. As it came into sight we were stunned by the horror of the place.

The church of St Denis is named after the first bishop of Paris, beheaded by the Romans on Mount Martyr – Montmartre. Legend says he picked up his severed head, tucked it beneath his arm like a cabbage and walked to the site where the basilica now stands, where he was buried.

Externally, in contrast to the cosmopolitan and colourful world on its doorstep, I found it sinister, and supremely ugly. It looks unfinished, because it is. I had expected something beautiful, like immaculate, creamy-stoned Fontevraud, where the French branch of the Plantagenets are buried. But the stone of St Denis is a sullen grey. The three Romanesque doorways on the front are blackened with the grime of ages. Badly damaged during the Revolution, the restoration of the church was subsequently begun but never completed, under Napoléon. The disastrous result of this project must be seen to be believed. One spire on the right-hand corner, and no spire on the left-hand corner gives it a most displeasing and lop-sided appearance.

In front of the entrance on a small, unkempt area of weedy grass lurked a few large grey concrete tubs. These accommodated some moribund plants vying for space with cigarette butts and empty beer cans. On the steps an Eastern European beggar clutched at us, pleading for support for her 15 little children.

Decapitating their erstwhile king and queen had failed to quench the wrath of the Revolutionaries. The sans culottes turned their attention to the royal residents of the necropolis who, they felt, although long dead, were not dead enough. They opened the tombs and tipped out the occupants into a pit, helping themselves to the odd finger or wisp of hair as talismans.

This meant that the mortal remains of almost every member of the French monarchy as far back as the 6th century AD all ended up in a jumble. The mass graves were opened up and the remains recovered and reburied at the time of the restoration. However, with everybody mixed up with everybody else, there was no possibility of knowing which parts belonged to whom. So they are all snuggled together now beneath the altar, and their magnificent marble tombs are empty memorials.

Inside the church the congregation was celebrating morning Mass. A fierce man held his finger to his lips and hissed "Shhh" as we walked in, so we walked back out and went to entertain ourselves for an hour.

Close to the basilica is the *Mairie* of St Denis, a clean, well-maintained building decorated with beautiful floral displays. There are one or two other attractive buildings in the vicinity – an immaculate little house painted all in pink, and a bank whose arched entrance doorway is topped by a splendidly carved stone peacock. But the area generally is, although colourful and interesting, run down and scruffy. In November 2005 it was the scene of wild rioting by the predominantly immigrant and unemployed population.

This is the milieu in which the church of St Denis stands, beside a particularly hideous glass-fronted building that looks like a pile of giant aquaria stacked upon and beside each other.

The market square was crammed with stalls. As the rain

fizzled out people began to appear, people of all different backgrounds who were noisy, and laughing, and wearing a variety of costumes. It did not feel at all like being in France, but rather in an exotic souk in a distant land. Lengths of beautifully embroidered saris in dramatic colours floated from rails. One stall sold nothing but nail varnishes in every colour of the spectrum, many hundreds of little bottles meticulously arranged in intricate patterns. There were rows and pyramids of exotic, mysterious fruits and vegetables. An enterprising man was roasting corncobs over a tray of charcoal that he pushed around in a supermarket trolley. A young woman with shrivelled legs and horribly twisted feet sat on a sheet of cardboard crying, holding out her hand for money. People stepped over her outstretched legs as if they were discarded cabbage leaves. Many of the shops in the streets were open, selling clothing and bed linen, cheap jewellery, take-away foods, leather goods, travel tickets.

The indoor market housed bloodied stalls covered in gory chunks of meat, fragrant piles of spices, breads in more shapes than you could count, polished fruit and vegetables. There were a variety of smelly cheeses whose prices ranged from the outrageous to the ridiculous. There were cheeses for €30 a kilo, and two-kilo boxes of mixed cheeses for €1. Strange fish gazed sadly from slabs, and crabs and lobsters tried to haul themselves up the glass walls and out of their tanks.

We succumbed to the €1 box of cheese and a crispy, still-warm baguette, and went in search of coffee. Just as we were about to step into one café a man slammed down a metal grille in our faces. Inside we could see two men chopping up the bar with a chainsaw. At the next establishment we were knocked back by the aroma of lavatories billowing from the door. There were no Michelin-stars in this part of town, so we settled for the least grubby café, where the coffee was good and the other customers all called out a welcome and raised their hands in greeting. From the way they watched us covertly I suspected that English customers were a novelty.

Walking back towards the church we were again appalled

by its unkempt and dismal appearance. One stained glass rose window was rich in colour, but many were just plain glass, and dirty. As soon as we stepped inside I was reminded of everything I dislike about churches. The gloom, the chill, the glowering 80 ft. high ceiling, the mustiness, centuries of penance, despair and suffering. I found it unspeakably depressing.

For lovers of funerary statuary, which we are not, the royal necropolis must be a Mecca. It is filled with tombs and effigies that are wondrous examples of sculpture at its most skilled. We, though, were only here on account of Louis and Marie-Antoinette who were down in the crypt.

Initially I could not decide whether or not this was a worse place than the floor above. Being underground went against it. I was fighting panic not to rush back up the stairs. But there was a less mournful atmosphere, less statuary, and very lovely vaulted ceilings. A small city of dead royalty in cosy caves, beautifully restored stonework, all bathed in a warm glow by subtle illumination.

In a well-lit cave of creamy stone we found the tombs of Louis and Marie-Antoinette. Their remains lie beneath heavy black marble slabs engraved with their names: Louis XVI and Marie-Antoinette, King and Queen of France and Navarre. They are not alone. Their neighbours include Louise of Lorraine, widow of Henri III; Louis VII, one-time husband of Eleanor of Aquitaine; and Louis XVIII, rather confusingly the brother of Louis XVI.

It was customary to embalm French monarchs. Behind a heavily barred iron grille is a small, dark room. Within, a row of boxes sits on a shelf. This macabre treasure trove contains the *"entrailles"* - internal organs - of defunct French royals. Whether the contents of those boxes survived the Revolution I don't know. I don't really like to think about them.

In a glass urn lies the desiccated heart of the little Dauphin. When the child died in the Temple prison, a doctor removed his heart. Preserved in alcohol, it had been hidden away for over 200 years until 2004, when DNA testing confirmed that it belonged to a child of Marie-Antoinette and Louis XVI. It's a grisly and pathetic little thing.

Upstairs is a very beautiful white marble statue of Louis and Marie-Antoinette kneeling beside each other. He wears full monarchical robes, the crown set on his head, his hands clasped piously and his eyes raised to heaven. The statue is kinder to him than any of his portraits.

His queen, exquisitely beautiful, with pearl drop earrings and a pearl necklace, wears a gown so décolleté that her bosom is almost falling out of it. I was surprised that it was allowed into a church. Her left hand appears to be about to pull down her dress and liberate what little of her shapely right breast is not already exposed. In contrast to the glowing whiteness of the rest of the statue, both breasts are brown and grubby. This is due to the thousands of hands that have caressed them in the belief that doing so brings luck.

Marie-Antoinette loved flowers. I thought she would have hated St Denis, the most flowerless and macabre church I have ever seen. Then I remembered the notice in La Chapelle Expiatoire that said: "The King and Queen's bodies (or at least the presumed bodies, at least for the King's) were excavated." A few handfuls of dust and a fragment of garter are hardly irrefutable evidence of pedigree. For all we know, some of it could be Robespierre or his satanic cronies.

I prefer to believe that whatever remains were removed from La Chapelle Expiatoire, they belonged to somebody else. And I hope that whatever is left of Marie Antoinette still lies in that small leafy square beside the Rue d'Anjou in central Paris, where the sunlight reaches, and clouds of white roses bloom.

When we first planned our journey our interest in France's most unfortunate royals had been superficial. I knew nothing of them except that they had both lost their heads and Marie-Antoinette had apparently made a remark about bread and cakes. It would be amusing to track our progress alongside theirs. So that we understood what had happened to them and why, I began reading about their lives. And then I was hooked. Following them through their marriage, their triumphs and trials to their deaths, they became real people instead of the comic opera characters they had once seemed to me. The thing is, I am not a royalist. The politics of their story did not interest me, but I could not help but be fascinated by their lives, and horrified by the way they had died.

Who was better placed to write about the intimate and daily life of the Queen than her first lady of the bedchamber, Madame de Campan? Nobody but the only surviving member of the family, the Princess Royal Marie-Thérèse could give a first-hand account of the family's ordeals during their escape attempt and imprisonment.

I particularly enjoyed Stefan Zweig's "Marie-Antoinette – The Portrait of an Average Woman" in which he concluded that she was neither a particularly bad woman nor a particularly good one, but an average person forced by circumstances to transcend her own mediocrity and become rather remarkable.

Louis seems often to be unkindly portrayed by history, his failings outweighing his virtues. But the more I read about him, the more I gained respect for his positive qualities – his kindness, courtesy, his love for his family, and the courage and dignity he displayed during the many humiliations and ordeals that he faced. Maybe he was greedy and indecisive. Perhaps he didn't have any idea how to command, and was clumsy and lacking in majestic appearance. But that didn't make him deserving of his fate. He was naïve enough to believe that to be a good king, it was sufficient to be a good man. I became quite fond of him.

Whatever their faults, from what I read they were two people without spite or malice, kind-hearted and well-meaning. Stefan Zweig describes them as "living in a circle of planetary admiration, fed on the subtle poison of flattery." Apart from their children and friends, and an abundance of courage, all they had in common was their unsuitability for the position into which they were thrust. If the fates had been kinder to them and not bumped off so many of his ancestors, Louis would have been no more than a minor *aristo* or

238

wealthy bourgeois. He could have lived in comfortable and undemanding obscurity, free to devote himself to the things he enjoyed. He would probably have broken his neck out hunting, or eaten himself into a heart attack.

Marie-Antoinette, had she not been her mother's daughter, could have been a sparkling wife for a wealthy man, spending her days in her garden, surrounded by children, a few little dogs and some pet lambs, and entertaining her friends with amusing soirées. She would have lived to a ripe old age.

And they would have both been forgotten by history...........

The End

BIBLIOGRAPHY
The extracts quoted in this book are taken from:

Memoirs of the Private Life of Marie Antoinette by Madame Campan, 1818, public domain.

Paris War Days by Charles Inman Bernard, Openlibrary.org., 1914, public domain.

Vive la France by E Alexander Powell, Charles Scribner's Sons, 1915; William Heinemann, London 1916 public domain.

Memoirs of Marie-Thérèse Charlotte, Duchess of Angoulême, first published by Librairie E. Plon, Nourrit Et Cie, Imprimeurs-Éditeurs, bibliothèque nationale de France. English translation by John Wilson Croker, pub. John Murray, London 1923, public domain.

La Route de Varennes, Alexandre Dumas *père,* Michel Lévy Frères, Paris, 1860, public domain.

A Popular History of France, François Guizot, translated by Robert Black, Estes and Lauriat, 1876, public domain.

There's A Girl In Château-Thierry words by E Ray Goetz, 1919, public domain.

Protest Against the Tower of Monsieur Eiffel, Le Temps 14 Feb 1887 public domain

Diary of Kurt Hesse Record of the Great War, Vol VI, ed Charles F. Horne, National Alumni 1923, public domain.

A Girl's Song from *'Flower of Youth: Poems in War Time'* Katherine Tynan. London: Sidgwick & Jackson, 1915 public domain.

Memories of Harry St Clare Wheeler Published on the website of his family, www.wheelerfolk.org and quoted with their permission.

The International Sommelier Guild, article published with their permission.

The Diaries of Louis XVI, public domain.

Further reading:

Marie-Antoinette – Portrait of an Average Woman by Stefan Zweig. First published by Insel Verlag, Leipzig, 1932; English translation by Eden and Cedar Paul 1933 The Viking Press, Inc.; current edition pub. Grove, 2002.
Treasures of the World – The French Kings by Frederic V Grunfeld, Stonehenge, 1982. Fr
Fighting the Flying Circus by Eddie Rickenbacker. First published by Frederick A Stokes Company, 1919. Kindle edition published by Doubleday, 2009.
Le Mouvement Perpétuel, Histoire de l'Hôpital Américain de Paris 1906-1989 Nicole Fouché, Pub Eres, Toulouse, 1992

The Maps:

The maps contained in this book are notional. Any attempt to use them for navigation purposes is inevitably doomed to frustration and failure.

SUSIE KELLY

Born a Londoner, Susie Kelly spent most of the first 25 years of her life in Kenya, and now lives in south-west France with her husband and assorted animals.

She believes that her explosive temper is a legacy from her Irish-American grandfather, but has no idea who to blame for her incompetence as a housewife. Still, she's very kind to animals, small children and elderly people.

The Valley of Heaven and Hell is her fourth non-fiction book. Best Foot Forward, Two Steps Backward and A Perfect Circle are all published by Transworld Publishers in Bantam Books.

Susie particularly enjoys exploring the road less travelled, discovering the lives and events of lesser-known places.

She is donating 25% of her royalties from "The Valley of Heaven and Hell" to be shared equally between Cancer Research and Tower Hill Stables Sanctuary in Essex.

* * * * *

Connect with Susie

Blog http://nodamnblog.wordpress.com/

Twitter: @WAPIFARASI

More Blackbirdebooks Digital Originals
The Dream Theatre (2011)
by Sarah Ball
Ten Good Reasons To Lie About Your Age (2011)
by Stephanie Zia

http://www.blackbirdebooks.com
mail@blackbirdebooks.com

Made in the USA
Lexington, KY
22 September 2011